Bad Girl
Gone Mom

Bad Girl
Gone Mom

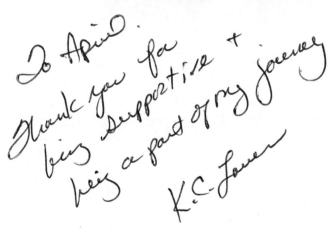

To April.
Thank you for
being supportive +
being a part of my journey

K.C. Lauer

K.C. Lauer

To order additional copies of this book, contact:
Xlibris Corporation
1-888-795-4274
www.Xlibris.com
Orders@Xlibris.com
89659

CONTENTS

Dedication

When Marie died in my arms, I had a choice to make. Would I keep my promise to her and live my life with no regrets, or would I allow fear to keep me hostage and keep me from living my dreams?

To those who want to be free

Dear Readers,

When I first read James Frey's *A Million Little Pieces*, his memoir about alcohol addiction, I identified with his rage and inability to believe in himself.

When I was done reading his book, I was reminded with how alone I had felt when I was a teenager and how terrible life had seemed at certain points in my life. I thought that if I had the guts to put my story down on paper and publish it, it might actually help somebody. So that is what I decided to do.

As I worked on this memoir, I used school records, photographs, medical records, and other pieces of memorabilia to construct the story with factual and accurate details to the best of my ability and recollection. I have not embellished the story, I did not feel I needed to; the actual events were raw enough on their own. However, because the events in this story are true, I have changed the names of individuals, characteristics, and places to provide anonymity for those involved.

This is a story about a girl who gets into trouble after traumatic events and does adult things, some of them illegal or immoral, and how it affects her and her family. It is a story of survival.

While some parents may deem this content inappropriate for young children and forbid kids from reading this book, what I think is *intolerable* are those teens and young adults that are committing suicide because of peer pressure, bullying, and an inability to come to grips with depression, their gender, sexual orientation, their name, their weight, their color, or their religion. If we do not provide them with a way out, they will surely make mistakes.

In this story, I reveal intimate details because these things happened to me when I was young, and they could happen to someone you know, even yourself or your kid, a fellow student, your granddaughter, your niece, or your older sister. Teenage suicide, alcoholism, drug addiction, anorexia, date rape, pornography, and STDs are real problems that affect real people. There is help and there is a way out. This memoir is a testament to the fact that even bad girls can turn out to be good moms.

K

Foreword

1980: The Twenty Questions

How do you know if you are an alcoholic or drug addict, or any other kind of addict?

AA has a list of twenty questions. The first time I learned about them, I was fifteen. Back then, they said if you answered four or more "correctly," as in the affirmative *yes*, you might be an alcoholic. Shit, I think I got fifteen out of the twenty correct the first time.

That was until I realized that it might mean that I was an alcoholic. I then devised the following list of disclaimers (in italics) to reduce my yes answers down to four.

1. Do you lose time from work due to your drinking? *No, not usually.*
2. Is drinking making your home life unhappy? *No, my life was unhappy at home before I started drinking.*
3. Do you drink because you are shy with other people? *No, I am obnoxious sober too.*
4. Is drinking affecting your reputation? *No, it is giving me a bigger one.*
5. Have you ever felt remorse after drinking? *I am always sad when I run out.*
6. Have you gotten into financial difficulties because of your drinking? *No, I work three jobs, so I can afford it.*
7. Do you turn to lower companions and an inferior environment when drinking? *No, I am usually hanging with the dregs of life anyway, might as well party with them.*
8. Does your drinking make you careless of your family's welfare? Nope, my *family disowned me.*

9. Has your ambition decreased since drinking? *Not at all, now I have ambitions to party like a rock star.*
10. Do you crave a drink at a definite time daily? *Any time of the day is good. I am not particular.*
11. Do you want a drink the next morning? *It depends on whether I have just woken up or had been up all night.*
12. Does drinking cause you to have difficulty in sleeping? *Not at all, I can pass out anywhere.*
13. Has your efficiency decreased since drinking? *No, actually I have become more efficient.*
14. Is drinking jeopardizing your job or business? *No, I do not think my arrest will matter.*
15. Do you drink to escape from worries or troubles? *Yes, but you would too if you were me.*
16. Do you drink alone? *Yes. I work a lot and I go to school. I do not have time for socialization; and besides, it is illegal because I am fifteen. If I were old enough, I would go to bars. However, since I am not allowed to go, I just carry a bottle or a dime bag in my purse, drink, and get high in school, at home, or at work.*
17. Have you ever had a complete loss of memory because of your drinking? *Yes, sometimes I cannot remember what happened; it can be very embarrassing I think I might have slept with my sister's boyfriend.*
18. Has your physician ever treated you for drinking? *No.*
19. Do you drink to build up your self-confidence? *Nope, I have plenty of confidence. I am cocky and cantankerous.*
20. Have you ever been in a hospital or institution because of drinking? *Yes, but that was only because my parents made me. It gave me a lighter sentence in court.*

If you have answered YES to any one of the questions, there is a definite warning that you may be an alcoholic.

If you have answered YES to any two, the chances are that you are an alcoholic.

If you have answered YES to three or more, you are definitely an alcoholic. (Lifeline)

AA Twenty Questions

Oh shit.

There are people that will tell you that alcoholism is insidious. What they mean by that is that it affects your body and mind slowly, entrapping you into its folds before you even realize you have the disease. At first, you want it, but then you feel like you need it. Then you feel like you can't live without it. At least that is what happened to me.

Chapter One

The End (January 14, 1983)

"If you want me to give you a ride home, you are gonna have to blow me."

We were sitting in his filthy red Ford pick-up truck in a dirt-covered parking lot behind some seedy country bar. I was not wearing a watch but knew the bar was closed and had been for a while. All the cars and trucks that were there when we arrived hours earlier are now gone; we are alone.

Ed has been trying to convince me to get out of his truck for the last thirty minutes as the lot emptied out, but I will not budge. "Please give me a ride back. Please!"

I was so drunk I could tell you my name and where I lived but that was about it at that moment. I had been drinking since he picked me up with his friend around 2:30 that afternoon. Now it was twelve hours later and I was plastered. I realized at that moment that I was out of control; it was one of those "oh shit" moments. Not unlike the ones I had had about a year and a half prior, when first introduced to Alcoholics Anonymous.

Earlier in the day, at my parents' house I had had another "oh shit" moment when I was scoping them out to see if maybe I could move home again. In fact, I had shown up with a peace offering but the meat had not made any difference in their response to my request.

Carrying the plastic bag of venison freshly killed and deliciously marinated, I had walked the entire way home to their house because no one would pick me up. I was enormously proud of my gift because I had helped hunt the deer, if you call jacking deer *hunting*. I had just held the flashlight in the buck's eyes. It had been enough to stun him for Frank to get the shot. Then he had brought me back to the house and gone with a friend of his to get the deer. When I got up a few hours later, Frank had gutted the organs from the deer and then pulled it up around the tree limb in front of the kitchen for it to bleed out.

It had to set there for twenty-four hours. We were vigilant banging pots around the kitchen to keep the vermin away during the day, and Frank had kept watch at night. "The hide was worth something providing the vermin did not get it," he had said.

Then that very morning, I had assisted with packaging the meat as Frank butchered the deer. Nothing was better than freshly butchered meat. Farm life was a new experience for me, and although I did not like everything about it, like having to clean the hog pens or feeding the hunting dogs first thing in the morning when the air was frigid, some things I actually did like. The meat was one, and singing on Friday nights with the local farmers was another.

I had called my parents the day before and warned them I was coming over to ask them something, but they were still not happy to see me. I was drinking and drugging, a situation that had caused my family a lot of grief. In fact, that was why they had thrown me out fifteen months earlier. Now, my mom was pregnant and the household had calmed down since my departure.

My younger brother and sister had been witnesses to my drinking, drugging, and promiscuity for years. I had messed up their lives too and I am sure my parents were not excited about the possibility of me ruining another one of their children.

My folks had tried to get me to stop drinking, but when I resisted they did not have any other choice. They went into the protective mode and adopted a tough-love stance.

I do not remember what happened to the meat. It was only after I handed it to my mother and she put it in the sink because it was bleeding through the bag that I realized I had ruined my favorite suede coat. It was another "oh shit" moment.

It was just the icing on the cake of another day in paradise, otherwise known as my life. I took offense immediately to my parents' desire to protect their home. How could they not see that I needed to be home?

"Mom, what do you think about me moving back home?"

"Well, K. C., you know we love you, but until you have stopped drinking we cannot let you disrupt this family anymore. We would like to help you but we cannot."

I felt as if I was the bag of raw meat, cast into the sink, bloody, and staining everything in its path. I would not beg and I could not apologize. How could they be so cold? Could they not see anything good about me? How could it be so easy for them to cast me onto the street after having put so much money and time into my well-being in my earlier years? How dare they tell me to get my priorities straight? I worked hard. I was an honor student pulling A's and B's at school and I had supported myself, on and off for a while. I was a decent kid with a wild streak.

"How are things going at Stephen's parents' house?"

I lied. "Everything is fine." The truth would have been too much for them to hear; it would have hurt them. Keeping secrets made things easier. I could not be who they wanted me to be. I was different, abnormal, and incomplete. I would never be a normal person; I had too many issues.

While I desperately wanted to be someone they could be proud of, my actions always caused them pain and despair. I had become a loser, a drunkard, and I was not even of legal age to be drinking yet.

I did not know where it came from; the rage was uninvited and at times flourished like a hurricane raging across the Atlantic. The anger I felt toward my parents and our relationship could have threatened the entire coast and inlands of the eastern seaboard if I released it.

If the swirling started, I was afraid there would be no stopping it. The only thing to hope for was a change in wind direction. I was ready to blow. Instead of spewing, I held it in. That was normally my way; it was easier to let people think they had no impact on me. Just pretend everything was all right and walk away. Do not ever let them see you cry, that was one of my mottos.

"Okay, well, thanks for considering it. I really appreciate it. I have got to get going."

"Let us know when you are sober, and then we will talk again."

"I will." Carefully not slamming the door, I let myself out of the front. I was a guest in this house after all, and an unwanted part of the family. They had made that clear when they changed the locks and refused to give me a key. They did not want me coming by unannounced. I was a threat and they did not trust me anymore.

They had good reason to keep me at a distance. I had stolen from them, lied to them, and ruined my little brother and sister's lives. Not to mention the shame I brought to our family.

Back then, I thumbed everywhere I went, because although I was old enough to drive, my parents refused to sign the approvals for me to get my license because I was not living at home. My life was busy, and if I could bum a ride, I would. Nevertheless, if I could not . . . well, I knew how to get around. Just stick out the old thumb.

It was amazing how many nice people you meet when you use your thumb as your major mode of transportation. I had many people pick me up and tell me they had stopped because I looked sweet, and they did not want somebody "bad" to pick me up. I would think to myself, explain "bad." Aloud, I would thank the nice people for picking me up and express my gratitude for the ride.

Is bad a relative term? It is not bad, badder, or baddest except in "baddest man in the whole damn town" in Leroy Brown. My bad might be good, and your worst might be badder than mine might. I had been thumbing for several years and been lucky but I knew all it would take would be that one time when I was not and it might mean my life.

That afternoon on the way to my parents' house, nobody had picked me up even though my thumb had remained up most of the way. It was probably because I was carrying a big bag of blood-red meat in a see-through plastic bag. It rarely happened to me that I had to walk the full distance anywhere I went, but on that winter day, it was warmer than normal and I did not mind walking at all. The interaction with my parents made me emotional and I began to sing.

There was always something to sing about; I sang for all sorts of reasons but mostly because it brought my heart peace. That was important because it seemed as if I was always fighting.

Most of the time, the fights were in my head. I would think about something, and then I would think about it repeatedly. I would replay conversations in my mind. I knew right from wrong but that did not mean I always acted accordingly. I would think about what I should have said. I would wish I had done something differently after the fact. I began wishing I had told my parents how I really felt, but I was not sure what I would have told them. "You hurt my feelings, poor me."

I wished I could be somebody different, somebody who was smarter, better looking, more adept at social interaction. I was stuck with myself, and that was a heavy burden to bear. How can you be with someone you hate twenty-four hours a day? When it is someone else, you can walk away, but when it is yourself, you are stuck.

The fact was I did not feel like singing at all when I first left my parents' house that day. I felt like screaming instead. Nothing was going my way and it never would. The one thing I was sure of was that I did not want to die. I had already been there and done that. I was not ready.

As the sun began creeping toward the horizon, I was chilled; and when I took off my coat and stuffed it under my arm, I got goose bumps. I knew nobody was going to pick up a girl with a big bloodstain all over the front of her jacket.

Can you imagine the possibilities? Maybe I had just left my parents' house after I murdered them. Headline reads, "Girl with bloodstained jacket found on the side of the road." I laughed at what passersby might have thought as I stuck out my thumb, started a verse from "Amazing Grace," and walked back to my rented room.

"Amazing grace, how sweet the sound, that saved a wretch like me, I once was lost, but now am found, was blind, but now I see." I hate religion but this song is spiritual and I do not mind that. Spirituality reminds me of maturity leading to Nirvana or self-awakening. Not that I was even remotely close to wisdom; I felt as if I was destined to be emotionally blind for the rest of my life, but the song still cheered me for some unknown reason.

As I sang, passing cars swerved to avoid me. I am sure the singing probably made them think I was high or drunk. I was not at this point, but I would not have minded a drink right then. Damn my parents, damn Frank, damn me.

I had my right arm out, walking backward with my thumb in the air while keeping the beat, snapping my fingers with my left. Moreover, of course, I danced to the music, swaying back and forth as the rhythm demanded. The people who lived along North Main Street were used to seeing me walking around town often with my thumb out. The resident state trooper pulled me over while I was walking one time. It had been nine o'clock at night and he wanted to know why my parents had not picked me up or loaned me their car after I told him I had just gotten off work. At the time, I had explained I did not live at home. I told him I could walk the two miles of the road to my boarding room and be home for 10:00 p.m., or I could stick my thumb out and hope to be home for 9:10.

He let me continue walking, telling me to be careful. What could he do really? I was a girl on my own.

On the third verse of "Amazing Grace," Ed and Jerry slowed down at the side of the road. They offered me a ride when Jerry stuck his head out and yelled, "Need a lift?"

Bales of hay and some shovels in the back of the medium-sized Ford farm truck validated what I was thinking. It looked safe enough to me, these were farming boys. After working all day, surely they meant me no harm.

We introduced ourselves and were already past where I was staying, by the time they asked me where I was going. I told them I wanted to go anywhere they were going. They told me they were going for some drinking, dancing, and fun. I laughed and told them I was running away from home for the night; their plan sounded good to me.

Jerry handed me a beer out of the cooler at his feet, and as an afterthought, inquired about my age. I assured him I was eighteen, which was the legal drinking age in Connecticut back then.

We drove along and talked. I told them where I worked and the fact that I was a singer/song writer and played guitar at the local restaurant. They never heard of the restaurant but that did not surprise me. It was a shithole diner in town, but the owners treated me like family.

Unfortunately, I was not very good to family or the people I loved. I worked hard but sometimes on the wrong things. I was always hurting somebody or a bunch of people, and they were not any different. Why could I not have been born as Tinkerbelle, just flitting about all sparkly and granting wishes to people? I was always the one left wishing; wishing I was prettier, more talented, smarter, faster, thinner, funnier, better, or best at something. I was nothing, a fraud, a liar and a waste—Tinker Buzz.

Getting high and being drunk was my way of rewarding the efforts I had made for working so hard. It was my release, a way to relinquish control of whom I was, which allowed me to become somebody else. I could become someone who was daring, attractive, and desirable. Creativity flowed when I was under the influence, limits evaporated. With each drink, toke, or pill, rational thought faded, and indulgent obsessive-compulsive self-destructive behavior commenced.

I told Jerry and Ed about my stint in a thirty-day alcohol rehab, and they were surprised.

Maybe it was not what they expected to hear from a girl like me. I was a freckly Irish/German girl with an innocent-looking face. One you might expect to see on the local cheerleading squad, or supermarket, ringing up your order. I was not particularly attractive, but not ugly either. With a little makeup and the right wardrobe, I could stand out as an eye-catcher, but most of the time I chose to fade into the background.

I was not a foo-foo girl. That was for sure. You would not catch me painting my nails except for an occasion like a wedding, funeral, or a job interview. I had little time for luxury. I had things to do, places to go to, people to see. Frivolity was for others. I was a straight shooter, kind of a bottom-line girl. I spent money on my hair on occasion and that was about it. My parents, on the other hand, had put a lot of money into me over the years. Being born with a cleft palate had required surgery, speech therapy, and in my teens, orthodontics. Although they had invested and I had a nice manmade smile, it was not my best feature, nor was it my worst. I was not self-conscious about my smile or the way I spoke and that was really what mattered.

Anyway, I guess my rehab story was not what they expected to come out of my mouth. They asked me how I had ended up in rehab and that led to "the time I got arrested" story. Since I had told them I was older, I was careful telling the story so that they would not realize I was still in high school. It felt good to have their attention. I was still feeling rejected by my parents' decision to hold off on my request to move back. I really had no options but I was not ready to give it up yet.

Relating the story, I realized that I was not proud of my actions, and in fact, in some parts I had been downright ashamed of what I had done. I pushed the guilty feelings out of my mind. Deny them and they do not exist; ignore them and they go away. Instead, I substituted laughter, making fun of the situation. I explained to them that I had been in love with one of the guys I was arrested with. He had begged me to see him in the stolen car before he returned it and turned himself in. Love is blind and being in love is stupid. "What's love got to do with it"? I sang them a few bars of Tina Turner's song and they laughed.

"Aren't you too young to be an alcoholic? I think of old men and street people. I do not think of someone like you." Jerry, the talker of the two was looking me up and down, shaking his head.

Smiling at him, I said, "Yeah, I am. It was easier for my parents and my lawyer to get me off without doing time if I went to the rehab. It worked. I got a year's probation." I was not going to admit I was an alcoholic to strangers, and besides, I was not planning to be sober anytime soon, so what difference did it make if I was a drunk or not?

The conversation was making me uncomfortable so then I did what I always did. I started flirting. At first, it was with both of them; Ed was driving and I did not want him to feel left out, but I really thought Jerry was the cuter of the two.

When they had stopped the truck to pick me up, Jerry had gotten out, letting me get in the middle since there was a hump where the shifter was located in the truck. Being small, I could sit scrunched up better than he could. As he was maneuvering in and out of the seat, it gave me a chance to check out his tight arms, tight legs, and tight ass. Thank goodness for farm boys, they were usually lean and almost never mean.

Jerry told me he grew up in Southwick, Massachusetts and that he and his pal Ed had met at a local farm where they were baling hay. They had just gotten off work, working for one of the farmers up in Granby, Connecticut and since it was Friday, they were off early and ready for some fun.

I was about halfway finished with my Budweiser when Jerry helped himself to another. When he pulled it out, he placed it on the seat between my legs. Although I had pants on, the coldness made me shiver.

"Brr," I said. "That is a bit chilly." He left it there and pushed it harder into my mons. I did not move or squirm away, just stared at him as he watched my face for any sense of reaction. I grinned and he knew instantly he was making me horny. After about a minute, he said, "Ooh, she's a wild one, Ed. She needs to cool off. Will you look at that?" I was holding the can in place on my own, pressing it against my body and gently bucking it.

Ed turned his head to catch a glimpse, and he chuckled. "Cool her off until we get there, huh, Jerry? She's going to need it." To me, he said, "You like that?"

I could not deny it. He had stirred something inside of me. The cold beer can hurt, but the longer I withstood the pain, the more they got excited and that got me excited. It was all about control.

The endorphins were kicking in and my puss was getting numb. The pain had passed as it often did if you could just tolerate it and work through it. I had learned to think about other things and ignore pain.

Ed copped a feel of my tits while Jerry kept the can on my clit. They were enjoying this ride. Jerry got himself another beer since I had warmed that one up, and while he was at it, he handed Ed and me another cold one. I drank my second beer without removing the cold beer can from between my legs.

We had been driving for about forty-five minutes, and I had no idea where we were but I was ready for some music, dancing, and who knew what else.

When we got to the bar, Jerry told me to go over and sit at a table with some other people he knew. I was sitting there when this pretty girl sat next to me and started talking. It turned out that Jerry had a girlfriend and she just loved him. They were going to get married next year she said as she showed me her engagement ring. After I introduced myself and told her where I was from, she wanted to know how I had met the boys.

I made up a story about meeting Ed somewhere and explained to her that he had invited me on a date to the bar. She did not question what I told her but seemed surprised Ed had a date. I did not tell her I had been hitting on her boyfriend and had managed to give him a rock hard-cock. I did not tell her that he had chilled down my cunt with a cold brew on the ride over either. Instead, I made up lies about breaking up with a boy and then meeting Ed. We commiserated over love and men. She and I danced and drank all night while the men just drank and watched us.

I do not know at what point I blacked out. We had maybe four or five rounds, and then I remembered going to the restroom. That was all I remembered. I came to in Ed's truck on the seat, leaning up against the passenger door. I had not eaten that day, and the alcohol had taken control.

Ed was outside the truck, banging on the window for me to unlock his door and let him in. He must have given me his keys so I could sleep it off, I thought as I let him in.

"Get out," he said as he climbed in. He was tired and wanted to go home.

"No! Please bring me home. C'mon, I am drunk; I cannot even hold my head up."

"You are not much of a drinker for someone who claims she is an alcoholic, and you know what else? I do not think you are really eighteen either. Colleen said she found you passed out in the bathroom. She looked in your purse and couldn't find an I.D. She thought it would be better for everyone if I let you sleep it off out here so I gave her my keys and she got you out of the bar."

I tried to remember but my head was fuzzy. I might have remembered somebody shutting the door before I slid against it, but I was not sure.

"Good thing she's a good girl, not like you. She and Jerry are going to get married. Did she tell you?"

I looked at him. Was he being sympathetic? No, the smirk told me that he thought it was funny.

"You know, it was hilarious watching you two girls dance out there. If she had known you were hitting on her old man, she would have scratched your eyes out. Obviously, you did not tell her the truth. So what did you tell her?"

What did I tell her? I could not remember for a minute. Then I remembered her face, her sweet, and naïve talk about getting married and living happily ever after. I remembered telling her love was for losers, and we had laughed.

"I told her you met me at work at the diner and had asked me for a date."

"Some date. Yeah, that is a hoot. There you were throwing yourself at him all during the ride over here like a whore. Kissing him, letting him feel you up, and then taking that cold can between your legs. That was something else, girl. Do not find 'em like you too much. Bet you could ride a bull as well. It is a shame you were not hitting on me. Otherwise, you might have had a ride home now, would you not? But you picked the wrong guy, and now you are shit out of luck because I am tired, and I must get up in the morning to go to work. You had enough time to sleep. You have been out here for a couple of hours already. So go on, it was nice meeting you but I have to get going. Get out."

The tears sprang to my eyes. Ordinarily I did not like to let other people see me cry but I did not know what else to do. I did not know where I was, and I had no idea how to get home. There was nobody else around. The parking lot was dark, and I was more afraid of being left alone in the dark in the middle of nowhere than I was of pissing Ed off.

"Ed, you're right. I am seventeen and a half. Not only did you give me alcohol, you took me over state lines. How about you give me a ride home and we'll forget this whole thing ever happened?"

"I tell you what, seeing you girls dance tonight made me horny, especially because I was thinking about how Jerry got you to chill in the truck on the ride over. You were an eager beaver, you know, like, all over him. Colleen would have slapped him if he had tried that with her, but then again, Colleen is a lady and you are not. You do not deserve a person like Jerry. On the way over here, you told us about all your boyfriends too. I am guessing you are no virgin."

If I had been sober, his comments might have hurt, but I was not and I did not care. "Jerry could not handle me," I laughed. "I probably would have given him a heart attack. He's better off with that domesticated chicken."

Ed laughed. "Look, I know what you wanted but since you did not get it, how about you suck my dick and I will give you a ride home and we'll forget this night ever happened; we'll call it even, and then I can get home and get some sleep."

I thought about it. How many cocks had I sucked by that point? I did not know, maybe fifty or sixty. Ed was probably thinking I would just as soon forget this night as he would. One more blowjob in a sea of blowjobs would not matter, but I did not want to do it. That was what was bothering me. I did not like Ed, his grimy hands or the beer belly he was sporting or his cocky fucking attitude, but he knew I was stuck.

Then again, if I looked at the situation realistically, it was not much as if I had a choice. Not that he was forcing me. I could get out of the truck of my own free will. Statutory rape maybe, but after any jury heard Jerry and Ed's testimony they would have said I was asking for it. They certainly would not have called it outright rape, maybe date rape, but I would never press charges and nobody else cared. We might as well just get it over with. I did not think I could stand up if I got out of the truck. That would be bad.

As I was deciding what to do, Tina Turner's "What's love got to do with it?" came on the radio. It was an omen.

"What's it going to be? You want a ride for a blow job or not?"

I had managed to straighten myself up some and was talking a bit more coherently but not by much.

"Start the truck and let my stomach settle first. I will give you a BJ when we get there. You can pull off the side street or something. I promise." Resigned to the fact that if I did not agree to his proposal I was going to be stuck out in the middle of nowhere, I thought the latter would be the worse of two evils.

"No, I am not starting the truck until you get busy, so let's get started here, honey, right now. It is not getting any earlier."

He undid his jean's button and unzipped the zipper. Then he shoved his underwear underneath his ball sack and slid his pants down around his thighs. He grabbed his penis. It was not hard and he was not stroking it. "C'mon." He was shaking it at me as if it was bait on a fishing line. "You gotta hold up your end of the bargain."

Images of people were flashing in my mind. I thought of my parents, the kids at school, Jim, Stephen and Frank, and even Vicky. I knew what they would think if they could see me now, I was glad they were not there. I had nobody I could call, and, even if there had been, I could not have called them. The situation was too embarrassing.

There was no getting around it. I was a drunken slut. Instead of being paid for sex as a whore might be, worse yet, I was giving it away free with no emotional attachments to get myself out of a jam. Unfortunately, I had gotten myself into this situation and it was time I got myself out. I vowed I would never put myself in this type of situation again.

I lay on my belly on the truck seat, putting my head between his legs. He was dank and I gagged, but he did not want to hear it. "Go ahead, suck it. I am not doing all the work here." He pressed my head down from between the steering wheel columns, and as I sank my lips around his dick, he started the truck. Well, at least he was good on his word.

The forty-five-minute ride was spent skull fucking. He did my mouth while he fucked with my mind. He told me that I should not thumb and take rides from strangers. He wanted to know if my parents had warned me about people picking me up and raping me.

Then he laughed. "But we had a deal didn't we? You begged to suck my cock. You wanted it. No, that is not actually true, you wanted Jerry's penis. Hah, I bet you are thinking about Jerry's cock right now, aren't you? I bet he and Colleen went to her house after the bar and Jerry made love to her, a nice girl, in a nice bed, nothing but the best for her. You are getting what you deserve too, aren't you now?"

He was getting himself excited talking this way. I just wanted to be home in my own bed, warm and safe. I did not hate him for giving me this ultimatum, but I hated myself for being a jackass, getting drunk, and not being able to come up with a better alternative than his proposition. I had no business in that bar at my age, and in fact, I knew I deserved what I was getting, but it did not make it any better. At least he had not been a total jerk. He was bringing me home, or at least I thought he was. My head was in his crotch the entire ride.

Fortunately, true to his word, when we got to the place where he had picked me up, Ed pulled at my shirt and let me up from underneath the steering wheel. I wanted to get out right there but Ed said, "Where do you live? I will drop you off."

"Not far from here, about four houses on the left," I replied, twisting my neck and pointing down the street; my back hurt, my neck was sore. My jaw was stiff and my head ached. It was still dark when I pointed out the driveway. He was driving slowly and there was no traffic behind us. "See, there, it is the big white farmhouse with the barn in the back. Park on the street, a little bit beyond the house, and I will walk back." The driveway had two entrances with a semi-circle surrounding the doghouse and some plants.

He pulled right into the driveway next to the house and left the truck and lights running. "Thanks for the ride," I said quickly as I put my hand on the door. He was going to wake everyone up. As I tried to pull the door handle to get out, he grasped my arm tightly, not letting me out.

"Oh no, no, no. You are not done yet. We had a bargain."

I tried to resist, telling him this was not cool, but he grabbed a handful of my hair and pulled my head toward his cock. "You owe me, cock-teaser. I still got an hour to drive home, and I need something to think about," he said as he held my hair and head firm, pushing my head down until I gagged. He let me up a bit to catch my breath, and then he did it again, pumping me up and down for about thirty seconds until he ejaculated.

"Don't spit it out until I pull out of the driveway, you fucking whore. Next time, you should think seriously about how you are going to get home before you get so damned drunk."

He was zipping up as I was opening the passenger door. I spit out his come on the driveway and turned around to head toward the door. I would not look back at him. My plan was to forget him by the time I woke up.

Then I saw Frank standing in the doorway with his loaded gun. I hung my head in shame. I was sure he had witnessed the whole event. He shook his head and smiled at me. "I see you been busy as usual. How is the drunken whore of East Granby today? You know the other day I said I thought I would give you a few weeks to become organized, get your act together, and find a place to live, but I think it is time you make plans to move on out tomorrow unless you can get yourself sober. We do not want any riff raff like you, he-ah." He meant *here*, but his Maine accent was heavy when he got mad.

"Okay." What more could I say as he stepped back and used his arm to gesture at me to come inside.

I had overstayed my welcome again. I was ready to move on. I just did not know where I was going or how I was going to get there. If suicide or alcohol and drugs were not the answer, what was? I knew if I was going to go home to my parent's house, I had to be sober and that would require me to pick up the phone and call AA. I knew if I was going to stay here, I had to do the same thing. I was out of choices. I had burned all my bridges. I needed to change my path.

Chapter Two

The Beginning (1965)

How does a middle-class white girl with a nice family, who grew up in a nice neighborhood, end up in an alcoholic rehabilitation center and in AA with the dregs of society at age fifteen and a half?

That is the question on some people's minds then and now. I am not sure even after thirty years that I have an answer. There is no one to blame but me. Someone exposed to the same factors may have chosen a different path. I take the blame for the paths I took and the choices I made.

What I do know is that if I had continued down certain roads, I would be dead now. Fortunately, eventually I was able to learn to face my fears head on.

If I start at the beginning, it will be easier to sort through. My parents were newlyweds and in their first year of marriage when I was conceived. On Christmas Eve of 1964, Mom ended up in the hospital. She was experiencing premature labor pains. Bed rest and medication relaxed her, and by the next day, she went home. On the last day of March 1965, mom went into labor and brought me into the world.

It was only after several miserable failed nursing attempts did Mom realize that something was wrong. On April Fools' Day, after an emergency ride to Boston Children's Hospital, the doctor informed her that the roof of my mouth was missing. I had an absent or what they called a cleft palate. Instead of nurturing and comforting me, her breast milk was running out of my nose and down my face.

Prior to and following cleft palate surgery, the doctor instructed my parents to keep my hands out of my mouth. Evidently, it was challenging, so I wore a washable long sleeved "straight jacket" that kept my arms from bending. Putting me into baby bondage was a hard thing to do for my caregivers. It was not natural and did not seem right, but it was medically necessary.

Chapter Three

The First Years (1966-1968)

In 1966, Mom got pregnant again, but unfortunately, she lost the baby. She was living with her parents in Littleton, Massachusetts when I went into Boston Children's for my oral surgery. For several weeks prior to the surgery, she conditioned me to strangers and family wearing nurse uniforms to feed me. The hopes were that I would not cry when I went into the hospital if I were accustomed to strangers in uniforms. Because the ears, eyes, nose, and mouth are connected, crying would be bad.

Banned from the hospital for two weeks during my hospitalization, Mom worked at Kimball's, the local ice cream parlor. Dad was traveling from job site to job site for his work, and she needed to keep busy.

After my hospital release, Dad came back up north to collect Mom and me. We joined him back on the road, moving every six to eight weeks, living in trailers as he serviced commercial boilers. My mom must have been devastated after having her second miscarriage, and then inexplicably, she had another.

I certainly do not remember those times, but when I was two and a half, she got pregnant again. My parents ended up living in a small apartment in Windsor Locks, CT while they saved money for a house. The doctors had told my parents that they needed to settle down if they wanted to have kids. Moving around had been too stressful for Mom.

The earliest recollection I have of my life was when we were living in that apartment. I was on top of a bunk bed, having a pillow fight with a friend at a neighbor's house and my pregnant mom was in the kitchen chatting with her friend. Dad was not home and I remember her crying.

Chapter Four

The Siblings (1969)

We moved into our first house. While we lived in Enfield, Connecticut, Mom gave birth to my sister, and then a year later, my brother. Both pregnancies went well with the doctor's instructions for us to "settle down" seeming to have made a difference. We were a family living in a little ranch house that was in a development near the Scitico section of Enfield. I walked to kindergarten with the other neighborhood kids, and I made friends with some of them. Dad was home every night and Mom was a lot happier.

Then my father got a chance for a better job, and we moved from Enfield, Connecticut to Spring City, Pennsylvania. We moved to a much bigger house, with a large yard in a neighborhood that was not a tract development. On the downside, we were about six hundred miles away from family. That meant during the holidays we would travel, have company, or sometimes we would celebrate the day with the neighbors.

I made the transition to Spring City, Pennsylvania's first grade smoothly. I was good at English and spelling but my hearing sometimes gave me problems. I sat in the first few rows of all my classes so that I would not miss anything, and as a result, I often was the teacher's pet.

Chapter Five

Speech Lessons (1970)

In first grade, I began taking speech lessons. At first it was like being the kid that has to ride the little yellow bus to school—you know, the ones for the physically, emotionally, or mentally challenged. That is how I felt when the parent helpers showed up in Mrs. Harrow's class to collect me to take me to speech lessons. I was special but not in a good way.

While the other kids went to recess and burned off their energy, I went to speech therapy and learned how to say "Sammy the Snake" without lisping. I struggled with S, T, R, Th, and Z sounds because of my cleft palate situation. The doctors had warned my parents that I would need assistance to be able to enunciate and learn these sounds.

The first time I went, I read with an older man. He was nice enough but I felt uncomfortable sitting in the little converted closet-to-classroom space. The speech therapy room barely contained a big bulky steel desk and two student chairs. The dark paneling was ominous began to feel better about speech lessons as I learned new words and read material that did not have "See Spot run" in it. After a few weeks, I walked myself to speech therapy, although I found the long hallways intimidating, the slick marbled green tile reflecting the bright-white overhead lights illuminating the hall. As I began walking myself to speech class, I started feeling independent and grown-up.

The truth of the matter was I was not physically inclined and struggled with jumping rope and foursquare anyway. I did not miss recess at all, and instead I became an avid reader, choosing words and the love of a book over conversations. I liked Nancy Drew mysteries the best, but I read the Hardy Boys mysteries too.

Chapter Six

Excruciating Earaches (1971)

At home, things were good though Dad had to travel with this job more than he had when we lived in Enfield. We had an aboveground swimming pool and it was great fun to spend the summers out in our yard with each other and an occasional friend.

As it is often the case with cleft palate babies, I had ear-drainage problems and constant earaches. The pain was excruciating. When you have an earache like that, you can hear the blood pumping through your head, almost like the sound of the tide coming in at the shore—slosh, break, retreat, slosh, break, retreat. The rhythmic sound would be comforting if it did not hurt so much to hear. It required silent tears.

You want your eyes to pop out of your head to relieve the pressure. Everywhere around you, people are laughing and having fun. Their piercing, shrieking sounds cut through your head like a knife and all you want to do is yell SHUT UP, but you cannot even whisper that because it hurts too much to say or do anything.

I should have been inside in my bed, but I did not want to miss the fun my brother and sister were having. They were such little fish in the blue water. The tears rolled out of my eyes uncontrollably as I lay with my reddened and sore ears on the pool deck on my beach towel. Mom had put in some eardrops, and I was waiting for them to take effect, wishing I were normal. She had just banned me from the pool until something changed, and I was heartsick. Store-bought earplugs did not stay in, and even though I was careful, somehow my ears kept aching.

The doctor explained it this way. The Eustachian tube is a narrow one-and-a-half-inch channel connecting the middle ear with the nasopharynx, the upper throat area above the palate, in the back of the nose. It functions as a pressure-equalizing valve for the middle ear, normally filled with air. Every three minutes or so, the tube opens quickly to equalize the pressure within the ear canal. If it becomes blocked or if water fills the cavity, it can cause hearing impairment. If the water in the middle ear becomes infected, it causes pain.

His solution was to perform a Myringotomy. This is a surgery where an otolaryngologist (ear, nose, and throat doctor) makes a small incision in the tympanic membrane of the ear and then installs temporary tubes (typanostomy tubes) in the eardrum to allow for drainage.

After speaking with the doctor, Mom scheduled me for surgery. I had had too many infections. The fluid was not draining. The antibiotics were not working. I was missing school. With hearing and speech affected, my constant earaches were causing a strain on the family and affecting my ability to socialize.

I do not remember being afraid of the hospital or the doctor. It was the first surgery that I remembered going through but my mom had prepped me for the experience by explaining what would happen. I had no reservations. I wanted the pain to go away. The surgery was uneventful, and afterward I felt so much better. The pressure, the ringing, the sensitivity to sound, listening to people talk as if they were in a tin can, all that and the headaches were gone.

I was *normal* again. Unfortunately, normal was short-lived and the temporary tubes fell out as they do as children age. I found one of the tubes on the tub floor after a shower, and I knew instantly what it was, a bad omen. Ear infections would return and they did. I had several tube replacement surgeries during the time we lived in Pennsylvania. The tubes would last six months to a year if I was lucky.

During this time, I had to be extremely careful showering not to get water in my ears. Swimming was out of the question, and after a period, I stopped fighting my mom on that one. It was not worth the pain and aggravation of being sick, although I do remember one time, hanging out in my neighbors' pool and telling my friend Lisa that I could breathe out of my ears. She did not believe me until I went under water and blew bubbles out of my ears. The next day, I was in agony again. That might have been the last instance of me fighting with mom about swimming.

Chapter Seven

Sex Education (1972)

I learned a lot about life from our paperboy. He was a few years older than I was and occasionally, if we were playing out in the front yard, he would stop on his bike and talk to us kids for a bit. My sister ate some glass from a busted television that was in front of our house because he told her she would just poop it out.

Stevie told us that my parents had fucked. I did not know what the word meant, but I knew it was a forbidden dirty word. I did not believe him at first and tried to make him take it back until he explained to me how things worked with penises and pussies. I was fascinated when he told me all the different words for it: fucking, fornicating, making love, getting busy, humping, fourth base, etc. I already knew that I loved words, but I discovered that I loved words about sex even more.

One time I snuck into my parents' room to see whatever I could, but a sheet covered them and they caught me staring between the closet doors. Dad boarded up the secret passageway in the closet before the weekend's end.

Chapter Eight

Outside Influences (1973)

Mom allowed me to walk to the bus stop and around the neighborhood on my own provided she knew where I was. One of the neighbors had an old-fashioned farmhouse that had three sets of stairs and arborvitae all along their stockade fence. Not only did they have the main house. They had a three-car garage and a workshop too. The garage had been servants' quarters in years past.

In the middle of their yard, they had an enormous weeping willow; the branches stretched almost the width of my house. I remember raking leaves with my friend and her mother, and then jumping in the piles. She had a radio plugged in the workshop, and the music was blasting across the yard.

We were having so much fun and then news came on that Jim Croce had died. It was September 20, 1973, and my friend's mom was devastated and went into the house, crying. I loved Jim's songs too, especially "Operator," "Time in a Bottle," and "Bad, Bad Leroy Brown." I took solace underneath the willow as I wept. It provided a safe haven, allowing me to deal with demons I did not yet understand.

Back then, my mom confided in me more than she probably should have, but I was too little to understand. Her marriage was lonely because Dad traveled frequently. Mom and I were friends and then almost overnight we became enemies. I was afraid my parents might divorce, and my dad and I were close too. I could not imagine what it might be like without our family together; I did not know anybody who was divorced.

One of the books I was fascinated with was the *Joy of Sex*. I had found it under my parents' bed, and it opened my eyes to a completely new world. I took it out to our tree house and shared it with the rest of the neighborhood kids. It was quite the popular afternoon discussion spot for a few days until my mother became curious as to why all the kids were in our playhouse, and found me in the clubhouse sharing the book.

I guess I must have been masturbating frequently; at least, that is what my mom says the doctor told her was happening when she took me in order to see him. My vulva swollen, he diagnosed me as having a vaginal infection and gave her a prescription.

Chapter Nine

The Color Purple (1974)

I remember lying on the bathroom counter. We had a full counter with big mirror over it, but I did not want to look in the mirror because I could see myself naked. The bathroom door was open slightly and my brother and sister were peeking in. I had no pants on, but my shirt covered my upper body.

My dad was squeezing purple medicine into my bum with an applicator. It was cold and I was physically and mentally uncomfortable. When he saw the kids, a term we used to refer to my brother and sister, peeking into the bathroom, he yelled at them that this was my private business, and he shut the door.

The purple medicine stained my ass and my underwear. Our gray porcelain tub had a purple ring around it that would not come off after I took the required bath. I do not know how long I had to take the medication; maybe it was a couple of days or a week or two, but it left an impression on me. My dad was administering the medicine because, apparently, I had told my mother to butt-out. I was discovering the differences of boys and girls, and I think I had a crush on my dad but the situation was embarrassing and not comfortable for either of us.

Mom was working nights at the local psych ward, working with the mentally challenged. I remember them fighting because my dad did not want her to work, but she was stir-crazy at home with us kids. We did not need the money, but she needed her sanity. Ironic that she could find it in a psych ward, but that was what happened.

After the application, I sat in the tub for twenty minutes, feeling and looking like a prune. The tub turns color from the purple medicine, and

I am embarrassed. My sister wants to know why the tub has stains. My brother tells her it is the medicine from my butt.

One day the neighborhood children and I are standing behind the neighbor's camper, and I tell them I have a purple butt. They do not believe me, so I drop my pants and show them. I might have turned the neighbor's kid gay for all I know. I was older than the rest of them and should have known better, but I could not keep my privates, private.

Dimetapp is a purple grape flavored medicine that reduces congestion. I begin taking it for my ears and sinuses. It tastes sticky sweet, and at first, I do not mind taking it but it seems like I am on it all the time and I start crying every time my mother says I need to take it. I do not like the color purple anymore, but I really cannot tell you why, I just do not.

Not long after that, I remember my brother's hands tied to his bed so he would not suck his thumbs. My mom was worried about him having an overbite and the doctor told her to add nasty tasting stuff to his nails so he would not suck them, but it did not stop him. Then the doctor suggested she keep my brother's hands away from his mouth by tying his hands to the rails.

I was so angry with Mom for tying him up. I thought it was wrong to restrain him. She told me it was doctor's orders. Maybe unconsciously I was sympathetically remembering my earlier years when I myself was in baby bondage. I do not know, but I remember being angry enough to scream, yell, slam the door to my room when she would not relent. I cried myself to sleep. The world was unfair.

When Nixon resigned, my parents and I watched it on television. They thought it would be one of those memorable moments in life. The kind of event that you would always remember exactly where you were and what you were doing at that moment. It was 1974, and although I did not understand Watergate, I knew that the president of the United States had been caught doing something he should not have been doing. I knew little about politics, but I vowed that when I got older, I would learn a little about it and vote; and if I ever did anything wrong, I would not be caught.

Chapter Ten

Boys vs. Girl (1975)

At age ten, I found out that one of my female friends, Tina, urinated while standing up. The school called her mother who was beside herself because her daughter wanted to be a boy.

I did not think that there was anything wrong with Tina wanting to stand while peeing, so I went over to her house to talk to her about it.

She was mad at me at first, and wanted to know how I had heard. I told her I had heard Janine's mom talking on the telephone when I was over there. She apparently had talked to Tina's mom first, and now she was blabbing it to the rest of the moms in the neighborhood.

"Look, I am sorry your mom went blabbing and then Janine's mom went blabbing, but do not pay attention to them. Lock the door and pee standing up if you want, who cares?" I asked her, "Do you want be a boy?" I sometimes wished I had been born a boy; they seemed to have an easier go of things in some ways, with little responsibility for anything but work.

"I do not know if I wish I was a boy, but I feel like I should pee standing up. Sitting is gross. That is all."

"Well, you do wear boy-looking clothes. I have never seen you in a skirt. Maybe you are gay?" I said.

"I do not know if I am gay. I don't even know what sex is, really. I am not attracted to anyone. I am only in fourth grade, and I wish everyone would leave me alone."

I was not worldly or anything, but I had a fierce drive for independence. "Do what you want. If you are gay, you can make your own choice when you move out; and if you ever want to become a boy, I hear you can do that with an operation." She says she has never been in a hospital except for the time that she was born. I tell her going through an operation is no big deal. I've done it several times and I tell her she'll be fine. I sense that she knows someday she will go down that route.

I can feel her pain. Her decision to stand up (pardon the pun) and make a conscious choice should have been supported by her teachers, her family, and those that loved her, but instead it was being debated by the entire neighborhood, and now she was embarrassed and humiliated. I knew what it was to feel different. I had gotten a taste of it with my speech lessons, and it was a lonely place.

Lisa, my next-door neighbor, was having trouble at home. Her dad was a drunk and beat up her mom. The cops came and took him away, and her mom was popping prescription pills to keep from killing herself. Her older brother came by and took her for a ride on his motorcycle. Mom would not let me go, but if she had, I would have tried to convince him to take me as far away from home as possible. Growing up sucked; I could see how life could get complicated.

Chapter Eleven

Moving North (1976)

The year that I was eleven, we went to see the Liberty Bell for our class trip in 1976. Philadelphia exhibited power as the official site for celebrating the Bicentennial. It was amazing how far we had come from 1776 when America had issued the Declaration of Independence and pulled away from England. In the two hundred years since then, the US had abolished slavery and women could vote. Public education and public utilities were common but people disagreed on occasion. I saw some black and some white boys fighting and our teacher made us get back on the bus. She might have been afraid of a riot.

One evening, Mom paid me a dollar to shut up and stop singing. She said she wanted to hear herself think. I am not sure how that happens, but I do remember the house smelled like burned fish and the realtor was on her way to the house to show the place. Frantically, Mom was trying to clean up the kitchen and remove the fish smell, and it was not working. She wanted the house to sell right away so that we could move home.

Dad had gotten a new job, and we were planning to move back to New England. I did not want to stay and I did not want to move. I was not close to anyone in particular but I was afraid of change.

One of the biographies of people I could relate to was Helen Keller's. Her life story was amazing. She ended up as an advocate for deaf, dumb, and blind people rather than living as a victim, although she had handicaps that made her life difficult.

I wanted to be like her some day. I loved the fact that she questioned everything and did not let her situation get in her way of living. She pushed her own limits and demanded that people listen to her. As a result, she changed life for so many people. In fact, she changed how people felt as a society about those that could not hear or speak. Her work allowed people to see that these characteristics did not always indicate mental retardation.

Another female that I admired was Anne Frank. Persecuted because of her family's religion, Anne lived several years in an annex or attic, hiding from the Nazis because of her Jewish heritage. It did not seem fair to me that God allowed discrimination. I was not yet wise enough to understand that the laws of man trumped God's wishes.

I related to the thirteen-year-old Anne's words.

"And finally I twist my heart round again, so that the bad is on the outside and the good is on the inside, and keep on trying to find a way of becoming what I would so like to be, and could be, if there were not any other people living in the world."—Anne Frank

I started questioning society, authority, and God. I wanted to be me, not someone discriminated against or cast aside because of differences. What was so bad about being Jewish? I had friends that were Jewish and they seemed pretty much like me except they had some different customs about what they ate and the day they worshipped. I did not understand how the world could have so many religions and belief systems that differed, yet each of them claimed to be "the one."

That summer after we moved, I made friends with some of the neighborhood kids and was excited to be in sixth grade. I would be going to the middle school while my siblings would be going to the elementary school. There were a couple of people in my grade in my neighborhood, so at least I knew a few people. I would not be alone.

By the end of my first day in my new school, I hated the fact that we had moved. I hated my parents for making us move. I hated the new school system. I hated the kids; some had been rude. Most of them had been in the same school system since they were in kindergarten, and I clearly did not fit in.

I was the new kid, and my name, K. C., stood out like a sore thumb. It stood for Karen Charlotte, and no, not of the *Charlotte Web* story. My parents' had named me after my godmother Karen, my mom's best friend from college; and they had picked out the name Charlotte because my dad wanted Sheila, my mom's name, and Charlotte sounded similar.

I thought Charlotte was better than Karen was, but both names were too formal for me. The names sounded like they would belong to somebody who was smart. That was not me. I was more of a smart-ass. I preferred just the single letter K, but some people could not handle that, and rather than confuse them, I told them it was Kay.

Unfortunately, when Mom registered me she gave the new school my nickname. Soon, everyone in the school was calling me K. C. instead of Kay. Several classmates told me that K. C. at the bat was okay, but KC and the Sunshine band was queer. On the other hand, maybe it stood for Casey Kasem, the disc jockey. What was I named after, the bat, the band, or the DJ?

I felt inadequate, lonely, and I hated my nickname even more than my real name. I had been afraid to move to the middle school in Pennsylvania, which is what I would have had to do if we had stayed. This was no better, and in some ways, much worse. I had not imagined that people would be so mean. I felt the need to be better than I was and I started embellishing things I told my classmates. What I was was not good enough and lying seemed easier than telling the truth.

Some of the girls were starting to wear make-up and had breasts. I had no breasts and even after begging her, my mom would not get me a padded bra. I was embarrassed to have my nipples stick out. The boys would notice when I got cold, and I could hear them whispering THOs (Titty Hard-Ons) under their breath.

I was even more embarrassed that Mr. Cleaver, our math teacher, seemed to like to sit at his desk and stare at the other girls' chests and me. I could see his hand moving under his desk, rubbing his balls and dick. It might have had something to do with my inability to concentrate on the problems. I was already behind in math but this new situation did not help matters. Instead of asking him for help, I would ask the other students for answers just to get by. I was not going to be a math genius.

I liked creativity and the only class I enjoyed being in was Mrs. Warren's English class. She was cool, enthusiastic, and encouraged the class to dream. I liked her and started making a few friends in her class.

I played my clarinet in the school band but was not very good with my tone. The reed was always dry or too wet. My foot would go up and down but it had nothing to do with the rhythm of the band. Not synchronized with the rest of the band, sometimes I would play at the wrong times. That would immediately bring the wrath of the conductor and the laughter of my fellow band members. Embarrassed, I would hang my head. I could not do so many things. It seemed useless to try.

I hated the clarinet. I did not want to play it but my doctor told my mom I had to play it to keep my palate soft. That way I could enunciate and be understood when I spoke. I had learned to say my S's, T's, A's, and Th's, but without playing the clarinet, my palate would harden, making it difficult for me to speak. I would have to play the clarinet for the rest of my life, and that just seemed to be too long. I started blowing off the band, hanging out in the parking lot or in the auditorium, sneaking smokes.

I had started smoking on a dare, and it just seemed like a cool thing to do. My parents had found my cigarettes and thrown them away countless times, but I bought more. I also thought drinking was something somewhat cool to do. I snuck alcohol here and there when I thought I could get away with it.

The first time I kissed a boy was at Susan's house. We were playing Spin the Bottle in the basement and each of us had to go in the closet for five minutes. By the end of the night, I had gone from first base to third with several different boys in the room. It had been an exciting night.

Before the next Spin the Bottle party, my mother had a discussion with me about sex education. By that point, Susan had already had an abortion. I knew what was up with sex. I received my education from the Pennsylvania paperboy and the *Joy of Sex* three years prior.

I probably could have taught her a thing or two if she had asked me. It was somewhat comical to me. Parents must live in a vacuum, I thought to myself. I intended on telling my kids about sex around first grade so that they would not have to hear about it from the paperboy.

I also was not going to lie to them about Santa Claus. I had been the laughing stock of my class the year prior when in fifth grade I was the only one, by a show of hands, that still believed in him. I was not going to lie to my kids no matter how bad the truth was. I hated lying. My parents had done enough of it. I was sure they had lied about God too.

My ears gave me problems again that year. Before we had moved from Pennsylvania, I had gone in for one more surgery. This time, the surgical procedure had left me with semi-permanent tubes that would not fall out on their own. Unfortunately, the tubes had ripped the eardrums, and my hearing loss was hovering around 80 percent. I learned to read lips, facial expressions and body language but my eyes were starting to give me problems around that time too. I started to wear glasses.

Along with the nervousness of being in a new school, the school system was testing the open-classroom concept. With no walls between classrooms, I found it difficult to concentrate and was easily distracted.

My hearing, with plastic reconstructive surgery on the eardrums, would greatly improve. Although I would still have a 10 percent hearing loss after surgery, it would be better than where I was at that moment. It was a no-brainer; during winter recess, the surgery was scheduled.

Right before surgery, I caught a cold. They postponed the surgery because I was running a fever and had upper respiratory congestion. I had been in and out of hospitals all my life and going in for surgery never bothered me, but the rescheduling did upset me. I had psyched myself up and was terribly disappointed. I screamed, punched the wall, and then cried when my mom told me the news over the telephone. It was not that I was looking forward to the surgery so much, though I was because I wanted to hear again, it was more that I had a hard time with change once I made my mind up on something.

When the cold was gone, Mom booked me for surgery again. With this operation, the nursing staff would shave my head around my ears so that the surgeon could slice behind my ear, open up the cavity, and get in there to perform the plastic surgery on my eardrum. With the tubes, they had just gone in through the ear canal but this was major surgery.

When I came around after the anesthesia wore off, I had an enormous white bandage wrapped around my head. I looked like one of those characters in a horror film, a partially unwrapped bloody mummy.

I felt awkward and self-conscious knowing the stitches and the bare patches where they had shaved off my hair behind my ears showed. The worst part was that I could not wash my hair for two weeks. It was horrible, particularly because I had to go back to school after a few days. I was embarrassed that my hair stank, and no matter how I tried to get it out, the powder caked against my greasy hair. It was the only time in my life where I begged my mother to let me stay home from school. I could not stand the smell of myself, and doubted that anyone else could either.

Out of all the comforts, the one I appreciate more than any other is the ability to take a shower with hot water and soap and not worry about getting water in my ears. A few days after surgery, all I wanted was to feel the water beating on my head, taking away the itch and smell.

Honestly, it could not have been a better ending to my sixth grade year. I was K. C., the new girl with stinky hair, freckles, double teeth, hairy arms, and no breasts from Pennsylvania. My favorite song at the time was "Constantinople, C-O-N-S-T-A-N-I-P-O-L-E." The song my grandfather had taught me came in handy one time in my sixth-grade social studies class when the teacher asked about the imperial capital of the Roman

Empire. In the middle Ages in Europe, Constantinople was the largest and wealthiest city. Later, the city was renamed Istanbul, but the song stuck in my head, and probably in the minds of my classmates too.

That was a memorable class because that was also the class that I broke my best friend's finger. Jenny and I had been playing football with an eraser and I had overshot the goal. When she went to snag it off the carpet, I got out of my chair and stepped on her hand. I thought she was kidding when she told me I broke her finger, but she was not. When I put my foot down on her hand against the carpeting, I broke her finger. Instead of doing the appropriate thing, which would have been to get her help, I laughed.

Laughing was not what I intended to do, it was not what I wanted to do, but it was the only thing I could do. I did not know what else to do. I was not able to control my emotions, which made it even worse. Fortunately, Jenny forgave me for my lack of social graces, and we remained best friends throughout the rest of my years in East Granby. She was a good friend, and I was lucky to have her.

Chapter Twelve

Adolescent Turmoil (1977)

At twelve, I fought with my parents and ran away to Tim and Jenny's house. Tim was away at the time, and Jenny was busy with school. Their mom, Norma, was kind to me and told me that I could stay after she called my parents to let them know where I was. Then, after a few days, she suggested it was time for me to make up with my parents and go home.

Chapter Thirteen

Babysitting (1978)

Thirteen is an unlucky number, and it was the traumatic year for me; I mean, it was a real life-changer. For starters, I fell in love for the first time. Tim was Jenny's older brother. I could see him in school if I snuck into the high school area, as he was a few grades ahead of me and the high school and middle school were connected. Sometimes, we would make out in the halls, and sometimes he would sneak into the middle school and meet me at my locker.

Tim would come to my house in the afternoons when my parents were working while I was supposed to be taking care of my brother and sister. He had beautiful brown eyes that would make me melt when I looked into them. His dirty blond hair felt soft on my face. He was gentle and kind when he kissed me, and he told me he did not care if I did not have breasts yet. He made my nipples erect with his touch, and I did something similar when I touched him.

Tim and I drank beers and ate popcorn after school. Sometimes we would get high, sharing a joint with my little brother and sister. I was thirteen, and that would have made my brother nine and my sister ten. They were still in grade school. They knew he and I spent a lot of time in my bedroom but Tim and I kept the door shut. I told them he was helping me with my homework.

One time, I was upstairs in my room with the door closed. When I finally came out, it was at the split second that my brother opened the front door, and Randy, a neighbor, kicked a soccer ball into the house. He had hit it high and my brother was afraid it was going to smash the winter storm window, so he opened the door. The ball came careening into the front hall and smashed into the hanging chandelier. Shattered glass exploded on the foyer, with pieces making it into the neighboring living room carpet.

There was no reasonable excuse as to how that happened. I was in trouble because I had been in charge. I should have been paying attention; if I had been, the ball should have never come toward the house. As usual, my brother and sister enabled me by not saying anything about Tim being there to my parents. It did not matter. They grounded me.

Another time, Tim thought it would be funny if he put the roast we were supposed to be having for dinner on my mother's velvet dining room chair. We got hot and heavy when I started begging him to tell me where the roast was and he thought it was fun teasing me. An hour later, my mother's chair was ruined, and again I had no reasonable explanation.

My love life was tumultuous because of Tim's drinking and drug use. He got into trouble and would steal cars and drive drunk. I drank with him when I could but it was rare that I could leave the house; I had responsibilities taking care of my siblings and my parents were strict.

Unfortunately, when he started drinking, he got sloppy; and when he got drunk, he became stubborn and dangerous. From my perspective, it was easy to see how his life got out of control when he drank. He clearly had a problem with alcohol and drugs but he refused to admit it.

I was afraid he would get in a car wreck or hurt somebody. We fought over his keys many times. I would beg him for his keys so that he would not drive, and he would say that he was fine. I would tell him he was not fine. Then sometimes we would physically struggle, or I would try to outsmart him by kissing him, trying to work my hands in his pockets to attempt to get to his keys. Most of the time, he would just get in his car and drive off and I would cry. He was bigger than I was, and I was afraid that if I pushed him too far he would get mad at me and drive with road rage really hurting himself or someone else.

I loved him when he was sober and hated him for how he made me feel when he was drinking. Most of the time, it felt like I cared more about him than he did. I hated feeling helpless. I hated his birth parents for giving him up.

Jenny and Tim were both adopted but from different families. Their adoptive parents loved them and did whatever they could for them, but it did not take away the sense of abandonment that they both harbored on some level. Jenny seemed to have a better time of it than

Tim did, for some reason. He was always getting into trouble in and out of school. He lacked motivation and his partying was more important. Jenny worked hard at her grades, was social, and seemed to be perfect for everything.

I wondered what it would be like to not know your real parents. I hated my parents for moving to the stupid state of Connecticut. I hated that I had to babysit my brother and sister and was not allowed to participate in after school activities. I hated how I felt when Tim left. I hated worrying about things I could not control. Sometimes I wished I could not feel at all.

One morning, at about 7:10 a.m., the phone rang. I knew it was about my grandmother. I had seen a vision of her ghost in my mind right before the phone rang. I knew she was dead and my mother's wails from the kitchen just confirmed it. I hated knowing things before other people said them. It was creepy, but sometimes it happened to me. I never knew if it was déjà vu or vuja de, but it was definitely a weird feeling.

Mom was a Girl Scout leader, and that day happened to be the last day of school before summer vacation. We were supposed to be going to the local amusement park for some fun. Our day at the park was cancelled, I knew it as soon as I heard mom sobbing.

When I got to school and told my friends about the situation with my grandmother's passing, one of my best friends, Debbie, tried to console me. I could see her eyes were puffy like she had been crying all night. She said she was sorry about my grandmother, but then she said she needed to talk to me about something just as bad.

We were in the library when she told me her father had given her some kind of horse potion that made her psycho and all woozy. Then she told me her brother and father had fucked her the night before while they were drunk.

I was in seventh grade. My grandmother had died the night before. My Girl Scout troop outing that I had been looking forward to for weeks and was to be this afternoon was also now canceled. To top it off, one of my best friends said her father and brother raped her. It was too much for me to handle in one day.

My hands sweat as the rage began to boil inside of me. It was just wrong. The librarian yelled at us for talking too loud, and I stood up in my chair and calmly said, "Shut the fuck up! You have no idea what we are talking about, and it is a lot more important than being fucking quiet in this fucking library." I sat back down waiting for her to scream at me. I almost wanted her to because if she did I was ready to release the rage.

How could she be so oblivious to life? Okay, *everybody whispers,* "Her father and brother raped Debbie last night. My grandmother died last night. Our Girl Scout troop trip is cancelled because of my family's problems and I feel guilty. There. Does that make it acceptable now?"

She sensed that I was on the edge, and instead of calling the principal to command discipline, she walked away in a huff. If she had responded, other teachers would have come to her aid in a second. I was not sure how much damage I could have done, but I had a hunch I could put the school in lock-down if I tried. I was beyond aggravated.

Debbie and I continued talking, more quietly this time. She asked me to go to court with her. She wanted to press charges and become an emancipated teen. She wanted to get the hell out of her father's house. I did not know her brother or her father, but I was ready to fight on her behalf. What had happened to her was wrong from every angle. It was obvious she had been crying. Her face was puffy and red but I did not see any marks on her.

"You should go to the doctor to be tested. You will need proof of intercourse. I hope you did not take a shower this morning. Did you tell your mother?"

"My mother takes sleeping pills. She does not hear a thing all night. She has no idea how sick my father is. I am afraid he might do this to my little sister. I tried to tell her I was afraid of him before but she would not listen. I cannot talk to her. I took a shower this morning. Of course I did. I was not going to come to school with their filthy stench on me. I scrubbed myself so hard but I still feel disgusting."

I left the library, storming up the hall. I had this tremendous amount of energy inside that needed letting out. I went into the cafeteria, picked up a chair, and threw it. There were two students in there and they barely looked up. I was not mad at them and realized I was not going to get the release I needed there. I didn't want an audience. I wanted to be alone. I was afraid I might hurt somebody.

I walked out of the cafeteria and entered into the ladies' room next door. I started slamming the stall door. It felt good, so I slammed it again. That felt better and I slammed it again. One of the hinges gave way, and the door tipped, held only by the top hinge. I kicked it as hard as I could into the cement wall and the door bounced off the wall and onto the floor, the remaining hinge landing on my foot.

That hurt and I slammed my fist into the cement wall. Finally, it was enough hurt to bring the tears that I had been holding back all morning to the front of my eyes. Through the onslaught of tears, I punched the cement wall again.

I let the tears flow, snot running out of my nose. I did not care. I did not care. I did not care. I did care. I cared a lot. I cared too damn much. Everything hurt. I did not want to care. I did not want to feel anything anymore.

The principal knocked on the door and walked into the restroom. The librarian must have told him I was acting crazy.

"Stop what you are doing right now, K. C. You are defacing school property and I will call the police if you do not stop."

I had already stopped but I glared at him anyway.

"Calm down and walk with me to the office. I want to hear what is going on with you". I was holding my right hand in the crook of my left arm. It was numb, though my shoulder ached.

We walked down the hall to his office and he told me to sit in the chair and tell him what was going on. I told him everything and he said he was going to call my mother, but I do not think he ever did.

I spent the rest of the day in the office chair outside his office. I think he realized my parents had enough on their plate with me, and that the day's events would have caused even normal people to stress out. The school let out early and I went home on the bus. I left Debbie to her own defenses; I could not deal with her pain too.

The next afternoon, we drove to my grandparents' house. My grandmother's cardiologist had given her a clean bill of health the afternoon of her death. Then, while watching a Red Sox game at around 11:30pm she had a heart attack and died. Being dead does not scare me; once you are dead, you are dead. However, the "how you die" part does scare me sometimes. Out of all the ways people can die, dying suddenly with those you love nearby is not a bad way to go. When we got to my grandmother's house, some of the family was there. My older cousins, recently adopted into the family by my aunt's marriage to their father, were also there. Their mom had committed suicide and it had messed the three of them up.

I thought my new cousins were cool and I was glad I was no longer the oldest grandchild. There is a lot of responsibility in that title, particularly when the rest of the kids are a bit younger.

When my cousin suggested we take in a movie at the drive-in, allowing our parents to grieve for their mom, everyone seemed to think it was a good idea. I was happy about it, especially when we stopped at the package store.

Since it was my first "adult" event, my cousins and friends chipped in and bought me my own bottle. I opted for blackberry brandy and that was the beginning of me choosing to use alcohol to drown out the pain.

I could not tell you what the movie was about, but I know I laughed and then I cried and then I puked, and then I laughed again as I downed the last of the bottle. I had found something, something that made me feel nothing. Feeling nothing was better than feeling something.

Rehashing the last twenty-four hours' events made me want to scream. Thinking of my mother's cries, my friend's cries, my boyfriend's cries—I just wanted to drown all that out, and the booze helped for a little while.

That night, I managed to sneak back into my grandmother's house after my parents had gone to sleep. Half the night, I slept with my head out the window; the other half I slept on the bed, with my foot on the floor because the room was spinning. It was only through sheer will that I managed not to vomit the next morning when I smelled the food cooking in the kitchen.

I wanted out of the house and took a walk as soon as I could. The fresh air was too much. I reached for a cigarette and re-played the evening's events in my head. I had vomited and then continued drinking afterward—was that normal? I did not know and I did not care. I thought that I would have to learn how to drink and not be sick. Then I could coast through life not feeling anything. I went up to the cabin that had been the home of one of my mother's friends. The home, abandoned since Mr. Masters died, was desolate and some kids had broken a few of the windows. I sat behind the house and smoked a joint and another cigarette. If I was going to start drinking, I was going to have to find a way to make more money.

When my oldest cousin came to live with us a few months later, she was trying to get her life in order but living in our house was no picnic. My folks were strict, religion and God's way was always the deciding factor, and us kids? Well, we were wild. My parents were losing control, and the harder they tried to rein us in the more stubborn we became in our defiance.

In a few months' time, I was getting high most days and drunk most nights. I was popping reds and yellows (uppers or speed), smoking hash, and sneaking out of the house after my parents went to sleep. As long as I was working, they let me come and go as I pleased, but when I was home, they expected me in bed early. I had a key to the house and when I was not working, sometimes I lied about working so I could stay out.

Chapter Fourteen

Television Gone Bye-bye (1979)

That was the summer our family started fighting over the television. My parents got sick of the constant bickering, and so they decided to limit our television watching, prohibiting it in the afternoons. That put a severe cramp in our afternoons of getting high and watching soap operas, so we would sneak it. It did not take long for Mom and Dad to find out that we were sneaking it.

To stop us, Dad cut the television cord off. That way, he could re-attach it if they permitted us to watch television at night and during the day, when they were not home, they could keep us from watching it.

That went on for a few weeks until one day Dad got home early from work and realized the television was hot. He looked behind it, and there he discovered that we, actually my brother upon my direction, had cut off the wire to the lamp and attached it to the television. That was the end of television in our house. It went to the dump. My parents were very upset that I allowed my brother to do this. We could have set the house on fire or worse, my brother could have been electrocuted. I remember being cavalier about the episode. In my mind, it was just another incidence of our parents saying no.

We were so bored for the next few weeks. I am sure we drove my parent's nuts. They wanted us to do something with ourselves instead of arguing over what programs we were going to watch. It was a reasonable request, but we were so far gone already that it just drove the wedge between us further. The kids at school could not believe our parents had thrown away our television. Even some of the teachers thought it was extreme.

I did not care. I watched television when I babysat. At home, I tried to learn the guitar. My brother started playing piano, and my sister started playing the flute. My father had wanted to be a conductor in his college years and had forgone his passion for something more practical that would earn him a steady living, engineering. Ever since he was a kid, he had always loved the woodwind instruments, and he began sharing his musical talents with our family.

To this day, when I hear the sound of a clarinet rift I think of my dad playing music in the family room. Sitting with his back erect and his feet spread just beyond the rungs of his chair, his right foot would tap the beat, and he would breathe in and out deeply. All the while, his fingers moved with precision as he carefully played the notes and measured his breaths to the time of the music.

When he hit the low notes, his cheeks got puffy with air. When he hit the high notes, his cheeks sucked in and his eyebrows rose. I loved to watch him play because you could tell it made him happy. Most of the time, Dad was fixing something one of us had broken; maintaining something that needed maintenance; working on the driveway, the lawn, the garden, the car; or going to work. Sometimes, he would read or play tennis, golf, or hockey; but when he was playing his clarinet, he was at peace.

Taking care of my brother and sister was starting to eat into my ability to make more money and party. I was not at peace. My parents did not pay as well as some of my other customers and I figured out that if I stopped watching my siblings, I could make more money.

My mom wanted to keep her job and have a life outside of the home, but if I stopped watching the kids, they could not afford to have someone else come in. Mom would have to stay home. I did not care. I was done with playing mommy to my brother and sister.

Mom got angry and told me I would have to pay rent if I stopped watching my siblings and I told her that I would gladly pay rent. I made up some flyers, and when I got the first job, I made sure I did it well. Soon, my schedule was full; I was working thirty to forty hours weekly cleaning houses and babysitting. I was so busy that if I got sick, my customers would have to wait a week to see me again because I had no spare time to accommodate them.

I was making around three hundred dollars a week and paying my mom $50 a month in rent for room and board. It worked out nicely for me, considering I was in seventh grade and did not have that many expenses. I chose to buy one pair of pants for that school year, and I wore them every day. Most of the rest of my money went to booze and drugs. My parents had no idea that I was drinking and drugging daily. They were oblivious because there were no indications. On the outside, things looked okay and I worked hard to sustain that image.

Chapter Fifteen

Emergency Room Visit (January 1979)

It was not long after that I ended up in the emergency ward; it was in the middle of January in the eighth grade.

I was lying on the carpet in my social studies class in a fetal position. My teacher had demanded that I get up off the floor and go to the office. The nurse was not at our school that day, so the principal looked me over. He did not know whether to believe me or not, but I was hunched over in his office chair. I did not want him to bother my mom at work because things were still prickly between us. The principal called her anyway and told her she needed to come get me.

She brought me home and told me I probably would be getting my period any day now. I had heard it all before. The cramping had started in sixth grade, right around the end of the school year when my tits started growing. I was tired of all this waiting.

Every month I would get a stomachache but nothing would happen. The other girls in my class were getting their periods; I knew because I heard them talking about needing tampons in the bathroom. Waiting for my "friend" was killing me.

Actually, literally, it was killing me, but we did not know that then.

One day, I could not get out of bed for school, and our house was so crazy that no one noticed. When my dad got home from work, he started yelling at me for skipping school, not doing my chores, and not cooking dinner. I explained to him that I could not get out of bed because of the pain. My mother came home a few minutes later and called the doctor because she knew I never missed school; I hated staying home. My mom explained my symptoms and my pediatrician thought that either I was pregnant or my appendix might have burst, so he sent us to the ER.

On the way to the hospital, I went in and out of consciousness. The pain was worse than anything I had ever felt before. My dad was yelling for me to hang on and my mom was telling him that I did not look good at all.

Chapter Sixteen

Surgeon's Notes

The following is the surgeon's notes following surgery at Mt. Sinai Hospital

—Lauer, Karen 340221—1/26/79 13—F—C

Dr. Ronald Czaja   Operation: Vaginotomy, Vaginal Reconstruction

Hematocolpos (accumulation of blood in the vagina), secondary to vaginal atresia, lower third of the vagina

Procedures: Under general anesthesia, the patient was prepped and draped in the usual manner. Pelvic exam revealed that the hymen was open and that the lower portion of the vagina was normal for about 3 cm.

Then a thick fibrous band of indurate tissue completely obliterated the vagina. A previously performed rectal examination on the floor prior to surgery showed that the Hematocolpos was a large cystic mass, approximately 8 cm in diameter and acutely impinged into the rectum.
  There was an area between the Hematocolpos, and the previously described vaginal stenotic area of about 4 cm. This stenotic area consisted of firm fibrous tissue, and the urethra was closely adherent to it anteriorly and the rectal anterior wall impinged this band posteriorly.
  The vaginal wall was carefully transected laterally in its upper third, staying close to the urethra into which a Foley catheter was placed.
  Upon opening the stenotic area, the tissue was very thick and dense, and the dissection had to be carried out sharply.

Great care was taken to stay anteriorly because it was felt that we would rather inadvertently open the urethral bladder rather than the contaminated rectum. The lower half of the urethra was carefully identified, and as the sharp dissection continued inwardly, an escape of urine was noted.

Hence, an opening was identified at the UV junction. The mucosal edges of this opening were identified and a layer of running interrupted sutures used to close this defect. It was in the midline and approximately 1 cm long. A second layer of interrupted sutures was used to re-enforce the area.

A fine probe was then placed into the urethra and the defect was completely closed.

The operator with another glove inserted one finger into the rectum, and using the anterior rectal wall as a guide very carefully continued the sharp dissection inwardly. After approximately 4 cm of this careful dissection, the tense wall of the Hematocolpos was identified. The operator then removed his finger from the rectum and re-gloved.

The rectal area had previously been very carefully covered with sterile towels. Prior to any dissection, a Voorhees type needle on a 10 cc syringe was directed inwardly. Hence, after 4-5 cm with aspiration the old clotted blood could be identified. This gave us the initial direction of the dissection.

When the wall of the Hematocolpos was seen, the needle puncture site could be seen in the direct center, and from it was oozing a little bit of the previously described gelatinous old blood.

By blunt dissection, the Hematocolpos wall was dissected away from the surrounding fascia, bladder, and rectum so that an area approximately 5 cm x 5 cm could be seen. Two lateral sutures were then placed with the wall of the Hematocolpos, which was approximately ½ cm in thickness.

A vertical incision of approximately 5 cm was then made into the Hematocolpos, and approximately 250 cc of thick gelatinous old blood was removed by suction and sponging. The bulb syringe with saline solution was introduced into the Hematocolpos and the rest of the old blood lavaged from the cavity.

A very careful digital examination was then performed, and a partially dilated small cervix could be identified at the deepest end of the Hematocolpos. The uterus was difficult to identify and felt quite small. No palpable masses in the adnexal areas were felt.

It was felt that now the Hematocolpos was reduced that the defect in the lower third of the vagina certainly had to be corrected. The previously placed lateral traction sutures were used to bring the opened edge of the upper 2/3 of the vagina down towards the introitus, and there was enough slack in the distended upper 2/3 of the vagina to reach the introitus.

It was felt that reconstructive vaginal plastic repair should be performed in order to recreate as normal a vagina as we could for this 13-year-old girl.

Vicryl suture was placed in the edges of the opened Hematocolpos, and these were sutured to the vaginal mucosa of the previously opened lower third of the vagina.

A series of interrupted vicryl sutures were placed in a progressive fashion until the upper 2/3 of the vagina was attached to the lower third of the vagina, thus in effect marsuplializing the Hematocolpos. Great care was taken to allow two-finger dilation at the lower third of the vagina.

There was a minimal amount of bleeding. The procedure was meticulously done and very time consuming but the results were extremely satisfactory.

The perineum had been previously bisected in a midline episiotomy fashion in order to allow more room to perform the vaginal surgery. This defect was closed in interrupted suture fashion, and it was closed in a transverse fashion thus enlarging the introitus as much as possible to correct the stenotic area.

A rectal exam was performed and there was no evidence of any paravaginal hematomas or any defects within the rectal wall. The urine that was passed was a small amount and did not contain any fresh blood.

The patient withstood the procedure well and was taken from the operation room in good condition.

Chapter Seventeen

Vaginal Agenesis (1979)

Cunt, twat, pussy, labia, clitoris, vagina—these are some of the terms we use to describe the female reproductive organs. Everybody over the age of twelve knows what those words mean.

However, what does the word "normal" mean?

When I woke up from the surgery, my mom was there as she usually was when I came out of surgery. She explained to me that they had had to do emergency surgery because I had been born without a vagina. She explained that I had had my period for several months, and after the surgeons got in there, they realized what was wrong. The infection from the backed up blood had been the cause of my pain, and we were lucky I was alive.

The thing was, I did not feel lucky. I felt violated and manmade. I did not understand how I could be missing parts and I did not fully understand human, embryonic development.

I was bedridden for five days, and on the sixth day, I could barely stand without help but there was no way I could walk. Atrophy had set in fast. I went to physical therapy to get my legs moving again. On day eight, my doctor released me, insisting that I must continue with the catheter to prevent infection.

On day ten, I stepped on the catheter and pulled it out with the balloon still inflated. I had been trying to move quickly up the hallway stairs because I was burning the lasagna that I was cooking in the kitchen. I should not have been doing it but the pain medication made me feel fine. When I pulled it out, I let out a guttural shriek. It hurt like hell and I was afraid I had pulled stitches!

I called my mother at work, and she came home and took me to the hospital right away. I begged the ER doctor to let me go home without the catheter, and he agreed so long as I was very careful. He was afraid of infection, but I told him I would be very careful, and if I had any problems going to the bathroom, I would call him. Even with the pain medication, I would never want to do that again.

At my first OB GYN doctor's consultation, I learned more about my situation. As far as they could tell, I had at least one ovary, and probably two. However, my cervix and uterus were very small and the likelihood of me ever getting pregnant was minuscule. Chances were slim to nothing but if on the off chance I were to get pregnant, I would have to have a planned cesarean. My vagina would never stretch to allow a full term baby to go through it. A natural childbirth would kill me.

I had made medical history and my case written up in the *Journal of Medicine*. I was not sure why, something to do with being born with a uterus and a missing vagina. Most women who were born that way were missing other parts. I knew I was odd. Now I had official medical documents to validate that fact. You would think that it might have made me feel better, but it only made me feel worse and more alone.

I guess that explained why there were tons of interns coming into my room at all hours of the day and night. At one point, twenty of them in my room were going over my chart and asking me questions.

I awoke to the sound of voices whispering. When I opened my eyes, there were about forty eyeballs staring at me.

My doctor's partner, the one who had shoved his hand up my ass in the emergency ward and told me it was no big deal, the one who made me pray that I would die so I could stop being in agony, was apparently a training doctor. He asked me if I would permit the students to ask questions. He wanted to show them the catheter, the incisions, and explained to them the McIndoe procedure. He drew back my covers haphazardly as he began talking to the students.

"This patient was admitted in the ER with acute abdominal pain." He was using medical jargon and spoke with a monotonous voice that belied the trauma I had experienced. He had no idea about me, and I already despised him. The only reason I had agreed to do this was that I thought maybe if I shared my experience, the interns would understand and be able to help another girl like me someday. I allowed my brain to shut him out, and instead I thought my own thoughts.

I wanted to tell the residents how I had waited for my period for months, and it never came. A simple check-up at birth would have changed my life and the last year of pain I had experienced. I wanted to tell them how I had endured pain lying on the floor in school because I could not get up or walk. I wanted to tell them that on the way to the hospital, as I lay in the back of my parents' station wagon, I had prayed to die and God had deserted me.

I wanted them to know that instead of me dying, the good-gloved doctor who was trying to save my life, humiliated and hurt me. I wondered if they would believe me if I said, he seemed to get satisfaction out of giving me the rectal exam that made me wish I had died and was burning in hell already. However, I could not tell them what I was thinking. I just answered their questions as my mind flew through the events that had led to the surgery.

My parents had been standing in the hallway beyond the sheet that acted as a privacy wall. The ER was busy that night and I was on a rollaway in the hall. The nurse had asked me questions like why did I look like I was three months pregnant. Had my father ever touched me inappropriately? Moreover, had I ever had sexual intercourse?

I told her I did not know why I was so bloated. My father was a good man and had never touched me inappropriately. Moreover, no, I had never had sexual intercourse. I knew my parents would have been devastated to find out the truth that Tim and I had been fooling around for months. I did not have my period, so I did not think it would matter. I was positive I was not pregnant.

"Just lie on your belly for a minute now. I just have to check one thing." I felt his finger on my asshole, and before I knew it, he shoved his fingers in me. Then it felt like he had shoved his entire hand into my rectum and was moving it around. I heard the blood-curdling scream before I realized it was I doing the screaming. "Leave me alone. Let me die. Please give me something to put me down."

"Calm down. Relax." It did not matter when he pulled his hand out because I was in agony physically, and now emotionally too. He had raped me. I didn't care that they called it a medical treatment. It was violently humiliating and excruciatingly painful.

His rectal exam had however given the doctors the answers they needed. Dr. Goodfella stepped out to talk to my parents, and the attendant pushed the rollaway bed to the operating room. They needed to operate right now. When I awoke, I found out I had been fixed.

I just looked at the residents with their eager faces and wondered what they thought of me. One of them asked if he could see my cleft palate and I opened my mouth wide. They formed a line and looked into my mouth, one by one. They thanked me for my time and then left the room.

I wondered if there was a relationship between the congenital birth defects. Alternatively, was it just that the medical students were trying to get all there was to see out of me in one visit? I was a circus sideshow. Whenever I went to a new doctor, they asked to see my mouth. I always got compliments on the surgeon's work, as if I had anything to do with it. Would doctors now be asking to see my vagina too?

Chapter Eighteen

Sexual Disorders (14 years old)

When I got home from the hospital, Tim gave me a gigantic bear to hug so that I would not be alone when he was not around. At first, I just told him I had had female problems, but when he pressed for more details, I had to explain.

"We were not fucking."

"What do you mean we were not fucking? Of course we were."

"We could not have been. It was impossible. I did not have a vagina. There was just a big wall of skin there." It was the first time that I realized how small his penis really was. I knew that it had bothered him when we had first gotten together but I had convinced him that size did not matter to me because it did not. He had never penetrated me deep enough for us to realize there was a problem. Unfortunately, that realization somehow made the entire situation worse.

I informed him that sex was off limits to me for a while. He kidded with me that I could dry hump the bear and think of him. Not long after that, the cops arrested him for drunk driving and then he began dating Sandy. She was older and could go out and drink with him. I bawled. Life was so unfair. It could have been good between us and it might have been perfect someday. Maybe we had been born to complement one another but I would never know. He stopped calling and I vowed I would never allow another man to break my heart. I would use them the way they used me.

When I went back to school, the rumor was that I had had an abortion. I did not confirm or deny it. I had been out of school for a month and I barely passed math that year. I became a loner, preferring to be by myself most of the time. I hated my body. I never ate breakfast, but I started skipping lunch and sometimes dinner. Even if my stomach would gurgle, I would ignore it, and try to remain focused on a task telling myself that I really didn't need to eat yet.

Toward the end of the year, when the officers came to school to talk about drugs, I dodged them. I had just picked up a dime bag. Fortunately, one of my friends had warned me that the drug-sniffing dogs were going to be there.

I did not fit in at the school. I second-guessed myself in every situation. I said things that were not cool socially, and as bad as I wanted to fit in, I felt like I never did. The daily smoking eased my tensions and helped me focus on what I needed to get done.

Chapter Nineteen

Dilators (March 1979)

A couple of weeks after the operation, the doctor handed me a box of six dilators. They were hard black plastic dildos that I was supposed to use to keep my vagina dilated. The smallest one was about the diameter of a pencil and the length of a pinky finger, and the largest was equivalent to a grown man's erect six-inch penis.

I had not asked for them and I did not want them. I hated the fact that I was required to use them. I did not want to know how to use them; they made me feel embarrassed and dirty. I was worried about the long-term implications of my surgery. What other surprises were in store for me? What would happen if I decided to do nothing?

Dr. Czaja, a lumbering rotund man in his sixties, was always professional when he dealt with me. He had been my mother's GYN and had helped deliver my brother and sister. His office was cold and impersonal with white walls and metal cabinets. His nurse was kind but out of shape and often running in and out of the patient rooms at his disposal.

The nurse or my mother was usually in the room with me because of my age, but I felt comfortable enough with him and would send them out or say I was fine by myself and occasionally I would be alone with him.

He was nice enough but I did not like him because he told me things I did not want to hear. For example, he said my vagina was limited in its elasticity, I would not be able to wear tampons, and I most likely would not get pregnant. He also told me having a uterus was rare for someone born with my condition and that I would probably never meet anyone who was born like me.

He cautioned me that if I were to get pregnant, I would have to have a planned cesarean. I was lucky to be alive, another few hours and I would have been gone. Unfortunately, dilation was a life-long obligation. As long as I had my period, I would have to engage in vaginal stretching through dilation or intercourse.

I felt like I did not have choices about the surgery or the subsequent treatment. I was angry that I could not have children but at the same time, I told myself I didn't care. The white box of intimidating black dilators sat in the top drawer of my bureau at first. Happy fucking fourteenth birthday, boy was I special; the insurance company had approved the claim and spent $400 on my dildos.

Maybe other girls can get over this experience without emotional trauma, but I could not. First was the reality that I was not normal. That led to thoughts that I was not a real woman. I was a partial woman. I was a manmade woman, manufactured, fabricated, a woman made possible for men through plastic surgery.

It also made me question what I was before surgery. Had I been an "It," lost between the sexes, congenitally deformed? So many talented doctors and nurses helped me become normal, but I still did not feel like I was. Was I a hermaphrodite, inter-sexed, partially baked, or genetically wired wrong?

Whereas the dark hair on my arms had caused me minor discomfort before my surgery, I began seeing it as a symbol of masculinity, and in a fit of despair I shaved it all off. Little did I know that it would grow back thicker and dark. I told myself that I wanted to travel, be in business, and have a career. I would not be the kind of woman that had a family. I did not deserve motherhood.

After a few days, my mother says as I am passing through the kitchen, "Did you use your dilators K. C.?"

"Not yet."

"Why not?" Mom asked me.

"I do not want to use them. It is weird."

"In what way is it weird?" Of course, she knows perfectly well that it is weird, but either she is trying to draw me out so I will talk about it or she legitimately wants me to tell her why I think it is weird. Either way, I am not talking.

"Forget it, I will do it. I promise."

How weird is it when your mother tells you to go fuck yourself? It would be funny if it was happening to somebody else, but it is happening to me and I hate it. I know she means well, but I just want her to leave me alone.

I cannot dilate myself at first. I was lying on the bed, but then I had to use KY jelly to lubricate the dilator and it was making a mess of my bed; everything was all sticky. I ended up streaking into the bathroom, putting a towel down on the cold floor, and then lying down in order to be able to get comfortable. I wanted to be able to wash up easily and not ruin my bed sheets.

The dilator was cold, and as soon as I tried to put it in, my vagina froze up. The harder I tried to push it in, the more it hurt and my body resisted. I felt sorry for myself and started to cry. I should not have to be doing this. It was not right, it was not normal. I was a sexual deviant. For the rest of my life, my vagina would have to take precedence in my thoughts.

My mind kept running the same question repeatedly: Where were you when you first lost your virginity? My doctor did me. I didn't have a chance to give it up to anyone, instead, it was taken from me.

After two weeks, I went back to the GYN and he was not satisfied with my progress. I just about jumped off the table when he stuck his fat pinky inside me. By that point, I should have been able to take it but I had not followed his instructions and my vaginal canal started closing up.

After my mother left the room, he asked me what the problem was and I told him that it hurt. He agreed that it would because of the nature of what we were trying to do. I had to stretch the area and it would be uncomfortable.

He suggested I take a warm bath and relax first, and then he suggested that if I masturbated while I was using the dilators, they might go in a bit easier. I would naturally lubricate and relax.

Afterward, we met with him in his office and Dr. Czaja told Mom that she might want to bring me for counseling. My resistance to the therapy meant that it was not going as well emotionally as they had hoped. If I refused physical treatment, it might mean that I would have to go back for subsequent surgeries. I needed to understand why the treatment was so important and work through my emotional issues. He had done everything right up to this point, but now it was up to me.

I was disgusted with his suggestion that I might need counseling. I did not need any help I argued with Mom on the way home but she insisted that she was going to find me a counselor. I was fine. I was pulling myself out of the depression. I was catching up on my schoolwork and was back working for my customers, cleaning houses and babysitting. I did not tell her I was smoking weed and drinking to ease the emotional pains. I did not tell her that I hated my body and felt like I had lost control over it. I did not tell her that I wanted to die.

After Dr. Czaja's talk, I decided to try his advice. I had a crush on my science teacher Mr. Martinson. He was usually dressed in a white dress shirt and dress slacks. I liked men who rolled up their dress shirt cuffs inside instead of out. I remembered my third-grade teacher Mr. Daws from Pennsylvania whom I adored. He had rolled his sleeve cuffs inward too, worn cowboy boots, and rode a motorcycle to school.

That afternoon, I masturbated thinking about the men in my life. The men that had become teachers or mentors, the ones who had guided me through my education or in some way had made me feel good about myself.

As I pressed the dilator in, and it began to hurt, I thought of these teachers goading me on, demanding that I do "it." Just rubbing did me no good. Then I pinched my labia until they hurt so bad I no longer felt the pain in my vagina, and that did it for me. I came up with a name for the process, calling it "pain transfer." I found that by hurting another place on my body I could stop thinking about the real source of pain.

During these times of pain, I chastised myself mentally. It was almost as if I became two people—one, the side of me that could feel the pain, saying please stop; and two, the other side of me that said, take it, take it. This thinking excited me and allowed me to get past the pain.

Sometimes, I hurt so bad I brought myself to orgasm with pain. On more than one occasion, I passed out alone on the bathroom floor. I would not realize I had pushed the dilator in all the way until I stopped quivering and came around to consciousness again.

Once, I figured out the process, I advanced from one size to the next on course with the doctor's prescription. Within about eighteen months after surgery, I had reached the six-inch dilator. Dr. Czaja was pleased with my progress. He explained that I would have to use the dilators until I got married, at which time I could commence having normal marital sex with my husband.

My mother brought me to a counselor and I would not open up. I could not verbalize my emotions or explain how self-destructive I was becoming. I did not trust anyone anymore, except for myself.

Chapter Twenty

The Dreaded Pads (Summer of 1979)

When I was a little girl, I used to get embarrassed when I was watching television and ads for Kotex, Tampons, or Maxi-pads would come on the television if there were men in the room. Desensitization to this came as I got older and realized that most adults understand about the facts of life. They know how the female body works, and they understand the fact that once a month, most women have to go through this tedious process of protecting their clothes from menstrual blood.

Because of my surgery, I would never be able to wear a tampon. My vaginal canal had no elasticity to hold the damn thing in and it was too small to accommodate most of the ones on the market. If I tried to wear one, it was extremely uncomfortable; it would slip out on its own.

I was stuck wearing the dreaded pads and I hated them. I was afraid they were noticeable through my clothing, as if I had a big old diaper between my legs. The worst fear I had was that the pad would leak and somebody would see it, and I would be mortified.

My worst fear came true; well, almost.

I was working as a blueberry picker up in the hills of Granby, CT. Most of my friends picked tobacco in the summer but that did not appeal to me. Instead, I picked blueberries. My dad would drop me off in the center of town at the dairy mart and I would catch the farm's bus to the blueberry farm and back again every day.

There were no bathrooms in the blueberry fields. You had to go off in the woods if you needed to relieve yourself. That day I had used the woods in the morning, but it must have been so hot, the soda I drank for lunch evaporated via perspiration and I had not needed to pee in the afternoon.

I boarded the bus to go home and sat with my legs on the seat, my back against the side of the bus. There were plenty of seats for each of us to have our own. A boy a little older than me, sat across the seat from me. I had short white shorts on, and although I was grimy and dirty, I caught him looking at my crotch. I thought he was checking me out because he found me attractive.

Wrong. He looked away and back again, and then he casually moved into my seat, forcing me to sit normally with my feet on the floor. Then he whispered into my ear that he thought I was bleeding.

I looked down and saw the bright red blood everywhere. I was mortified and wanted to sink under the seat of the bus. He was wonderful though, and acted like a big brother to me, graciously handing me his flannel work shirt so I could cover myself up.

I wrapped it around my waist so that it covered both the front and back of me and my shorts, and when the bus finally hit my stop, I got off the bus feeling as if everyone knew, although they probably did not. I was so grateful to this kid for saying something to me and not making a big deal of it. It was worse than a pad leaking. It was a case of me being unprepared. He could have easily embarrassed the hell out of me, but he did not.

My dad was there waiting for me as he always was. I could not tell him what had happened. I was just too embarrassed. I sat in his car, hoping I would not bleed through the flannel and ruin the car seat. After waiting so long to have my period, getting the monthly cramps but no bleeding, you would have thought I would have been excited but I was not. I was surprised that it had come without any awareness on my part.

After that, I made sure I was always prepared with a pad. I would check my underwear in the morning and afternoons faithfully to make sure there were no signs of blood. Sometimes, I would wear a panty-liner just in case. I did not want to be unprepared again.

Chapter Twenty-One

Eighth-Grade Prom (1979)

Along with all the bad that year, there was some good. Mom made my eighth-grade prom gown, and miraculously I won as part of the queen's court. I say miraculously because I was not one of the popular girls, nor was I particularly pretty. The aquamarine dress was clingy and highlighted my slender shape, making me feel beautiful and chic. Most of my female classmates were wearing prom dresses with puffy sleeves, frills, and were displaying their cleavage. I called them nightgown dresses. I had no cleavage and I was not a frilly kind of girl. My mom's efforts paid off; the dress fit me perfectly, physically and mentally.

Mom noticed that from the time she had done my first fitting to my last fitting, I had lost some weight. She began getting concerned and started policing my eating habits, nagging me to make sure I ate. I loved the dress, I loved her, but I was fine. She just needed to leave me alone.

Most of prom night I had spent alienating or trying to dodge Allan. He had asked me early but I had kept him waiting, hoping the boy I liked would ask me. When he did not, I decided it would be better to go with Allan than to go alone. I felt bad about the way I treated him but it didn't stop me. Allan was a nice person and deserved better. Unfortunately, I did not want a nice guy. I wanted somebody who was going to be bad.

Where would I find him?

Well, the bad guy I wanted happened to live right next door.

Chapter Twenty-Two

Arrested (Fall of 1980)

My cousin Carolyn moved out after a disagreement with my parents. They felt she was a bad influence on my brother, sister, and me, but we were capable of our own destruction with or without her. They just did not know it yet.

One of the neighborhood parents kicked their kid out and my parents took him in. The only thing was, they did not know that we were dating. If they had, I am sure they would not have permitted it, but we lied. In fact, we came up with this great big cover-up story so that they would think he was dating another girl.

My parents' had a five-bedroom house. Jim stayed in the guestroom next to my parents' room. In fact, he could see into his parents' house from his room. My bedroom was on the opposite side of the house and you had to go through my sister's room to get to it.

Jim was taller than most of the kids his age. Even with his blond curly hair and a killer smile, his comments had a way of cutting you to the bone. He was rude, crude, a manipulator, and a liar; and in fact, his disrespect for authority was what I loved most about him.

At first, we were very careful. He would go out on dates, and he encouraged me to have boys call the house so my parents would never think that we were an item. We would sneak kisses here and there in the hall as we passed one another. Occasionally he would come in my room when nobody was around and we would fool around.

One time, I snuck into his room after my parents went to bed. I thought maybe we would lie on the bed and cuddle. We had to be very quiet so as not to wake them. They would have punished me if they saw me in there. Being in Jim's room with the door closed was against the house rules.

I knew what I was doing was wrong but I did it anyway. Jim's mood intensified as the situation played out, the fear of being caught enhancing his senses. He insisted I leave the light on, saying he wanted to see me. I was afraid if my parents knocked on the door I would not have time to get clothed again before the door opened, but I did not want to argue with him because I never knew what he would do. He was brutal when he wanted to get his way. Instead, I appeased him and did what he wanted.

He sat on the bed and managed to remove my nightgown while he was kissing and hugging me. Normally, I was the kind of girl who fucked my men in the woods, in the backyard, on the soccer field at school, or on the stage in the auditorium. Tim and I had fooled around in my room many times but this was different; for one thing, because my parents normally were not home, and for another thing, the lights were never on. With the lights on and my parents sleeping in the next room, it seemed different and dangerous.

I guess I thought he loved me until he said, "You are quite the slut, aren't you?" He had my wrists in his hands, and although he was not squeezing, his grasp was firm.

"I guess."

"No, there is no guessing about it. What do you think your mom would say if she could see you right now? She is right on the other side of that wall. I could call her if I just spoke her name loudly. Do you want me to?"

"No, Jim, quit fooling around," I whispered in his ear, nuzzling his neck as I felt the hairs on my back and ass stand up. I should not have come to his room and I knew it before but I felt it now, this had been a stupid idea.

I should put my nightgown back on and go back to my room but I knew he would not just let me go. "From now on, every time your mom calls you K. C. I am going to think of my new nickname for you, Kinky Cunt. That is what you are, a kinky cunt."

He was, of course, right. Judging by my own actions, there was no doubting it. Did I agree? He wanted to know. "Aren't you a kinky cunt?"

I nodded though I wanted to kick him in the nuts and get away from his grasp.

"Good, let's make this interesting, K. C. the kinky cunt," he said.

He opened the guestroom window that faced his mother's house carefully. It was about three feet from the closed window in my parents' bedroom. I was grateful it was cold out.

Jim twisted me around until my wrists were behind my back. He then pushed me toward the window and kept pushing me forward until my head and tits were outside in the cold. Bending me over the windowsill, the whole time he fucked me, he was repeating the words, "K. C. is a kinky cunt."

It was one of the few times in my life that I remember praying. I prayed that my parents would not hear us and that his mother or father would not come into the kitchen and see me hanging out my parents' guestroom window stark naked. I prayed that Jim would not get any louder. Then I prayed that Jim would have an orgasm very quickly. It was clear he was enjoying the power he had over me. Some say, "Be careful what you wish for." I had wished for the excitement but not the embarrassment and the inability to make the situation stop.

Jim ejaculated almost as soon as he saw his mother come into the kitchen. She was standing in front of the refrigerator with the door open. If her eyes moved from the interior of the refrigerator to looking out her kitchen window, she would have seen us. It was intensely humiliating for me, and extensively exciting for him.

"Kinky Cunt is getting fucked in the window. Look, Mom, aren't you glad you kicked me out?" Saying the words aloud, as if his mother could hear him, made him come. As soon as he came, he released me and I ducked out of the light of the window and then pulled the shade. Then I was dressed and walked out of his room without saying a word. I was pissed at him for putting me into that position but I had not felt like I could do anything about it without jeopardizing my own situation.

The next day, I told him I did not want him calling me K. C. anymore and that I thought we should stop seeing each other. I did not like the way he had treated me, but he said, "You know you wanted it." I told him I did not like it but then he asked me why my pussy had gotten wet. I admitted I had been excited but the situation was wrong. He said that I was a kinky cunt and that was why I liked it. "I think I am going to tell your mom that she should call you kinky instead of K. C."

Every time somebody would call me K. C. within his earshot, he would say, "Kinky Cunt." Sometimes, he would whisper it or sometimes he would sing it in a way so no one would get what he was saying. One time, he told a bunch of kids in the neighborhood that it was his secret name for me. In school, he would miraculously appear just as a teacher would be calling on me, and I could read his lips as he walked by, "Kinky Cunt."

I hated him. He was ruining my life. I asked my family to stop calling me K. C., telling them, "I hate that name. Just call me Kay, please!"

After that, things were not so good between Jim and me anymore. He would try to catch me in the hall upstairs or in the kitchen when my parents were in another room. I would try to dodge him or give him a quick peck without the usual fondling but he knew what I was doing and would squeeze my breasts crushingly hard, tweak my nipples viciously, or he would slap my ass to try to get a rise out of me. I wished he would move out but I could not say anything to my parents because of my guilt and complicity.

I was afraid to push him too far away because I was afraid he would say or do something that would be even more awful. It was like walking on thin ice, I had to keep moving a few steps ahead or behind him.

I kept up with my cold shoulder routine and it did not take him long before he started dating Elizabeth again. She was another neighborhood girl that he had dated before me, and I was glad to be rid of him. One night, though, he came into my room while I was sleeping.

Liz and he had been drinking together. He was sexually frustrated because she had not been able to get him off even though he had tried fucking her. The door between my room and my sister's was open but he had closed the door from her room to the hall. As soon as I opened my eyes and saw him standing there with his big shit-eating grin, I knew I was in trouble.

"Jim, get out of my room. I will see you in the morning. C'mon, I am sleeping right now. You are going to wake Cathy," I whispered.

His answer to that was to shut the door between my room and my sisters. As he turned toward the bed, I saw that he already had his cock out of his pants.

"C'mon, Kinky Cunt, just get me off so I can go to sleep," he told me, "You are better than Liz."

"I do not want to get you off, Jim. That is your girlfriend's job now. Leave me alone. Get out of my room."

"No, I cannot do that, Kinky Cunt." He grabbed my hair and stuck his cock in my face but I clenched my lips closed. I could smell where he had been. He slapped my face hard enough to bring tears to my eyes but I still would not open my mouth. "Do not be like that, Kinky Cunt. You know you want it, K.C."

"I will bite it off," I whispered through clenched teeth, staring at him with hatred in my eyes.

I was not going to respond as I wanted to because if I did, I would have screamed and the whole house would have known something was wrong. I was in a mess again and did not know what to do about it. I would have liked to believe my parents would have come to my aid, but I was not sure they would. I was afraid they would kick me out.

"That is okay, Kinky Cunt. I know what you like." He did not give me much of a chance to think. He pushed me back on the bed and lifted my legs and flipped me over on my stomach so fast, I did not have time to react. Then the covers wrapped my body as I tried to struggle and push him off and then he pinned me down and I could not move.

"Stop it, Jim." I was whispering loudly and it was apparently enough to make him worry. As he pushed the covers and my nightgown up, he put the pillow over my head after whispering to me, "Be quiet, Kinky Cunt, I have got some work to do on your ass."

I thought about the consequences of what I had done to get myself in that position and I laid there as he sodomized me, calling me his whore. I cried silently and tried to push him off, but the more I struggled, the more he became aroused.

When he was done, he turned me over and slapped my face until I licked his penis. He then petted me on the head and called me a good bitch before pulling his pants up and leaving my room.

I snuck out of my bedroom, went into the bathroom, and washed up. Then I passed out in my bed and awoke to my sister coming in my room the next morning.

"Jim said he needs to talk to you, he is in the bathroom." She went downstairs to have breakfast with the parents.

Why I went in there, I will never know. I was so angry with him I wanted to beat him to death. I snuck in there and started berating him about what had happened the night before. We had a laundry chute that connected to the laundry room next to the kitchen. I shut it, hoping my parents would not hear us talking together.

I told him we were over and how dare he do that to me. He got all sad-eyed and then he wrapped his arms around me and I thought he was going to kiss me, but then he held me tightly, with his head pulled back, and said, "Kinky Cunt's got shitty dog breath this morning."

I tried to pull away from him but he was too strong. I tried to pinch his nuts and as we were struggling, he spun me around and twisted my arm until the next thing I knew my face was close to being in the toilet bowl.

"Don't do it, Jim!"

"Let's wash your face."

"You are a fucking asshole," I said as he pushed my head in the bowl and held it there. My parents were laughing downstairs and I should have just screamed. They would have come running to my rescue, but I did not. He let me up a bit and then pushed my head in again. He used his long legs to spread my legs so I could not move and he held me there with one hand until he blew his load on my back. He released me quickly, laughing, and hopped into the running shower. He was stronger than I thought he was. However, it was his mental power over me that I hated the most.

I sat on the toilet crying while I waited for him to finish showering. Then I stepped in one side as he stepped out the other. He left the room quietly as I tried to wash every orifice I had; I felt so dirty and used.

As I got dressed in my room, I could hear him making fun of something with my parents downstairs at the breakfast table. I found my bad boy, and now I could not get rid of him.

Chapter Twenty-Three

Arrested (April 1981)

Not long after that, my parents kicked Jim out and I was glad to see him go. He had gotten himself a job at the local hamburger joint on Route 75 in Windsor Locks. In fact, he was still cooking on the grill about six months later, when I applied there right after I turned 16. I got a job as a cashier.

He was trying to go to high school and work but money was tight, so he was picking up as many hours as he could. I had gotten over being angry with him. When he asked me to help him make some money, I did not refuse. Occasionally, we would move some pot through the drive-through together.

A few weeks later, he was caught stealing from the register and the manager fired him. It seemed trouble followed him everywhere. I had distanced myself on some level from Jim, but I felt sorry for him on another.

A few days later while I was at work, the supervisor called me to the phone; it was Jim on the other end. He asked me to leave work early to meet him. He admitted to me that he had stolen a neighbor's car, as we all had surmised he had done, and he said he was going to turn himself in but he wanted to see me first.

What had happened was his mother was watching a neighbor's house while they were on vacation, and his little brother Evan had mentioned to Jim that he knew where the key was. Jim, who was on the streets and living in hotel rooms, felt desperate. He and his friend Stephen had decided to check out the house. While they were in there, they decided to steal some stuff and take off with the neighbor's car.

They had intended on going to Florida to meet up with Jim's aunt and try to make new lives for themselves since they were both in trouble with their parents and the law. They had made it all the way to Pennsylvania, dining and dashing and filling up the car without paying, but decided they were being foolish and turned back.

They were back in town now and were going to go to the police department as soon as Jim got a chance to say goodbye to me. He said he loved me and had been wrong to do the things he had done.

"Kay, please, I need to see you."

I knew I should have stayed at work, but almost as if in a fog, I heard my own voice asking my supervisor if I could go home early because I was feeling sick and was getting a headache. She told me to sit and get some water, and I did, but I assured her I still felt sick and needed to go home. She finally relented, though I did not think she believed me. Ignoring the sense of impending doom I felt inside, I walked outside. I was becoming a frequent liar, and it bothered me.

Stephen and Jim were waiting for me on the side of the restaurant where employees parked, in the stolen car. I saw Stephen first and gave him a hug as he got out of the car. He was one of my best friend's older brothers. Then Jim got out and I gave him a big hug and a passionate kiss. I was glad to see them safe and unharmed. Standing by the hood of the car, they were telling me what had made them turn back on their journey when a copper pulled into the drive-through.

Stephen immediately said, "We should not stay here," and got back in the driver seat. Jim opened the passenger door and motioned for me to climb in the back. As I climbed into the back of the car, I was thinking, "I cannot believe I am getting into a stolen car with a cop right there, almost looking at me," but I did it anyway.

Jim jumped in behind me and Stephen started the car, slowly backing out. We pulled out of the driveway, past the police car, and onto Route 75 heading toward Southwick, Massachusetts. I changed out of my work uniform and back into my school clothes in the back of the car while they filled me in on their escapade.

Behind the driver's seat, the backseat shouldered the weight of the stolen stereo, some silver and jewelry, and a box of partially filled booze bottles. I helped myself to one of them and began drinking. The boys were doing the same in the front seat. We passed around a joint and I gave them cash to fill up. My goal was to fulfill Jim's wish of hanging out before he turned himself in, but now that I was with them, what was the rush?

We ended up at the lake, watching the sunset. It was a normal day. It was around 4:00 p.m., everyone was doing normal things, and yet here I was, with fugitives running from the law with stolen property and getting drunk out in public.

Jim finally said it was not cool for us to be sitting there like that, so we got back in the car. I suggested we head back toward East Granby and that it was time to turn themselves in, but Jim said he was not ready.

We headed toward Barkhamstead, and as we passed over the bridge, I started feeling queasy. "You need to pull over, Stephen, I feel like I am going to be sick."

The sun had faded behind the mountains but the dusk light was enough for us to see. Stephen pulled off into a picnic area, and Jim got out so that I could sit down for a minute at a picnic table. He and I were sitting there, and Stephen was standing in front of us, talking, when we saw the cruiser coming into the rest area up the hill. Stephen said, "It is time to go." He climbed into the driver seat nonchalantly and started the car.

Jim agreed. "C'mon, Kay, we need to go." He opened the car door, I climbed in behind the passenger seat, and he got in, deftly shutting his door. He was whispering, "Oh Fuck," as the officer pulled directly behind us.

"He's running the plate. We are so fucked." Stephen was freaking out. He already had a record.

"Just chill out and be cool, man, maybe not. Ever drive a racecar before?" Jim was cool.

"No," Stephen replied, and at the same moment the officer got out of his car and headed toward us, Jim shifted the vehicle into drive and slammed his long leg from the passenger seat into the driver's area and onto the accelerator.

"Drive, goddamn it," Jim was yelling at Stephen because we had shot off like a bullet and were heading toward a tree. As I glanced back, I saw the surprise on the officer's face. I was just as surprised.

"Oh shit. Pull over," I yelled. "This is fucking crazy."

"Shut the fuck up and let him drive," Jim yelled at me over his shoulder and told Stephen he was going to pull his foot off the accelerator and that Stephen needed to take over.

"I am not going to do it." Stephen was trying to manage the wheel but he knew that if he hit the brakes we would spin out if Jim did not let up on the accelerator.

"Yes, you are. We can do this. We can get away. Do not be a pussy, man, drive." Jim had a condescending tone to his voice. He never cared about anyone's feelings.

"Okay, back off. Let me drive the pedals." They were switching and Stephen took over. With him managing the pedals and the wheel, things were a lot less rocky.

The cruiser behind us was flashing its lights and the siren was blasting at us as we made the turns and twists of the mountainous road. The incident had sobered me up, and although we were driving at a fast clip, rounding corners at breakneck speed, my stomach had calmed and the adrenalin kicked in.

If you had asked me just five hours previously if I ever thought I would be involved in a high-speed police chase, I would have adamantly said no; but here I was, in a stolen car, running from the law.

The chase lasted twenty minutes and we went through several towns. It seemed like an eternity, but at least I was alive to talk about it. After Stephen took over, we were going a little over the speed limit but not crazy like we had been when Jim was using his feet on the pedals.

I thought for sure we would die, and it might have been the better fate. Instead, we crashed into a hill. The road dead-ended and we should have taken a left or right but there were cop cars and lights flashing in all directions; we literally had nowhere to go.

The stolen car came to a stall as it went head first into the dirt barrier the homeowners had built specifically to protect their home from disasters of incoming traffic like this. The crash jostled us hard but nobody was seriously hurt.

Uniformed police officers and detectives swarmed our car and one cop told us to put up our hands. I did what they told me to do. This was not going to be a good night after all. As the passenger door opened and one of the police officers hauled Jim out of the car, I felt the cold; and instead of thinking, I reacted and reached for my jacket that was on the seat next to me.

I heard the crash and looked to my right to see what was happening as I saw the Billy-club retract, and in its place a loaded gun pointed at my temple.

"Do not move. Keep your hands where we can see them."

I learned afterward that the officer thought I was going for a gun but I was only trying to get my jacket. I tried to explain that I was cold but he did not want to hear it. He was mad and told me to shut up.

"You'll have a chance to explain later when we take your statement. You almost got yourself killed right there. Now get out of the car, keeping your hands where I can see them."

He cuffed my hands behind my back while we were on the side of the car and then he walked me over to the street. Stephen was cuffed and docile, talking to another cop. He had his head down and looked sad. Jim on the other hand, also cuffed, was animated. I could see him shaking his head up and down and looking around, casing out the situation as he talked to a different cop.

In the center of the scene was a family. There was a daddy and a mommy, and two young children standing in their pajamas above the mound of dirt that contained the front of the car. I heard the father tell the officer that he was just glad to see that nobody had gotten hurt. He gathered his family and they went back in the house as the officer in charge of me read me my rights.

After reading me my rights, the cop told me that he was arresting me for being in possession of a stolen vehicle, fleeing, and eluding for starters. He wanted to hear my side of the story but I did not want to talk. He gave me a cigarette by lighting it and sticking it in my mouth. I started to open up to him a little by saying that I had not stolen the car but admitted that I had gotten into it knowing that it was stolen property.

Once I told him who I was, he ran my name and I was clean, never having been in trouble before. He told me that because of my stupidity of having gotten into the car that night, he left his girlfriend, who was still lying naked on his bear rug. He said she was waiting for him, as he had to take the police call. In fact, if it were not for my friends and I out joyriding in the stolen car, he would be home getting some action right now.

My attitude turned on a dime. I hated his smugness. How dare he insinuate that it was my fault he was not being laid? I felt his comments were inappropriate and uncalled for and I wanted to slap him, but I could not because of the handcuffs.

I do not know how it happened but my foot connected with his balls hard enough to hunch him over and make him gasp. It was the highlight of my night actually, until another cop came over and roughly put me in the back of his cruiser. It seemed each of us was going to have our own ride to the county jail.

Who would have thought I would have ever been in the back of a police car in cuffs? I was a nice girl, a hard worker, an honor student; but here I was, drunk, in a stolen car, and arrested. As I realized how bad the situation was, I surmised that my parents were going to kill me. I thought about the car chase and realized somebody could have gotten hurt. I had seen television shows portraying police chases where people died. I was glad that Stephen had taken over the wheel. With Jim and his reckless ways, we could have easily been dead.

As the officer headed toward the precinct, he told me that I should not have kicked the other officer. Assaulting an officer of the law was serious business and it was going to add more charges. Now they would require me to be in foot shackles because I posed a threat.

I told him I was not a threat and that if the police officer had respected me I would have respected him back. He wanted to know what I meant by that and I told him the comments the officer had made.

Upon hearing my side, he said I had a point and that he would talk to the captain about it, but because the rest of the officers had seen what I had done, I would have to wear the cuffs and foot shackles in jail.

"Whatever, okay? I get it, and I fucked up again. I understand. I will be good. I do not want to be bad but I always end up doing bad things. I do not know why. I am sorry." I am numb as he drives us to the station. I do not cry and I am not scared.

What was happening to my life? What was wrong with me? I knew better but I still got into that car. Even after I got in the car, I could have continued to sit on the rest-stop picnic bench and refused to get in when the cop showed up and the outcome of tonight might have been different. Now I was facing criminal charges, I would have a record and possible jail time. I had nothing to do with the robbery, but now I was smack dab in the middle of it because of my own stupidity.

The remorse was setting in, but I was still on the fence. If it had happened again, with Jim asking for my help, I still might have shown up. He was my friend and we had a history. If I had called him and asked him for help, he would have been there for me. Maybe, depending upon what was in it for him. I was starting to see him for what he was, a user and abuser, but I was still attracted to him for some unknown reason.

Maybe I felt bad because he was in trouble again; I did not really know why I got in that car. Whatever I was thinking at the time, I obviously did not think it through, nor did I think about the effect it might have on my own life. My original concern was only for Jim.

Now, when I was in trouble, I was thinking about me, and it was not looking very good. An accomplice is an accomplice, no matter why they get involved. The officer booked me, taking my mug shot and fingerprints. He led me to a waiting area where a female officer came in.

The cop was a big black woman whose ass almost broke the seams of her uniform. Her hair was greasy, long, and dyed red in some places and I immediately wondered if she was a dyke. Would she try to rape me? I had heard stories about rape and lesbian guards in prison.

Then I noticed her wedding ring and it relaxed me. She started at the top of me, and ran her hands through my hair, and then she worked her way down, under my pits and around my chest, asking me to open my mouth as her hands continued down my torso to my feet, patting me down. She brought me into the bathroom, shut the door, and un-cuffed me. She asked me to pee but not to flush the toilet as she turned her back to give me privacy. When I was done, she checked the toilet and then flushed it.

"I am going to have to do a cavity search on you." I had pulled up my pants but her words stopped me from trying to zip or button them up. I dropped my pants as she put her gloves on and asked me to lean against the sink and bend over. There was no mirror in the room and I was petrified but she was professional getting right down to business. I felt her gloved fingers checking my private places but there were no surprises on either side.

After giving me prison clothes to change into, she turned her back again allowing me to change. When I was done, she put my clothes in a plastic bag. She re-cuffed my hands in front of me and walked me out of the bathroom where the other male officer was waiting.

"She's clean." Nodding to her, the awaiting officer led me to my jail cell. After I sat on the cot, he asked me to remove my shoes. When he removed my shoelaces, I asked him why he was doing that.

"She should have done it, but I guess she missed it," referring to the female officer who had frisked me. "We do not want anybody to get hurt." I did not think I was a suicide risk but apparently, he did. He sat on the cot next to me, after putting the laces in his shirt pocket.

"Do you want to go to Niantic Women's Prison or should I call your parents?"

"I would rather go to prison than see my parents."

"You do not want that. Really, these women are on the wrong paths. You screwed up, and sure, your parents will be upset but they will get over it. Let me call your parents."

"No, please do not call them. Take me to Niantic." He shook his head and left my cell. A few minutes later, I heard voices in the block of cells around me.

Chapter Twenty-Four

Jail Time (April 18th 1981)

"Hey, Jim, Stephen, is that you, guys?"

They responded almost in unison and we laughed, grateful we were all together again.

"How did it go? What are you being charged with?" I asked.

"Just shut up, Kay. We'll talk about it when we get out." That was Jim, the almighty wise one.

When we had three cruisers on our tail during the chase, we had spent the last few minutes theorizing what might happen. They had told me I would probably get off on probation since I had not had much to do with the robbery. Each of them had had priors and they were looking at doing some kind of time. The question was how much. Stephen was pissed that Jim had put his foot on the accelerator and Jim was pissed that Stephen had not taken the initiative himself and gotten us out of this mess by being a more aggressive driver.

I had a five-page paper that was due for school for Mrs. Cornish's English class in about four hours. I had planned to work on it after I got out of work that afternoon, or rather, the day before as it was now 3:00 a.m. I wondered if I would ever see my classmates again. I did not know that it actually mattered. I did not care one way or the other but right now, I was in deep shit.

As it often did when I was troubled, singing appeased my soul. I began a rendition of Amazing Grace that would have made churchgoers weep. The guard went by and asked me to quiet down because the rest of the prisoners were sleeping but I did not care, I got louder and louder until I started to cry. When that happened, the snot choked me up and upset my stomach.

There was nothing in the room but an ashtray. Believe me when I say it was a bad idea. A few minutes later, the guard came by again, wondering why I had become quiet. He saw me covered in puke and cigarette ashes and called for the female guard to take me into the bathroom so that I could wash myself up.

When she got me in the ladies' room, she told me to chill out. I was full of energy but flushed from a chill. She handed me a face cloth and I washed my face.

"You are lucky that Niantic is all backed up tonight. Your parents will be here in a few hours."

There was no hot water in the restroom, so I used the cold to wet the face cloth. "Get cleaned up and get a hold of yourself. You can make this better or you can make this worse. You strike me as somebody who should not be in this kind of place."

She was standing on the side of me, against the wall. I looked at her, and she said, "Get your hair too. You got ashes and vomit everywhere," shaking her head with disgust. "You gotta get your life together, girl, before it is too late. Do not be choosing guys like these guys. They ain't right for you. If you learn a lesson out of this, it ain't all bad. You can do better with your life than this. I know you can."

I felt sorry for her for some stupid reason. She was obviously somebody who was trying to help others through her work and she thought I might be somebody she could help. She had no idea how fucked up I really was. I would be better off in prison. Maybe I would become somebody's bitch. Who knew?

The male officer walked me back to my cell as they swapped spots again. He told me the female officer covered the desk most of the time but they kept her on staff to assist with the female prisoners. It was three hours later before he came back to the cell. My parents had decided to come for me after they had breakfast. It was after all, their seventeenth wedding anniversary.

When I first saw their faces, I wanted to crawl in a hole and die a sudden horrifying death because it would have been easier. If I was in a box dropped from the top of a building and smashed into a million pieces, would it make up for how I had embarrassed the family?

I knew I had acted very irresponsibly and made some bad decisions. What was I thinking? How could I be so stupid? They knew I knew better. This was all going through my head, but they said nothing until we pulled up to the main entrance of my high school forty minutes later. It was about 6:30 a.m., classes started at 7:15.

My mother told me, "We do not understand you or why you did this. We have contacted Maria, our attorney, for her help."

"We have an appointment for 2:30 at her office in Hartford. We will be back at 2:00 to pick you up. Do not keep us waiting." My dad's voice, delivered through clenched teeth, belied his frustration with me.

I wanted to apologize but I could not bring myself to do it, and even if I had, words were words and actions were actions—two entirely different things. I did not know why I did what I did; I had no good or reasonable answer. I was crazy, stupid and messed up, and I smelled.

"It would be nice if I could go home and take a shower." I was still covered in puke and cigarette ashes and wearing the jacket I had torn during that incident with the officer pointing a gun to my head. Stale alcohol and cigarettes permeated my personal space.

"No, your mother and I do not feel comfortable with you in our house anymore K. C. We are not sure what we are going to do yet. We will talk about it this afternoon when we see Maria," Dad said.

With not much of a choice, I got out of the car. I certainly had not imagined this outcome. Not knowing what to do, I turned and went into the school, awakening to the fact that they were treating me as an adult and not a kid anymore.

I had no idea what was going to happen next. I went to the gym, took a shower, and debated about putting on my dirty clothes or my work uniform. I ended up with my dirty clothes back on. The fast food uniform was nastier.

Chapter Twenty-Five

Legal Advice (1981)

School that day was a blur. I did not want people to know what had happened but it was obvious it had not been a good night for me. Neither Stephen nor Jim was in school. The arrest hit the papers and one of the teachers brought in the newspaper clip.

The school guidance counselor pulled me out of my first class. My mother had called the school and they had been through my locker but had not found anything illegal. I never left anything in my locker. I always carried my stash on me, but that day I had nothing. Mr. Martinson said he was aware of my situation and wanted to know what was going to happen. I told him I did not know but that I had an appointment with a lawyer for that afternoon.

I was waiting by the curb outside the main doors of the school at 2:00 when my parents arrived in their Honda. I was jealous that they smelled clean because I knew I was still a stinky mess. Maria, a petite Chilean woman, their attorney, greeted us in her small office with a prestigious address in Hartford. She mostly handled real estate and trusts but she assured us she would do what she could to help my parents, as this was an emergency.

She asked me what happened and I told her. She had already pulled the report from the public records, so she knew my charges. It was obvious, if you looked at the circumstances and knew the events leading up to the robbery, that I was a mess.

Jim and Stephen had burglarized the house three days prior but I had not been involved at all in that. I had witnesses at home, school, and at work.

I had no knowledge of the crime prior or during the event. It was not my idea nor was I involved in anything but being in the stolen car, aiding and abetting fugitives, and destroying personal property by drinking the stolen alcohol.

Apparently assaulting an officer had come off my sheet because she did not ask me about that, and I did not tell. She asked me why I had put myself in that position and I could not explain.

"I do not know. I was trying to help Jim return the car."

"What did you think you were going to accomplish by getting in the stolen car?"

Grilling me now, I began shrinking in the large leather chair she had offered me to the side of her desk. My parents were looking at me as if I had committed murder and they did not want to know me.

"Do you think drinking alcohol helped that situation?" Maria wanted to know. The police report says you were inebriated, and by the smell of you this afternoon, I believe that is true."

"K. C., how much did you drink last night?" She used a trigger word; I hated that name and my defenses kicked in.

I was exhausted and answered snidely, "I don't know, a bottle and a half maybe. They were all partials. I threw up at that rest stop right before the cop came. Then, when we were in the police chase I took a swig or two, but I was too nervous to put the bottle near my lips—I thought it might crack my teeth. Stephen was trying to drive while Jim was yelling at him to go faster. It was awful. We were going so fast over those bumpy roads and Stephen was trying to brake while Jim had his foot on the gas. I wanted them to stop but they were not listening to me. Finally, Stephen took over the foot pedals and the ride started to calm down and then we crashed."

"So how much do you drink on a daily basis?"

Deliberately evasive, "I don't know. Here and there, a little bit, I guess."

"How much is a little bit?"

Little is a relative term. My little is maybe different from your little. To her, I said, "Maybe a pint a day; sometimes, a pint and a half."

"Your mom tells me that she went through your room today and found a pipe, a few empty and partially filled bottles, and a bag of marijuana."

"Oh shit."

"What did you say?"

"Nothing, I did not say anything." My parents did not permit swearing—as if that mattered much at the moment.

Maria continued, "Judging from what I see here and what your parents have told me over the phone, I think you have a problem with drugs and alcohol. After reviewing your record, it appears that this is your first offense. The judge will go easier on you if he thinks you are going to get some help. That is why I am recommending that you to go to an alcoholic rehabilitation center and get sober. K. C., you need to wake up because you are headed down a seriously bad path."

I could not bear looking at my parents but I did and they were nodding their heads vigorously in agreement with Maria. They looked like strangers at me. It was clear they did not think they knew me anymore.

Well, they did not really. I had so many secrets, but apparently, a few less after they found my stash. All day long I had told myself I could get through the day knowing that when I got home I would get high to erase the last forty-eight hours of events from my mind. That was not going to happen now.

I needed a hot shower and clean clothes desperately, and it was my intention that after I took my shower, I would then take refuge up on the roof. My bedroom was next to the garage, and if you climbed out my window, you could sit on the garage roof, which is often what I did when I wanted to get high or smoke a cigarette. I was exhausted, my mom had taken my pot, I was not going home, and this was not going well.

Maria was still talking. "I have called up Spofford Hall in New Hampshire and related the details of your situation. They have agreed to admit you tonight, provided you arrive before 10:00 p.m."

Evidently, Maria had briefed my parents beforehand because I did not see a glint of surprise in their eyes. Instead, I saw disgust, determination, and a little bit of relief. They had a plan of action and I would not be sleeping at home tonight.

"This is for the best for all concerned," Dad said. That was the end of it. There was no discussion. He did not want to hear anything I had to say.

When we got back in the car, my mother informed me she had come across my stash because she was attempting to pack a bag for me for the rehab. She normally respected my privacy, but when she found the first bottle, she continued to search; and I figured she had found everything. I was glad she had packed my guitar. It felt like my only friend.

On the ride up to Spofford, Mom talked about her disappointment in me, and the fact that she did not understand why I had put myself in that situation. She hoped that I would try to get some help because she thought I really needed it. She was afraid for my future.

The rest of the trip was silent. My father never said a word, containing his rage and disappointment, but that was worse. It would have been better if he had screamed and let it out. I hated that my actions had caused them embarrassment. I wished I were dead. It would have been better if I were never born.

I did not know why, but that was always my reaction. When things got bad, I wanted to die or run away. I was not good at dealing with things as they came and when I reacted, it was usually to the extreme.

We drove the hour and a half to Spofford New Hampshire with a quick stop to go through a drive-through, eat a burger, and get some cigarettes because I refused to go to rehab without them. By the time we arrived, the sun was setting. The place had a dome shaped entrance, and I saw Spofford Lake glistening under the lights of the gazebo. The sprawling yard, meticulously kept, was reminiscent of a five-star resort. There were no fences surrounding the grounds, nor were there bars on the windows. It was better than I had expected.

I relaxed a little. I did not know what to think but at least from the outside it didn't seem that bad. As soon as we pulled up to the curb, a uniformed nurse came out to the driveway and escorted my parents and me inside.

"Do you know why you are here, dear?" The white-haired nurse with the hairy upper lip was talking to me. We were sitting in her office.

"Yes, because my lawyer said I have to come here." She looked at my parents with raised faded blonde eyebrows that did not match her white hair color. Her uniform top was colorful and bright, and she wore clog shoes. I liked the casualness of the uniform rather than the stark whites of years past.

"Why did your lawyer recommend you come here?"

"Because she thinks I have a problem with alcohol." Maria had told us she had called this place. I wondered if the nurse had spoken to her directly or whether or not someone else had just given her a message. She did not seem to know what was going on.

"I see." She smiled at me, and then glanced at my parents before asking me, "Do you think you have a problem with alcohol?"

"I don't know." I did not know. All I knew was that my arrest was causing big trouble.

"That is not good enough, I am afraid. If you do not think you have a problem with alcohol, maybe this is not the place for you."

My mother was glaring at me. "K. C., in Maria's office you agreed that you would get help with your alcohol and drug problem."

"I know I did, Mom." To the nurse, I said, "I think I might have a problem, but I am not sure. If I have a problem, I know I need to get help." I was not being deliberately obtuse. I really was not sure. My dad's exasperated sigh of defeat led me to the decisive factor.

"If I really look at the situation, I guess I do have a problem; otherwise, I would not be here, right? I need help." I thought about being dramatic and saying, "Please help me," but I was not in the mood. The last part was true anyway. School that day had not been fun. I had a few months to wait before my court date, and I really did need to figure out what I was doing with my life. In a way, this might work out well. My parents would have time to chill out and I would have time away to think.

Chapter Twenty-Six

Admitted to Rehab (1981)

It had been over twenty-four hours since I had a drop of alcohol, but the nurse's quick blood test revealed that I still had an abundance of it in my blood stream. My parents said goodbye, telling me they would call me on the weekend during visiting hours. They turned and left; there was none of the usual hugs or kisses. They were exhausted and emotionally drained.

A new girl came to fetch me at the nurse's request, and she led me to my room. She told me I would be bunking with another girl recently admitted. I was glad I was not going to be alone, but then it turned out I was alone after all. The other new girl signed herself out of the facility early the next morning; she had reconsidered.

That afternoon, I met Carol. Carol was bizarre with her unmanageable straw-like blonde hair and oversized sweatshirts and pants rolled up and dragging. She did not care what she looked like at all.

I introduced myself as Kay and she told me the nurse had told her my name was K. C. My mother had done it to me again, telling the nurses about my nickname. Carol said she had come close to killing herself with downers, pot, coke, and booze but she did not want to die. She told me she just wanted to "Get down Tonight" and "Shake her Booty."

I thought she was making fun of me when she began reciting the KC and the Sunshine Band songs, but she said she was a fan. She knew their hits, and after we talked for a while, she said she thought I was a hit too.

Carol was glad I brought my guitar, and I played a bit for her until it became obvious that her repertoire of songs was bigger than mine was. She wanted Bob Dillon and all I could give her was John Denver. At fifteen, I was just learning and that was about all I could play. She was not sure about my guitar playing but she encouraged me to keep singing and said I had a sweet voice. I was fine with her honesty; I knew what she said was true. My eardrum plastic surgery had helped improve my voice because I could hear when I was off-key again.

Being roomies with her was fun because I never knew what was going to come out of her mouth. If she got frustrated, she thought nothing of letting out a wail at the top of her lungs, just as if she were home. Sometimes, the nurses would come running to find her frustrated, combing out her hair or angry at trying to make a corner out of her top sheet on the bed. She was a two-year-old in a twenty-three-year-old woman's body.

I learned from a counselor that when you start drinking at a young age, your emotional growth is stunted and you fail to mature. That might explain Carol's tantrums. She had started drinking when she was fifteen. I had started at twelve. I wondered what that meant for me.

I was the youngest person in the rehab. Most of the patients were a lot older, and the majority of them were men. There was one older woman who played cards in the kitchen. She hung out there because it was a "smoking permitted" area.

I smoked cigarettes with her and watched her play cards as she beat the pants off most of her competitors. I did not notice the slits on her wrists until she went to get herself a drink out of the faucet and pulled up the sleeve on her shirt so she would not get it wet. That is when I started paying attention and noticed that the slits on both arms were plentiful. I wondered how she could still be alive. Was it a cry for help because of her alcoholism, or was depression the true cause of her troubles? She had been in an abusive relationship, she told me, and could not imagine getting out alive. Instead of him doing it to her, she had tried doing it to herself. I would never do that.

Another old man was kindly. His wife had kicked him out of the house; she had had enough. He did not know what he would do without her; she always picked him up after a bender, but not anymore. He had burned his bridges.

There was this tall white guy with dark hair that struck me as kind of sleazy. He had jailhouse tats on his hands, arms, neck, and face and I did not trust him. He was about forty-five and chronically in and out of jail. My skin prickled when he walked by and I made sure I was not caught in the kitchen alone with him after I heard he had been put away one time for kidnapping and rape charges.

In the daylight hours, the rehab looked even more like a high-class resort. It had a workout room and pool area. It had an arcade and a pool table in the great rooms. The patients were encouraged to walk around the complex and enjoy the lake as they contemplated their new sober lives.

I stayed in detoxification for seven days before they moved me into the main rehabilitation area. During those first few nights, I read the Big Book or AA bible from cover to cover. My first night in Spofford, the girl who had walked me to my room had given me a copy of the Big Book and had even signed it so I would remember her name.

Since I did not have anything else to do that first week, I read the book. I had heard about AA meetings before from Tim. He had had to go one time for stealing a vehicle; it was part of his sentence.

I still was not convinced that I had an alcohol or drug problem and thought my problems related more to circumstances and situations rather than smoking or drinking; but I realized, wisely, that if other people thought I might be an alcoholic, then maybe I should at least consider it. I had never tried to quit drinking before but I did not think it would be a problem. I had maintained my grades and my lifestyle, and held it all together; at least, until everything had fallen apart.

Jim called me during my second week in rehab, but I did not feel like talking to him. I asked him for Stephen's number, which he gave me, and then I told him not to call me anymore. I called Stephen and told him that I was going to tell the truth during my hearing. If Jim had not put his foot on the accelerator, and if we had gotten out of the car when he wanted to, things would not have been so bad. Stephen was nice and I let him know I thought he was hot to look at too.

Every day I went to group therapy and individual therapy. I ate three fantastic gourmet meals in the dining area that was set up daily. In the evenings, I walked the grounds and played my guitar, singing in the gazebo out on the lake. I met many people and heard their stories. Some had lost jobs, others families, many their self respect. Some were sicker than others were. It was amazing how much drinking could ruin a life. I was fortunate that I was getting help at a young age.

I began to warm to the idea that I might be an alcoholic. I did not get in trouble every time I drank but I could see that every time I got into trouble, drinking was involved. I had lost the respect of my family over this one. I had been in other situations where I had lost the respect of my friends. I certainly had little self-respect and my counselor pointed out the correlation.

My behavior led to drinking, which led to bad decisions, which led to feeling guilty, which led to more drinking and ended with bad results. It was a simple formula. Stop drinking and my life would get better.

My parents came to visit on the second weekend and it was uncomfortable, but at least I smelled better. My eyes were clearer than they had been in years and I was worried about my court case. My sister and brother came up the following week for a weeklong program on Al-Anon, alcoholism, and Family Addictions: How to Stop Enabling. My brother and sister had been my biggest enablers. I relied on them to take care of me even though I knew it was wrong.

They told me they were going to stop enabling me and it made me angry and scared.

A few days before my release, Ronnie started hitting on me. He was in rehab for cocaine mostly, though he drank a lot when he snorted, he told me. I told him I had never tried coke, explaining it was one of my YETs. He recommended I never start because it caused a whole lot of trouble.

His girlfriend of two years had come up on visiting day and told him that she was leaving him. He had figured as much as she had caught him in their bed, with two girls. She was supposed to be away on business but she had come home early and surprised him. He explained to me that he was a coke dealer and the girls had offered him a trade he could not pass up, but now he did not know where he was going to go.

I commiserated with him. Everybody had issues in rehab. No one's future was secure.

"Have you ever been with a black guy?" he wanted to know.

"Nope, it is one of my YETs," I replied. We both laughed at my use of the AA slogan "You Are Eligible Too," and then I explained, "It is not that I have anything against black guys. It is just that I have never had the opportunity to be with a black man." I did not want to tell him how sheltered I was but we only had three black kids in my entire school, and two of them were girls.

He was twenty-three and told me that black guys had bigger dicks than white men did. I could not help myself and said they had bigger lips too. His lips were huge and he told me they were good for kissing.

"Show me," I told him, he kissed me quickly and I laughed. He was afraid we might be caught, as women and men were not supposed to fraternize in the rehab. We tried to look for a place to hook up and we attempted to get busy in the gym, but it lacked privacy and a counselor chased us out. We ended up on the main floor of the rehab center, behind the stairwell that took the steps from the first floor to the second. He was right; not only did black men have big black lips that were good for kissing, they had big cocks too.

Coming home from rehab was better than going up was, but things were still very stifled between my parents and me. I had managed to be a good liar up to that point but now they knew my secrets and they were not condoning my behavior. They started policing my every move.

Chapter Twenty-Seven

Foster Babies (1981)

Mom had quit her job a few years earlier but she was restless. She applied and became a foster mom. Suddenly, we were a foster family to babies who were being given up for adoption or for those babies whose mothers were too sick to care for them, such as drug addicts who were trying to get clean. Mom converted the guestroom into a nursery and loved every single baby that came into our home.

Some of the babies were sickly, with jaundice or infections. Others were jovial and peaceful; all left better than when they came in. Mom was good with babies.

I loved having the babies in the house. It took the focus off me.

Chapter Twenty-Eight

Struggling for Sobriety (1982)

The battle of independence was raging in me. I wanted to be able to party all the time and not worry about parents and rules.

What was the magic number of lovers that turned a girl into a slut? One, two, or five—even if I knew what the magic number was, I doubted it would have mattered. I was a girl hungry for a grown-up world.

Upon my release from rehab, they assigned me an aftercare counselor. I could have gone into a halfway house but I was still in school and begged my mom to let me stay at home. My parents agreed to let me stay with them as long as I followed their rules and stayed sober. I got out of rehab at the end of May and only had a few weeks before summer.

I lasted a few weeks and then I was smoking pot again.

I continued to go to meetings after I got out of rehab, but on the last day of school in 10th grade, one of my friends, Robin, had a keg party and I could not resist taking a beer from the tap.

Another of my friends noticed that I was drinking a beer and he made a big deal out of it. "I thought you could not drink anymore, K. C." It was a small town where everybody knew your business. The kids in my class had been surprised to hear that I had been arrested in a stolen car, and even more surprised to learn that I was an alcoholic and drug addict. I never got into trouble.

"I am just having one, I will be fine," I answered him, but I drank the beer down quickly and got myself another. By the time I was finished with the second drink, I was feeling light headed. It had been almost two months since I had a drink and my tolerance had changed. I left the party because I was afraid I would make an ass out of myself, and instead, stopped off at the package store and got myself a bottle, and went home and drank in my room.

When I went to court in July, the judge, as our lawyer Maria had predicted he would be, was glad to see that I had gotten some help for my alcoholism. My criminal charges reduced, I got off on Youthful Offender status, with a year's probation and a recommendation to continue with my alcohol and drug rehab.

Stephen did not fare so well. He had previous offenses and was older, and the judge told him he would have to do ninety days in jail.

One of my house-cleaning clients, Gerry and Mary, wanted me to go on vacation with them in August. Mary had a colostomy bag and could not do certain things like lift anything over ten pounds. Gerry would love to be able to relax on vacation with Mary but he was usually stuck doing all the things she cannot do.

If I agree to go on vacation with them, I can cook and clean during the day and then have the evenings to myself. My parents gave their permission, my probation officer gave me permission, and I was off to Hawke's Nest beach with Mary and Gerry.

I had been dating Rod before I left for the beach but I broke up with him on the off chance I would want to be available for someone else. He had been upset with me, professing his love, but I was beyond the point of loving a man for his sensitivity and caring. Rod was not for me, he was too passive and good—natured. I had been looking for a way to get out of the relationship and this seemed easiest.

I had told him when I broke it off with him, "I do not want to cheat on you, and I am afraid if I meet someone at the beach I might."

I just was not ready to settle down, and he was getting too serious for me. The truth was I did not think I would ever be able to settle down with anyone. I was a free spirit and focused on the next sexual adventure. I wanted it more than just about anything else besides drinking and smoking dope.

The cottage Mary and Gerry rented was typical of the beach area. Clapboards painted barn red, white trim, with a white picket fence surrounding the house. The front of the cottage sported a screened-in porch. The inside of the cottage was painted sea foam green, furnished inexpensively with wrought iron and wicker furniture. I had the small bedroom that contained a chair, a bed, and a dresser. They took the master suite, which was not much larger.

I had worked for them for over a year by the time we left for the beach. They had had other housecleaners before me but none had been as efficient as I had been. Mary appreciated the fact that I listened to her instructions and did precisely what she asked me to do.

The first night we were at the cottage, I learned about Mary's tests. In the beginning of our working relationship, she thought I might steal from her, so she had left money and valuables around the house. I just moved them to dust and put them back where I found them, or I put them on her bureau and told her I found such and such here or there. She was paying me twelve dollars an hour and I gave her what she paid for. I was not a thief (except for what I stole from my parents), and for the most part, I was a decent hard-working kid with a few issues.

She realized that now, she said, which is why as she got to know me better she began leaving me snacks and told me to help myself to what was in the refrigerator. I took the school bus to her house and worked afternoons, and then either she or Gerry would drive me home after they got home from work and my work was completed.

Sometimes if there was a special project, like the refrigerator or oven, I would work later and eat dinner with them. They were the first adults I felt I could talk to about life in general. They knew I was not happy living at home but I was not old enough to move out. I told them about my surgery and the fact that I felt weird.

They told me they were sure it was a tough experience to go through but that my life would get better and to keep doing what I was doing. I was performing well in school and education would be important to my future success. Mary had a doctorate in psychology and Gerry was an insurance man, I agreed with their advice.

That week at the beach, during the day, I cooked, cleaned, swept, and did laundry. In the afternoons, I played Scrabble with them. After dinner was my time. The first night, I went down on the beach and walked it alone. The second night, I met Howie. Howie was twenty-five and had a lifeguard tan, because that was what he did during the day. He was a part-time professional weight lifter who waxed his body for competitions. I had never met a man who felt so smooth. I only had six days left. We fucked on the beach that night, and I was back at the cottage at midnight with plans to meet him the next evening.

On the fourth night, we fell asleep on the beach. I barely made it into the cottage before Mary and Gerry awoke. It turns out, they had not slept all night; they were waiting for me to come home. When I had had dinner with them in their apartment before vacation, we had had wine with dinner. When we were at the cottage the first few nights, they allowed me to have beers as long as I stayed inside the cottage and did not tell anyone they had given me alcohol.

Up until the fourth night, I had managed to hide my alcoholism from them; but on the last few days of the trip, I messed up and they saw me for the wreck I really was and they became worried. They did not want me to have any more beer.

When we got back to town, they introduced me to one of Mary's friends, Pat. He came to dinner one night and I stayed to visit. Pat had been to school and was a psychologist too, one who specialized in adolescents. Mary did not think it would be appropriate given our closeness for her to try to treat me. Pat seemed nice. He was forty-one years old, had grown up in Longmeadow, Massachusetts, and I was instantly at ease with him. I began writing letters to him, and when my parents had a Labor Day picnic, I invited the three of them to come.

He caught me alone as people were getting ready to fill up their plates with food. "Look, I got your last letter. I am concerned about your smoking, and I think I can help."

I had written him, "I get high. It helps me zone out. Otherwise, my mind spins and will not let me sleep."

We were in my parent's front hall, with most of the guests still outside but a few in the kitchen, gathering the salads out of the refrigerator.

"If I showed you a way to calm down, will you promise me you'll stop smoking at night?"

"I do not think it will work. My mind races like crazy all the time; but sometimes, when I am lying in bed at night, it is the worst."

"Look, I promise this will work if you are willing to try it."

"I do not believe you, but what the heck, I will try anything once."

I lay down on the living room floor and he sat about a foot away from me by my feet. He was sitting Indian style and telling me to relax my breathing.

"Picture a safe place in your mind."

I tried like hell but I could not think of one, so he gave me the homework of creating a haven that I could go to in the future that would provide me peace in stressful situations.

Then, we started at my toes. He had me flex then squeeze them and hold the squeeze for a count of ten and then release. Then, he coached me to move to my ankles, doing the same thing. We were on my knees when my dad happened by and saw us in the living room.

"No way, no, I am sorry. Why don't you come out and eat with the rest of us?" Dad did not know what we were doing and he did not want to know. He and Pat had known each other from high school and Dad was uncomfortable with my alliance with him. Dad did not come out and say it but I could tell he did not want Pat hitting on me. I tried to tell Dad that it was not like that, but he did not want to hear it. I got angry but complied with his wishes, and after that, I never saw or spoke with Pat again.

That fall I became exhausted again. I had not fared well at the fast food restaurant and had taken up with my customers again. I was working different hours every day and allowed myself about an hour of down time a week. My phone kept ringing, people wanted my services, and I did not have enough hours in the day to give them everything they needed. I was tired of the strain of being self-employed.

Every day was different, yet every other week was the same. One family wanted their socks folded one way, another wanted them folded another way. One set of children could not watch television, while another set of children had the television as their babysitter and were put in front of the television deliberately. I did my best and my clients were happy, but I was not. I wanted to go to one place and have one boss rather than thirty of them.

I sold my business for a profit on my seventeenth birthday. At the same time, I applied for and got a "real" job at the local diner. I started washing dishes and then ended up working as a server and host. The owners liked me and let me play my guitar and sing in the restaurant, entertaining their guests Friday nights. The only problem was I could not do it sober. I began to sneak smoking grass behind the building or grabbing a quick beer in the ladies' room before I could play. I was taking home less money now because of taxes but I had enough to live on and I liked my employers, Nancy and Hyde.

During the day, I went to high school pretending to be normal. My friends were talking about writing a children's book, becoming a clothes designer in New York, becoming a professor of history; I had no clue what I would do with my life, and it was starting to bother me.

Chapter Twenty-Nine

The Father Factor (1982)

How does a father deal with a daughter's sexuality? I have embarrassed my father by what I have become.

I arranged to meet a neighbor boy in the woods. We were going to party but he brought his brother and a few of his friends. I sat in the circle with them and we passed the bottle and laughed as we talked about school and the neighborhood. I heard my father yelling my name but I ignored him. I was not ready to go home yet.

Then, I was kissing John, and then after another swig of the bottle, I kissed his brother. This was getting fun, and I heard my father yelling for me again. I ignored him, hoping he would go away and leave me to my vices.

My father, though, was persistent. He got on the moped and rode it around the neighborhood. I knew I should leave and come out of the woods and go home, but I did not. I did not care that he was worried about me. He was wasting his time. The boys told me I should go, and I know they are right, but I did not want to go.

It was dark in the woods and we did not see him until he was practically standing over us. I was screwed.

"K. C., I have been calling you and calling you. It is time to go home NOW." My father was livid when he found me in the woods with these boys. He knew what they wanted from me. The same thing all men want from women: sex.

He grabbed my arm and roughly escorted me out of the woods. When he asked me why I did not answer him, I gave him a wiseass remark and he punched me in the mouth. My lips bled from the impact of his hand against the braces in my mouth. He rode the moped home and I walked behind him dejectedly. I will never be daddy's little girl again.

Chapter Thirty

Fall Bonfire (1982)

I was sitting alone at school. People were talking about going to the bonfire. I had been sober once but it only lasted about a month and a half and now I was off the wagon. I was a people pleaser by nature. I learned that in rehab. I went above-and-beyond in most situations because I hated myself and wanted others to like me.

At the same time, no matter what I did, it never seemed to be good enough. I judged myself harshly; I was a lonely girl living in a mixed up crazy world. Nancy had given me the night off, saying I was working too hard. She called me cantankerous and told me I needed to have a little fun in my life and to stop being so serious.

I had started making my own rules about life, and at this age, I think it was a hell of a lot easier to live life that way. I did not trust anybody anymore. I was not going to make it to my eighteenth birthday. I wanted to be free as a bird. I wanted to fly away but I was trapped and angry. I allowed my mind to escape but my body was stuck here.

I was supposed to meet Drew at the bonfire, and I did see him, but what I saw was that he was trying to dog some other girl. That is not what he said, of course, but I knew him well enough to know what he was doing. We had been seeing each other secretly on and off for the last three years, mostly in the woods or in my parents' backyard.

Sometimes, he would swing by when I was up on the roof smoking. We would go off and hook up and then I would have to try to sneak in the house or sleep on the front porch until my brother, David got up to do his paper route. Dave would go out the front door and I would go in, catching a few hours of sleep before school.

Drew had said he was going to hang out with some of his friends that night, but when I got close enough, I realized he had washed and combed his hair. I went up to the group he was with and smelled his cologne. He had even scraped the usual dirt from underneath his fingernails. Men just do not do these things when they are going to hang out with other guys.

He walked with me around the bonfire, telling me he had a change in plans and would not be spending time with me. I was okay with it, I told him at first. I wanted a kiss to walk away but he would not give me one. "Please, just a quick one." I wanted people to see me with him, but he refused.

"Maybe I will swing by later tonight. Will you be around?"

"I would be," I told him, and I walked away feeling dejected.

A few minutes later, I saw him with his arm around Melissa. I was humiliated and pissed. He was blowing me off. I was just a piece of fuck meat to him and his actions confirmed it. He would never consider me a girlfriend; I was just fooling myself if I thought anything different. I knew because he never wanted people to know that we had been together. If I told anybody, he threatened he would stop seeing me. I could not bear that because I really liked him, and because I did not have to put on any airs with him; he knew me for what I was.

Normally, I was good at keeping secrets, but this secret hurt to keep.

I thought about how I could hurt him but I like him too much. He had been fun and honest this whole time. I could not fault him for that. I had a reputation for being easy, and we both knew it was true. I was not the girlfriend type, he had joked with me before.

I walked around the schoolyard for a while. I did not have that many friends and those that I did have, I had been working to alienate. Sometimes, it was just easier when people kept their distance. I had no desire for people to know what was going on in my life in every aspect. I was like Sybil, with multiple lives.

I was not going to stay in town after graduation anyway. I hated this town and I always have. I wanted to live in the city, maybe New York or Boston. I did not fit in a small town. Too many people knew your business, not enough privacy in a town like this. There was no getting past mistakes; everybody knew.

An hour later, I was sitting on the bleachers next to a soccer field with two of my male high school classmates. We had a joint but mostly I was the one smoking it. We also had a six-pack of Bud.

I was sitting between them and my hand was on each of their legs. I was being a cock-teaser. I kissed each of them one at a time as I rubbed up against the other. At first, they wanted me to choose one or the other but I was greedy, I wanted both.

"Why not?" I said innocently as I looked up the hill. "We have the place to ourselves."

The fire was raging and many of the high school students, as well as some of the middle school students, were roaming the school grounds in honor of the beginning of football season. There were maybe a couple hundred kids, some drunk, others high, but most just ready to do the rah, rah boomsdia, siss boom bah.

"I couldn't care less about the team," I told them, "but I would not mind playing with a few balls."

The boys were excited about my proposition, but nervous at the same time. One of them I had made out with before in Susan's basement closet. The other I had never been with before and I knew he did not particularly like me. It was a power trip and I insisted they unzip their pants. Sitting between them, with our backs to the crowd, I fondled each of them until they were both rock solid.

We made small talk and I teased them some more. "What do you say we do something with those things?" I stood up, squatting low so my head was not visible over the bleachers, and bent over.

They were nervous at first, but Cy positioned himself behind me while I blew Allan. Then, after a bit, I had them switch. I was being tag-teamed and it felt spontaneous but that was about it. What turned me on was not the boys I was with, but that we might be caught. That, and the fact that I could see Drew and Melissa walking around the fire, arm in arm. I bet he would come by tonight after she got him all worked up.

Some boys worried about pregnancy, but I told them it did not matter. I told them I could not get pregnant, and not to worry about that. When they asked why, I would go into this explanation of how I had been born without a vagina and how doctors had created one but it would not stretch and it was tight. The doctors were not sure I had all my parts. That was usually enough to get them off the subject of safe sex and asking me questions.

Carpe diem was my motto. This *ménage-a-trois* was not the first time I had been with two boys. I liked being in the middle and had no problems sharing. After about ten minutes, both of them had gotten off and there was an uncomfortable silence. I was not looking to cuddle or profess my love for either one of them. We decided to go up to the hill to see how the fire was going. Each of us ran into other people we knew and we went off individually.

When my dad picked me up that night after the bonfire wound down, he asked me how my night went. I told him I had fun, and I had.

I knew he wanted to know what I wanted to do after high school but I had not given it that much thought. I had no burning desire to do anything specific. I wanted to travel and see the world but I was not sure how I would afford that. Maybe I would be a paid whore. I loved sex, and why not be paid to do something you love? No, I could not say that aloud. Maybe I could become a dancer. Maybe a writer—I would love to write someday, if I only had something to say. Perhaps I could be a musician. I knew I sucked at dance, writing, and music, but those are my passions. No. No. No. That is all I ever heard as a kid.

No, you cannot do that. No, you will not be good at that. No, you cannot make money at that. No, you need to do it this way. No, you cannot wear that. No, you cannot go there. No. No. No.

I needed a Yes.

Chapter Thirty-One

Stephen (1982)

Drew never came over that night, but the next day, Stephen phoned me and we agreed we would go to a meeting together. Stephen was one of my friends' older brothers.

I did not really know Stephen until that night of our arrest in April. I never pictured that we would become a couple, but as we talked while I was in rehab and then after I got out, I discovered that not only was he gorgeous with his thick brown hair that matched his dark eyes and olive complexion, he was a sweetheart, not to mention, a gentleman.

Whereas Jim had done things and said things to make me feel bad about myself, Stephen always tried to make me feel good. He was supportive and he said he cared about me, wanting me to get my life on the right path, and not follow the path he was on already.

My eating disorders counselor had gotten through to me on some level. He made me realize that anorexia was a sickness in which people acted out controlling their food intake because they felt that another area of their life was out of control. It was hard for me to give myself permission to eat. Every time I looked in the mirror I thought I looked terrible but it wasn't the outside I was seeing, it was the inside. I couldn't look in the mirror without hating myself and that had to change. The psychologist suggested I go back to therapy with a sexual counselor but I refused and promised I would start eating more, and I did. I hated when people told me I looked too thin. It was none of their business, and at least by eating more, that kind of harassment stopped.

When Stephen came home from jail in October, we tried to get sober together, but one night we ended up drunk and in my bed. When my father came in to wake me up for school, he found us and he was so upset with me that he kicked me out.

My thirty-second plan was to live in the cabin in the woods. The abandoned hunting cabin was great to party and screw around in even though it had no plumbing. It had windows and doors and I thought I could stay there long enough to graduate high school; I did not have any other options, so I told Stephen that was what I was going to do. He ran home and told his dad, Frank, what had happened.

As I said, Stephen was a gentleman. I think Frank felt somewhat responsible that I had gotten in trouble with his son. I lugged my belongings from my parents' to the end of the road; attempting to carry them up to the cabin one by one. Frank told me I was being ridiculous and I could not live in the woods. He began loading my plastic bags into the back of his pick up, saying I could rent a room from him and his wife, Vicky. That was how I began living on the farm with Stephen and his family.

On one of our drinking nights, Stephen and I went to a party up in Hartland and our ride home left without us. We tried to hitch a ride back home but we walked the twenty miles because no one would pick us up.

The next day, I had my scheduled meeting with my probation officer in Simsbury and then I was supposed to go to the other side of town to have my pictures taken for the senior yearbook. I had no problem thumbing all over town and getting to Simsbury that day. It was easy to get a ride when you were a girl thumbing alone.

Then during a warmer than normal October day, Stephen and I went to an AA meeting together, but as soon as we got to the church, we decided we were thirsty and went to the package store for some booze. Stephen wanted to show me a local watering hole that he swam in when he was a kid with his dad. It was just up the street a ways, he told me, so we walked.

We got there and skinny-dipped for a while until the owner of the farm that owned the creek came out with a shotgun and escorted us off his property. I hurried to get my clothes back on while standing on his beach but he hollered for me to keep moving, so I finished getting dressed on the side of the highway where the river met the road. The farmer stayed there until we began walking away.

It took us awhile to walk the mile and a half, but we made it back downtown. I knew if I were alone I could get a ride, but I speculated that, together, we would be walking; and that was what we did.

Back in the center of town, we decided to hang out behind the elementary school. There were six bikers throwing Frisbees and they looked like they might have some weed. We went over and sat on the grass watching them throw and catch. There were three guys and three girls with Harleys out having a good time.

The biker's drank and offered us beers from a case that was on the back of one of the bikes. We gladly accepted their offer as our booze was gone. Then we mentioned smoke and they said we should go back to their place, as smoking weed on public school grounds was not cool. We agreed. Secretly, I did not think drinking beers on elementary school grounds was that cool either.

They had friends that were up at the package store with a car, so two of the guys brought two of the guys over there and they restocked on the booze and dropped off the riders. Then the two bikers came back to get Stephen and me and we formed a caravan with the car and bikes as we travelled to Tarriffville where Jason's apartment was.

The Indian summer night air was humid. The fan pushed the hot air from one side of the room to the other but offered no relief. We drank beers, ate pizza, and watched a movie. After eating, I felt ill and asked if I could lie down. Jason told Stephen and me that we could crash in his spare room and I thought that that was awesome.

Keeping the bedroom door open for air, I lay down on the bed as they popped in another movie. I felt better in a few minutes. Then, Stephen came in, lay down next to me, and we started getting it on. He had not bothered to close the door, although he had shut it enough to give us privacy. As he was kissing me and removing my shirt, Jason and his old lady, Pam, came in and sat on the bed.

We ignored them for a minute but then Stephen copped an attitude when Jason began rubbing my leg. I was fine with it, but Stephen was not. Pam insisted we could all have fun, and she tried to rub Stephen's leg but he pushed her off. They left the bedroom, and Stephen glared at me for several minutes before deciding that we were leaving.

He told me to get dressed and then he apologized to our host and hostess. He did not want any part of swinging. He was sorry if we had led them on in any way. We were grateful for their hospitality, but we were going home.

We stuck our thumbs out as we had on our trip from Hartland, but just like before, we got no offer for a ride. It took us about three hours to walk back to his house in East Granby, and the entire trip Stephen kept saying, "I cannot believe you were willing to have sex with them."

To me, it was no big deal. I thought it would be fun, but I could tell I had crossed the line with him. He no longer thought of me as a nice girl. He had known about Jim but I had not informed him of my entire sexual history. It was easier to stay quiet than spill the secrets and risk rejection.

He would not make love to me when we got home, even though I tried all my tricks. He pushed me away and told me to go to sleep. I slept on top of the bed, fully clothed.

A few days later, Stephen went back to jail and I stayed on with his family. I was smoking pot and drinking, mainly. If I was working a lot, I did amphetamines, and occasionally I would smoke some hash. I tried acid a few times but I got into trouble with it.

Hours before he went back to jail, Stephen asked me to marry him and he gave me his pot-leaf chain as a symbol of our engagement. He told me he had forgiven me for my sexual indiscretions and chalked up my behavior to our involvement with alcohol. He said that when he got out of jail we would live sober together and build a life for ourselves.

Stephen's sisters and parents were hard working, strong loving maniacs. They were kind to me, and on Sundays, Vicky would drive her girls and me to the prison to see Stephen. Several times, I slipped him joints wrapped in cellophane that I would pass to him when I kissed him before we sat down at the visitation table. I was doing the wrong things again, and if caught, it would be considered a violation of my probation and I would have had to do some time.

Meanwhile, on the farm, Frank, their dad, taught me how to hunt deer with flashlights, skin a hide, and trade furs or meat for eggs, milk, and cash. I helped with the chores, such as feeding their pigs Grote and Weigel and the coon dogs, also used for hunting.

I enjoyed kicking through mud, throwing the slop, and jumping from the lofts onto the swing and singing at the top of my lungs over the hay bales like any farm girl might. Friday or Saturday nights would often be spent eating venison or pork chops while friends came over with their banjos and spoons and we laughed and sang the night away. I wanted to belong and they did their best to make me feel like a special girl, but I fucked it up. I have a tendency of doing that, especially when things do not go my way.

In the dead of winter, I was the only one that slept upstairs in the big farmhouse because some of the windowpanes were missing in some of the bedrooms and it was really cold. I slept in my long underwear, pants, coat, mittens, and hat in my sleeping bag. I was just grateful to not have to be outside.

Chapter Thirty-Two

Broken Engagement (November1982)

At work one afternoon, I started partying with the line chef after the owners left for the night. We drank beers and I got my first taste of cocaine. I was sucking it off his cock in the booth in the front when we thought we heard somebody come in the back, and we did; it was the bug spray guy. Long story short, the line chef left his beer in the microwave when we got disturbed and the owner found it and fired him. He took the wrap for me and I felt bad about it. I went to his house and fucked his brains out while we listened to Jethro Tull. Fucking him was my way of saying thank you. A few weeks later, I missed my period. That was a first. I did not think I could have kids, and it was freaking me out.

So anyway, there I was, Ethan said he would help pay for the abortion if I was pregnant but turns out it was just a false alarm. Unfortunately, Frank overheard me talking on the telephone about the possibility that I might be pregnant. Seeing how his son and I were engaged and he was in jail, it was not a conversation I should have been having.

Frank let me know that just as soon as I hung up the phone. He wanted me to break up with his son and move out. I called Stephen in jail that night and told him the truth. He agreed that if I could not be faithful to him, we should end our plans to get married. He wished me well and had no hard feelings.

That night, I tried to kill myself. I snuck into Frank and Vicky's bedroom and got the loaded shotgun that he always kept by his bed and brought it up to my room. Frank had taught me how to clean a gun and load it. I checked the chamber; there was a bullet in there. If it had been a pistol, I might not be here to talk about it, but the damn thing was a rifle and it was heavy. I tried to hold it up to my head but the barrel on the.22 was so long, I could not reach the trigger with my arm without having the barrel point somewhere other than my head. I did not want to miss the shot and risk paralysis for life. That would have been worse. If I was going to do this, I wanted to do it right.

I set the gun down on the bed and took my shoe off. If I could use my toe to pull the trigger, then maybe I could be successful. The gun kept moving and I was afraid I would shoot it off unsuccessfully and be worse off. I did not hear Frank's footsteps on the stairs or walking up the hall, but all of a sudden my door flew open and he was there, yelling at me, "What do you think you are doing?"

"Trying to kill myself."

"Well, go ahead then. Do it." His reaction was not what I expected, and when he slammed my door and walked away, I put the gun down and I sobbed feeling sorry for myself. I could not even kill myself the right way.

I did not want to die; I just did not know how to live.

I walked the gun back down the stairs and set it in his room. Vicky was sleeping but Frank was at the table. He watched me return the gun to his room and then he beckoned me into the kitchen where he was sitting.

"Look, it has been an emotional day. You made the right decision to put the gun away. You made the right decision to end your engagement but I still think you need some help. Get some help and you can stay here until you graduate from high school. Otherwise, you are going to have to find another place to live."

Chapter Thirty-Three

Confession (December, 1982)

I sat in a confessional. I did not want to tell this man priest what I had done. How could he know how I feel or understand what I have been through? He has been programmed by the church to discount behavior like mine. He will sit in judgment. All men do. They judge and ridicule, and then they go off and play with themselves, thinking of the sinners as they rehash the stories in their minds.

My parents had picked me up at Stephen's house for a family photo they wanted done for the holidays. On the way to the shoot, they stopped at church and insisted I go to confession.

"Bless me, Father, for I have sinned. It has been about a year since my last confession. I have been very bad. I have not listened to my parents, and I have lied to them. I took the Lord's name in vain. I have been a drunken slut and a bad influence on my brother and sister."

My mind is racing again. I have been a whore every day and sold my soul along the way. I am in trouble, Father, but you cannot help me. Do not worry, Father, I do not believe in God anyway. You do not have to forgive me. Forgive my parents. Forgive yourself. Forgive God. I do not need forgiveness from you or them.

I explained to the parish priest, a man I have known and liked for several years, that I was here to appease my parents and that I am supposed to make a confession but I really don't believe in it.

He wants to know if I am sorry for the bad things I have done.

"Am I sorry for the things I have done? I am not sure, Father." I am always sorry when I am caught, if that is what you mean. Yes, I am always very sorry then.

"Penance, Father? I never believed that men could grant forgiveness to other mortals." I don't mean to slam his profession, but I think the whole thing is a farce.

I think to myself, you know what they say, once a whore always a whore. People do change but others never forget. According to the laws of religion, I will go straight to hell. I do not have to worry about being stuck in purgatory. They do not allow people like me in heaven, the rules are clear. Nevertheless, thanks anyway, Father.

To him I say, "Have yourself a great day."

I did not feel any better when I left, but I bet he was glad that the Catholic religion forbade him to be married; otherwise, he might have a daughter just like me.

Christmas that year was unmemorable. I went to my grandmother's for dinner with my parents and siblings. The conversation was stilted and I didn't feel like I belonged. Then I got back to the farm and I didn't feel like I belonged there either. I didn't want to be away from my bottle or a joint for very long. They comforted me more than people and yet left me beyond needy. I recognized the signs that I had become addicted.

Chapter Thirty-Four

First Day of Sobriety (January 15, 1983)

That January morning, I thought I would forget Ed by the time I woke up, but after my exchange with Frank after the red truck pulled out of his driveway, I could not sleep, tossed, and turned all night long. My life was going nowhere fast. I was ruining every relationship I had. People that had loved me at one time are now repulsed by me.

I remembered how I had felt when Tim drank. I wanted to shake him and get him to stop but he wouldn't. I imagined that that was how the people around me felt too. They couldn't make me stop. I was the only one that could do it. I was so afraid. I was afraid to grow up. I was afraid to feel. I was afraid to face the wrath of those I had hurt.

I decided that I would honestly attempt to try to change my ways. I had hit my bottom. I was lucky. Being that drunk and out of control thumbing and taking rides with strangers could have cost me my life. I had had a bad ride but I had survived. Now I had burned all of my bridges just as that old man in the rehab had done.

Embarrassed by my behavior, I recalled the disdain in Frank's voice. "We do not want riff-raff like you around he-ah." There was no doubt in my mind that had I not gotten drunk the night before, I would not have found myself in that situation. I did not blame Ed for doing what he did, nor did I blame Frank for threatening to kick me out after watching me in the driveway either.

It was time for me to change the path of my life. It was the end of the beginning.

At eight o'clock in the morning, I called the AA hotline and the man that answered hooked me up with someone who called me right back.

That man, Harry, agreed to pick me up and take me to a meeting at noon. I did not tell him I had been drinking the night before and that I was hung over. I assumed he could figure it out on his own. People do not call the AA hotline when things are going well.

I knew about speaking from my time in Spofford Hall, the rehab I had been at for five weeks after my arrest. Speaking or telling your story in AA was supposed to help the audience realize they were not alone. By sharing stories, it was supposed to help the alcoholic face their past, their fears, and get on with living in the present.

When we arrived at my brother and sister's school, I began to shake. He thought I was nervous to speak but I was actually petrified someone in the classroom would know me or my brother or sister. Technically, I should not have opened my mouth at that meeting but he was insistent I share. It was Saturday and I was surprised there was an AA meeting going on at the school but there we were and even though I kept pinching myself, I couldn't wake up.

I did not want to say anything about what was going on in my life for fear of it coming back to haunt them. I spoke in general terms, and when I was finished, I felt a little better. Afterward, Harry took me for coffee and we talked about my arrest. I never told him what had made me pick up the phone. I was too embarrassed to share with him the fact that I had had to give a blowjob for a ride home, and that the whole situation was enough for me to say I had hit bottom.

The next time Harry invited me to a meeting, I went to his house to meet his wife and kids. Later in the week, I babysat his kids while he and his wife went out. He came on to me in the car on the ride home and I gave him a blowjob. It was my way of saying thank you. I did not feel obligated to him as I had to Ed. Harry was happy, he had indoctrinated another person into the folds of AA. They had a name for what he did. They called it 13-Stepping and it was frowned upon.

It did not matter to me how I got back in the program, I felt lucky to be alive, and I was ready to change.

After my call to AA, Frank and Vicky talked to me one more time and told me that if I stayed sober I could keep renting my room. I had one last chance and I was not going to ruin it this time. They had been very good to me and I desperately wanted them to be proud of me. They wanted me to finish high school so I could support myself someday.

I will not lie to you and say getting into AA, staying sober, and being a senior in high school out on my own was easy, because it was not. I was ashamed of who I became when I was drinking but I was not sure how to change. At first, I was afraid people would know I was in AA, but then I realized that they had known I was a drunken loser before, so trying to get help had to be a step in the right direction.

Taking that first step and admitting that I was an alcoholic was a big achievement for me, and it rapidly led to steps two and three. That is where I ran into a major obstacle. I could not reconcile my emotions with my desire for sexuality and a belief in God. I thought if I could face my fears head on, I could overcome them. Inside, I still did not feel like a woman.

Chapter Thirty-Five

The God Factor in AA (1983)

I began questioning God somewhere between the fifth and sixth grade. Raised Catholic, I celebrated the holidays because of my parents' teachings but I felt like the Catholic religion was a farce and I did not want to be a part of it. The older I got, the more I despised religions and what they stood for; they divided people. I felt that the rules of the church were for people living 1500 years earlier, the church had not kept up to the changing times.

I gradually found a sense of community within the rooms of AA meetings that became my church. I was a popular speaker, probably because, at the time, I was one of the youngest females around, I was a straight shooter, and had a memorable story. I went to meetings in Manchester, Southwick, Granby, South Windsor, East Granby, and Enfield, meeting people and hearing their stories.

Besides my alcoholism, I battled with depression. My normal energy levels were manic. I never wanted to stop for sleep even though I had to. I wanted to cram as much of life and living in every waking hour I could. My head would reel but I kept moving trying to stay ahead of it. I started to try new things.

I met Diane in AA. She was three years older than I was, and we began to spend more time together. We took mini vacations once a month, taking off from work on a Friday or Monday so we could have three days for an adventure. She was driving a piece of shit car but she had a friend in Cape Cod, Massachusetts who agreed to sell her his car for cheap. We took a ride out there for a weekend, hung with her friend, and brought home an old blue Pinto with a sunroof.

K.C. LAUER

We drove everywhere in that car together. One time, we went to Salisbury Beach on the Massachusetts/New Hampshire border. We walked along the boardwalk, holding hands. Some people made fun of us and called us gay. Diane pulled her hand away but I was not ashamed of our friendship and so I grabbed her hand back. I was not gay, but even if I was, who had the right to judge me? "Fuck them," I told her.

We enjoyed our weekend at the beach, on the boardwalk, and playing Scrabble in our room in the bed-and-breakfast that had about twenty rocking chairs on its wide planked white washed porch.

Another time, Diane and I went up to upper New York to visit her cousin. We hung out with her during the day, playing ball, sharing stories, and then that night we went to an AA meeting. It was cool to go anywhere in the world and instantly find people we had something in common with. We went to a dance and found some guys to hang out with that night.

One time, we decided to take a whole week together and we went to Lake George. We rented an efficiency apartment from some French Canadians who had a quaint motel that contained sixteen units. They lent us fishing poles and we went fishing one day. Another day, we went out on the lake and Diane tried to convince me to parasail. I was petrified, and although she convinced me to get into the jumpsuit harness, I panicked and would not let the attendant clip the sail attachment to the boat, which meant I was not sailing. She was so mad at me that day we barely talked on the ride back to the motel. When we got there, she took off, saying she needed some time away from me. I felt bad that she was mad at me but the terror had been overwhelming.

In 1982, Connecticut changed its legal drinking age from eighteen to nineteen; and then in 1983, they raised it to twenty. I was seventeen and sober but wanted to go bar hopping to dance and meet men. Diane and I went to the motor vehicles department together. I used her social security card and birth certificate and they took my picture and put it on a license. Within minutes, she went through the line and updated her license, giving the attendant the same information I had just provided. I sweat bullets the whole time, waiting for a uniformed officer to take me to jail, but nothing happened. Getting a fake ID was easier than I ever thought possible.

After that, we went bar hopping sometimes after going to AA meetings. We were playing on the tracks, so to speak, but we were not there for the booze. We were there doing collections. Diane was a bookie and sometimes she had to chase people down to collect. She had a mouth like a sailor, and even though she was shorter than I was, she was stocky; and if push came to shove, she could take all five-feet-two-inches of her stature and make grown men cry and plead for mercy. She would threaten them with telling their wives or girlfriends how much money they had lost on a bet, and usually they would pay up. If she had too many problems with a guy, she would enlist the aid of her dad or brother, both bookmakers themselves.

Her mom was sweet and gentle, and always happy to see us when we came into the house. She had no idea what was going on in her house and that made Diane feel guilty. Her mom wanted her to settle down with a nice boy, but Diane was not ready.

One night, Diane wanted to go to the Cape and watch the sunrise over the ocean, but we were broke. We had stopped in at her house but Diane's dad was out of the house and her mom did not have any money to lend us. We went to the I-90. It was ladies' night and we got in free. We found a couple of guys to dance with, and even though we did not drink, they offered to buy us Cokes and we accepted. About a half hour later, Diane found me dancing on the dance floor and grabbed my arm.

"C'mon, we gotta go."

"What are you talking about? The bar does not close for another two hours and I am having fun. I do not want to go yet."

"Kay, we have to go, and we have to go now. C'mon."

Normally Diane was soft with me, allowing me to be the dominant one on what we were going to do and when, but this time she was insistent.

As soon as we got in the car, we pulled away. Normally Diane would fool with the radio for a few minutes before we ever pulled out of anywhere, but this time she was not waiting for the perfect song. I fiddled with the radio and was silent, waiting for her to tell me what had happened.

When we hit the highway headed back toward Springfield, she reached into her purse and pulled out a wad of cash.

"What the hell? Where did you get that money? I thought you were broke?"

"I was but I'm not anymore." She had picked the pockets of one of the guys she had danced with and hit a homerun. We had three hundred dollars, more than enough for gas money to go to the Cape.

At first, I was angry with her. "How can you just take money from people? It's not yours to take."

She did not make excuses. "The guy was an asshole to carry that much cash to a bar. Somebody might have rolled him in the parking lot, but he does not have to worry about that now. He got off easy with me; I even gave him a kiss."

"Did he know it was a $300 kiss?"

"No way, I was careful. And not to pat myself on the back or anything, but I am pretty good. He did not feel a thing."

She was proud of her thievery and I was stunned. "Diane, I do not want to be a part of this kind of thing. C'mon, we are sober now. I do not want to be involved with stealing from people. I never stole while I was drinking, and I am not going to be a thief in sobriety. You should go back and return the money to that guy."

"Now you are the one being crazy. You are carrying a fake ID with my information on it. We are not going back there. If it makes you feel better, I promise I will never do it again, but we have the money now and I am not returning it. I want to go to the Cape. Are you going with me or not?"

It was a little after one in the morning, and if we were going to see the sunrise, we had better skedaddle. Instead of dropping me off as I wanted her to, she went by my exit and continued on her way toward Hartford and the highway that would take us northeast toward the Cape. When I did not ask her to turn around, she took my compliance as acceptance, and we drove the four hours in three and a half.

The sky was starting to lighten as we pulled into Buzzard's Bay. We pulled into the rest area just beyond the bridge and got out of the car. We lay on the front hood of the car against the glass, with a blanket around us, drinking Tab, and toasting to the sunrise. It was glorious.

I had never gone anywhere specifically to see the sunrise. It was an important day. Diane told me about her grandfather's sexual abuse and it explained her anger and hatred of men in a new way. I was sad for her, and as I listened to her story and then related mine., I reminded myself at the end of the day that you could never trust anyone but yourself. The awareness made me sad.

Life was not fair, and yet as youngsters, our elders tell us that if we work hard, mind our manners, and listen to our parents' things would be okay. It was not the truth. Parents could not protect us from demons that they did not know about or refused to see.

About the same time as I met Diane, I met Pat and asked him to become my sponsor. Pat and his wife became dear friends and introduced me to many others who also became good friends of mine. They were nudists and enjoyed life and that was what attracted me to him, and later to them, in the first place. They were both bleach-blond, buffed-up people in their fifties, and made no bones about their swinging lifestyle. I envied that they could stay sober and be honest with who they were. That was what I wanted.

I wanted to progress in AA, so I explained to Pat about my issues with God. He was an atheist too and said he used the power of the rooms as his God.

I knew it was a requirement for me to choose one singular god or recognize a power greater than myself. I had to recognize that I only had control of my actions, not my thoughts, not other people's actions, or anyone's feelings. I needed to relinquish control to a higher power. And so it was that a Group of Drunks (GOD) became my higher power.

Many in AA had hardships far worse than mine. Sometimes, I would think I might be too young to be in the rooms after all, I only got drunk and drugged for five years, but then I would remember where I ended up. I knew I did not want to go back there.

I met Mike through Pat and Wini. He was a nudist too. He and his wife were going through some rough times because he had had an affair. He and his mistress, Becky, were getting sober together. She was a paralegal and we hit it off, chatting together when we saw each other in meetings.

Then, I met Alex through the young people's meeting in Enfield. I adored his mother and she thought he would adore me. He was four years older than I was, which made me jailbait when we first hooked up.

He was cocky and outspoken, calling himself a slut. We had that in common. I thought he had a great body, a fast wit, a funny sarcastic sense of humor, and he loved to dance. He was as broken as I was in many ways, and we agreed that since we were newly sober, we would just be fuck-buddies. Neither of us was ready to be in a relationship but we were definitely into having sex.

Chapter Thirty-Six

Senior Year (February 1983)

One day when I was with Alex at his mom's house, he joked about giving me to his brother as a welcome home present when he got home from the navy. I was game.

The morning of his brother's arrival, Alex spanked my ass and made me promise to treat his brother as I would him, giving him an excellent blowjob, and doing whatever it was he wanted me to do. I promised Alex I would give Joe the best present I could.

Alex left for the airport and instructed me to lie naked in the bed, waiting for the two of them.

I was so nervous lying there, waiting. Part of me was surprised that I had agreed to do this and part of me was nervous about whether I would even like Joe. It did not matter whether I liked him or not, I was doing this for Alex, and that excited me even more than being with someone new.

I talked to one of my girlfriends about Alex's proposition and she thought I was crazy even to consider it. "How can you think about having sex with someone you do not even know? And your boyfriend cannot love you if he wants to share you with his brother. He is just using you for sex."

"Using me for sex? Of course he is. That is what our relationship is all about. We fuck. I am not looking for love, and I am not looking for a lifetime commitment. He is a lot of fun, believe me. Even if I do not hit it off with his brother, I am sure it will be an experience to remember."

"I do not know about you, Kay. I could never sleep with someone unless I loved them and knew that they loved me back."

That was not me. I could easily detach from my body and separate my emotions. I knew how to stimulate men; I had been designed for them.

I heard the kitchen door slam and then Joe came up the stairs first. Alex wanted the effect of him seeing me lying there waiting, nude under the sheet.

As we were in the middle of saying hello to each other, Alex wrenched off the sheet and exposed me.

"Welcome home from the navy, Joe! Look what I got you!"

Joe was pleased with the gift. I could tell, as he looked me up and down, beaming.

"Awesome. I want to take a shower first though." Joe explained to us that he had travelled for half the night coming home and felt disgusting.

When he left the room, I voiced some reservations, but Alex was perceptive enough to get me in the mood, spanking me with the hairbrush over his knee, and then making me suck his cock as I knelt between his legs.

Joe was back in five minutes and happy to watch. Alex joked that he was priming me for Joe and we all laughed.

Joe sat on the bed and watched me suck his brother. I was looking up at Alex when I felt Joe's hands on my left breast and then running his hands through my hair. He was pushing me harder on Alex's cock and it made me gag.

"Ooh, she is a good cocksucker. What else does she do?"

They were talking as if I was not in the room with them. Alex took the hairbrush off the nightstand and threw it across the room. "She plays fetch too. Go get it, K. C." We had a routine we did where Alex would treat me like a bitch.

When I came back to the bed with the brush between my teeth, I felt very humiliated as I saw them laughing at me. I tried to drop the brush in Alex's lap but he insisted I give it to Joe instead.

When I did, Joe petted me on the head and said, "Good girl."

Most of my boyfriends were jealous of other men, but not Alex. He got off on knowing that I would do whatever he wanted, even if it meant he would share me.

Chapter Thirty-Seven

AA Steps (May 1983)

The twelve steps of AA:

1. We admitted we were powerless over alcohol—that our lives had become unmanageable.
2. Came to believe that a Power greater than ourselves could restore us to sanity.
3. Made a decision to turn our will and our lives over to the care of God, as we understood Him.
4. Made a searching and fearless moral inventory of ourselves.
5. Admitted to God, to ourselves and to another human being the exact nature of our wrongs.
6. Were entirely ready to have God remove all these defects of character.
7. Humbly asked Him to remove our shortcomings.
8. Made a list of all persons we had harmed, and became willing to make amends to them all.
9. Made direct amends to such people wherever possible, except when to do so would injure them or others.
10. Continued to take personal inventory and when we were wrong promptly admitted it.
11. Sought through prayer and meditation to improve our conscious contact with God, as we understood Him, praying only for knowledge of His will for us and the power to carry that out.

12. Having had a spiritual awakening as the result of these steps, we tried to carry this message to alcoholics and to practice these principles in all our affairs.

Step Four requires that you look back at your past. You write it all down on paper and face your demons head on. In step five, you have to tell your sponsor about the rotten things you have done, whom you have hurt and why, and they walk with you through your journey as you create a plan of action to right your wrongs and make amends.

By the time I got to those steps, the ones called the action steps, I had moved from a male to a female sponsor. In the beginning, it is suggested that girls pick girls and guys pick guys for sponsors but I was a non-conformist and did things my own way at first until I realized I wasn't getting any better.

Chapter Thirty-Eight

STDs (February 1983)

Tony and I were seeing each other while Alex and I were seeing each other. Alex was banging this other chick and Tony was sleeping with two other girls besides me. Then one day Tony called me up and asked me if I was itching. He said this chick had given him the crabs.

I had already been to the doctor because I realized I had gotten them but I thought the other guy, Chris, whom I had seen for one night, was the one who had given them to me. I had not told anyone, but when I realized that the problem was bigger than I thought, I contacted everyone involved.

Though I knew better, I never actually thought about the ramifications of having multiple sex partners and STDs.

What I did not know at the time was that I had borrowed a business suit from my mother's closet, wore it all day and put it back in her closet without having it cleaned. She came down with the crabs too and my father accused her of having an affair. It almost ended their marriage but I was oblivious at the time because I never told my family what was going on. It was only twenty years later that I realized the damage I had done.

Chapter Thirty-Nine

Eighteenth Birthday (March 1983)

"Tell them not to expect you at home tonight, say you are going to be sleeping over at Diane's house," he had told me a week in advance. I was not living at home anyway and still renting a room at Stephen's house, but Alex did not want anyone calling the cops or becoming worried if I did not come home. I told him not to worry; I rented a room, came, and went as I pleased.

Stephen's family was civil to me but the warmth and generosity that I had encountered when I first moved in as his girlfriend and then later as his fiancée were now gone. I would never be a part of the family again, and I had resigned myself to that fact. They had graciously allowed me to stay there and finish high school now that I was sober, but my dating caused problems.

Alex arrived at my place in his car. I had packed an overnight bag and he asked me what I was planning to wear as we cruised along the highway. I showed him the black pants and loose fitting black top I had packed.

"Oh no," he said. "That will not do. Tonight is your eighteenth birthday; we are going to do it up so you remember it for the rest of your life. We are going to have to take you shopping."

Part of his surprise was that Joe, his older brother, was going to be celebrating with us. Alex said that because he had been in the navy for a long time he was having trouble acclimating back to civilian life. Alex thought that Joe needed to have some fun too, so he invited him along for the event.

We went back to their mom's house and picked up Joe. Our first stop was a local sex shop where the three of us went in together. I had never been in a sex shop before and it was even naughtier because I was with two guys and not just one. They were like two kids in a candy store, pointing out toys that they would like to use on me. In the end, they bought just a pocket rocket vibrator and a dildo, but it had been quite the experience.

Next, we drove to the mall. Joe had a friend who worked at the JC Penny clothing store and he introduced me to her. Then he told her he wanted me to look virginal.

"Be sure whatever she gets is white." The store clerk and I blushed at his request but she obligingly brought several dresses into the dressing room for me to try on until I found one that made me look innocent and fit well enough.

Along with the dress, Joe asked the clerk to supply me with a garter belt, white stockings, white shoes, a purse, and a new push-up underwire bra. I was going in style.

I felt like Cinderella getting ready for a ball as I carefully carried my purchases to the car. From there, we went back to their mom's house, showered, and then dressed for dinner. Alex had told me to take my belongings as we would not be coming back to the house. As we were walking out the door, Alex asked me where my new toys were, and I told him that I had left them in his room.

He told me to go get them and put them in my purse. Carrying a dildo and a vibrator in my purse was a new adventure. We looked like we were ready for a night on the town. The men dressed in dark jackets, dress shirts, pants, and me in my white everything. If the neighbors had been paying attention, it might have looked odd to them. However, nobody was watching and I was ready for the night of my life.

Dinner was delicious; we dined on a seven-course meal, all the while the guys ordering for me and making me feel special, pulling out my chair, handing me my napkin, and occasionally spooning something in my mouth. We had a lively conversation about our previous sexual experience, laughing because I was finally legal and they no longer had to worry about prosecution for statutory rape.

After dinner, we went on a scenic drive and then to a local bar for some dancing. We were all sober but we were still crazy. I loved dirty dancing. In fact, Alex and I had won some dance contests at the AA dances in the last month or so doing our dirty dancing.

Our server brought us to a booth and Alex let me slide in first so I was sitting between him and Joe. Alex put his hand up my dress, and pinched my labia while the server took our drink orders. I had a hard time holding a straight face and not squirming. He loved teasing me like that.

I was eager to dance with Alex but he said, "I want you to dance with Joe. He never has a good time because nobody will ever dance with him. I want you to make him feel like he is the only one here tonight, make him feel special."

Joe caught Alex's hand under the table, surmised what he was doing, and put his hand in there too.

I was uncomfortable in the position and wanted to get out of the booth. "C'mon, Joe. Let's dance."

Joe was bigger than his little brother in every way. On the dance floor, he held me tight, grinding his groin against mine. He used his hand to press my back against him even more. "Hold still," he told me as he rubbed to the music. "I do not know where Alex found you, but I am glad he does not mind sharing."

After dancing a few dances, I said, "Let's go back to the table." There we found Alex casually flirting with the server who was cleaning up the table.

"What do you say, big brother, time to put this birthday girl to bed?" Alex asked Joe. Joe laughed loudly. "Yes, it most definitely is."

We piled into the car and arrived at a local hotel. I stayed in the car with Alex as Joe made the reservation. When he came back out to the car, we got out, Alex locked up the car, and the three of us grabbed our stuff and walked to the room together.

Joe went in first, then Alex. Alex turned around and put his hand up. "Hang on," he said, as he closed the door in my face.

I waited a few seconds but it was obvious they were not going to open up the door. I knocked and they laughed.

"Open up, let me in." I was ready to party.

They were laughing again and I finally heard the door lock click and the door opened a crack.

"Do you want to come in, little girl?" Alex asked me.

"Yes please!" There was no one in the hall and we had not encountered other guests on our way. I was grateful. Had I run into anyone I knew, my nerves would have prickled. Wearing the virginal white outfit felt uncomfortable as I stood alone in the hall. Was it *What color is your Parachute*? or some other self-help book about colors and how they affected people's perceptions? I never wore white. Black was easy to match, it reflected power and strength, and evil. Wearing white made me feel vulnerable and I didn't like it.

"Are you sure, little girl?" he asked me.

"C'mon, open up. Of course I want to come in." Alex and I enjoyed bondage, dominance, sadism, and masochistic (BDSM) role-playing and this night was going to be no different.

When I got in the door, Alex was removing his shirt, pants, and underwear, making himself comfortable in the lounger by the table at the other end of the room. Joe was sitting on the double bed near him, naked already.

"Why don't you take off your dress and join the party?" Joe's eyes were undressing me already. I looked at Alex and he nodded. I went to him and turned my back so he could unzip me.

Lifting the dress shyly, I did a little dance as I brought the dress over my shoulders and up over my head. I tossed it into the corner behind Alex's chair.

Right away, Joe looked at Alex and said, "She is a pig, huh, no manners and no respect?"

I knew I was in trouble. Alex told me to walk to the corner, bend, not stoop, and pick up the dress. Wrestling to get behind his chair, I was keenly aware of both sets of eyes on my torso. I still had the white heels, garter, and stockings on. I wondered if they were admiring my ass as I began to stoop. Taking my time, I lifted the dress from the floor and brought it around Alex's chair.

"Come here," he said, pointing directly to the right of his chair. I stood for a moment until he grabbed my arm and forced me over his knee.

"Put your hands behind your head, little girl," he told me, and as I did, he whacked my ass hard with his hand three times. I looked at Joe and he was playing with himself on the bed. The sting on my ass accentuated the embarrassment I felt, and the tinge of a red mark represented the excitement that rose from my groin.

"How dare you throw that beautiful dress on the floor after we bought it for you? Hang it up nicely right now and show us a little respect," he demanded with a stern voice.

Walking across the carpeting in the heels was a bit more challenging than bending over. Trying for a sexy walk, I almost tipped. My hand against the bureau kept me from falling. I was a novice and way out of my league. Knowing their eyes were on me made me anxious and nervous, I felt like a little girl playing dress up.

Before I even made it to the clothing rack that stood by the door, Joe said, "Seems the little girl's got a hygiene problem too."

He didn't like my hairy bush. They shaved my beaver bald and then we spent the night fucking, sucking, and role-playing. I never knew how competitive brothers could be. Unlike the evening prior, we ran into other people as we checked out, and I looked like I felt, used, and abused. My stockings had runs, my heels had scuffs, and my dress, still white, slightly crumpled revealed my reddened ass and tortured sensitive nipples. I was eighteen, legal and ready to take on the world.

Chapter Forty

The Color White (April 1983)

How do you get confidence? Practice, practice, practice.

Two weeks after my eighteenth birthday, I made a porn flick.

One weekend, Alex and I went to his gay friend Jimmy's house, and Jimmy filmed us while we screwed around. It had been exciting. We watched the movie afterward a few times and it turned me on.

Then, Alex suggested we make a film with a bunch of guys. He suggested that I arrive in my nurse's uniform after my Friday night shift at Jimmy's apartment. I was to pretend to be an "all-call" nurse.

I would graduate high school in just a few weeks and I was in my prime, and sober. I wanted to live life to the fullest. Jimmy had said to me one time, "You can do anything you want to do in life, as long as you are willing to pay the consequences." I thought I could handle anything that life had to offer. I had conquered anorexia and alcoholism.

Making a porn flick was something that I never thought I would do but then I never thought I would be sober either. What was the worst thing that could happen if I did it? People would see it. People would think badly of me. People might be shocked, or some turned on or turned off. I knew I had seen plenty of porn that turned me off. Our agreement was that we would make the film and Alex and I would get a copy, and Jimmy would keep the original.

"What the hell," I told him. I had had sex with many men already, what was a few more. Besides, having sex with multiple partners had always been a fantasy of mine. "Set it up."

We agreed on the date and time, and Jimmy and Alex took on the mission of finding suitable studs.

Alex had asked me to wear white stockings and the garter he and Joe had bought me for my birthday to work. All that night, I was hot, thinking about making my planned house call the next morning.

When my shift was over, the sun was just barely coming up and the morning was crisp. I felt the lack of pantyhose as I made my way across the parking lot to my car. Normally I wore pants, and the garter hooks were cold against my legs. Because I had been up for twenty-four hours already, I stopped and got myself a coffee at Dunkin Donuts. I gave myself a few minutes to think about it, knowing I was running late. Was I really going to do this? Yes, I was. I was sober, and I was an empowered female who took charge of her sexual life.

Jimmy's house in West Springfield, Massachusetts was a twenty-minute drive. Tiptoeing up the stairs to his balcony on the second floor of the duplex rooming house, I rang the bell. The door opened quickly and I stepped into the front hall. Alex told me I could use the bathroom if I wanted to freshen up.

As I made my way from the hall to the bathroom, I caught sight of the room full of men from the mirror Jimmy had hanging in the hall. I could see them, but I was not sure if they could see me. I got jittery, went into the bathroom, and closed the door.

Removing my clothes, I took a quick shower, removing the nursing home smell from my skin while carefully keeping my hair dry. Then I got dressed in the nurse's uniform again. I could hear them talking and laughing. The noise factor was elevating as the caffeine from the coffee they were drinking kicked in. In about half an hour, I was ready and opened the bathroom door.

I noticed the camera and Jimmy as soon as I came out of the bathroom. He had it panned on me, and I was instantly aware of being watched. All eyes were on me as I came around the hall wall and I counted; there were seven men ready for this "nurse's session," not including Jimmy, and Alex.

Alex suggested I pour another round of coffee and then Jimmy suggested I serve donuts to everyone. Jimmy set up the room with more lighting as he reviewed the tape of me walking in the hall and into the kitchen. Finally, I got myself a cup of coffee and sat down on the floor in front of Alex.

After brief introductions and some uncomfortable joking, Jimmy said we should get started. Alex took his cock out and told me that it was hurting and he asked me to make it feel better. I knelt down in between his legs and kissed him, looking up at him. I smiled, and he smiled back. Our relationship was intense; he forced my head onto his cock hard enough to make me gag.

"Easy there, you need to slow down with your treatment," he laughed, and asked his friends if anyone else's cock hurt. Of course, you know it, there were a few complainers. Before long, clothes were in bunches on the floor, and I was trying to take care of several patients at once.

Reading that *Joy of Sex* book when I was younger finally had paid off. It took me six hours, and when I was finally done, I was exhausted. I had no idea how hard it would be to make everyone happy. A few were greedy and got more than their fair share, but one guy just kept hanging on and it took the other guys goading him before he finally came. Most of them had deposited their gifts on me, and I was quite mess. I had brought a change of clothes, but Jimmy had other ideas as part of the film.

He turned sadistic and said he did not want me using his bathroom and then determined that it was time for me to get dressed and go home. This was supposed to be a house call. I had done what I had set out to do, it was getting late, and it was time for me to leave.

Talk about a walk of shame. My makeup had run, and my hose had runs in them. I was a filthy mess. I begged Alex to let me clean up and he tried to change Jimmy's mind but he would not have it. It was time for me to go.

The downstairs neighbor was out raking leaves and I could not meet his eyes as I walked by. I am sure he must have heard the ruckus we were making and had gone outside to avoid the noise. I got into my Pinto and drove home.

Alex and I watched the movie a few times after that and it excited and repulsed me at the same time. While actually having the sex had been exciting, seeing myself on camera was very revealing and it made me feel vulnerable. I did not like the way I looked, but I liked to watch the role-playing and the effect it had on my partners.

Feeling vulnerable to Alex was part of the allure in the relationship. He enjoyed oral sex in the car on long trips, and he enjoyed making me wait to pee, sometimes to the point where I would almost pee my pants.

Chapter Forty-One

The Herpes Situation (April 1983)

The thing with herpes is that you do not know you have it right away. You can be contagious before you show any symptoms. That is why it is easy to contract if you do not use protection. I am not exactly sure how I contracted herpes; I think it was Joe but it could have been Alex. The bottom line was, the three of us broke out at the same time. Right after I made the porn movie, and that meant I had to reconcile the situation with several people.

After going through the crab's ordeal, I knew how quickly things could get out of control with STDs if people waited to tell you what was going on. When I found out I had herpes, I vowed I had to be honest with anyone I might have had the potential to infect.

Physically, I hurt so bad I wanted to die. It felt like someone had used sandpaper on the inside of my labia and vulva and then sprinkled salt in the open wounds. I could not walk. I had to waddle to the doctors, and I was mortified when he told me what I had. I felt like a leper.

For the next few days, I arranged to talk to each of these individuals in person and explain the situation. There were twelve men and Stephen's family. I did not know much about herpes until the doctor gave me pamphlets that explained it. Suddenly, I was becoming an educator to a bunch of people about a disease I had unwittingly acquired.

Naturally, many of the guys wanted more information; they had really no idea about the ramifications of the virus, nor did I until I contracted it. Almost all of them were gracious and thanked me for being honest with them. One guy named Jack was extremely upset with me. He was Irish/Italian and I had gone to his house to tell him.

We were in his room and he wanted to try to get busy but I pushed him away and said what I had to say. He started screaming at me and throwing things around the room. He took me by the arm and walked me down the stairs and out his front door, right by his mother.

He told me, "You are not welcome here anymore. We do not appreciate your kind of trash."

I was trash. I knew it, he knew it, now his mother knew it, and his whole neighborhood knew it. I walked to my car with my head down. I felt horrible. He later apologized to me, but it made me realize that by my careless sexual behavior I could cost somebody more than a good time, and that they might just be enraged enough to hurt me.

Chapter Forty-Two

Moving Home (April 1983)

The morning after I told Vicky I had herpes, Frank wanted me out.

I came down the stairs and Frank was sitting at the table. I averted my eyes. I could not look at him. He did not say anything as I made my coffee but I could feel his steel eyes boring through my soul. He saw me for what I was and he was making me look too. I hated him for it.

As I turned to go back to my room, he stopped me in my tracks.

"Just a second there, Kay. Vicky told me what is going on with you and I want you out of here today. This is the last straw. You could infect my family with your dirty ways. Do you hear me?"

He was not one to mince words under normal circumstances and his cutting tone made me feel like I was an ant. I knew that if he attempted it he could hurt or even kill me. He knew the woods; he was a farmer, a hunter, and a rebel.

He had done jail time for almost killing somebody who was screwing his first wife. When he got out, she had wanted nothing to do with him, which was how he met Vicky and her kids. I knew he had a violent temper and yet I was not frightened of him, because for some reason, I knew he loved me despite what I had done and despite how I had disrespected him and his family.

I sensed that Frank was restraining himself because of that paternal love, a love we had forged as he taught me about the land, the farming, the hunting, and about living within our means and enjoying the simple things in life. There were good times and that was what he wanted to remember.

I would never forget those jam sessions. We did not need much to have a good time; some spoons, a harmonica, a banjo or two, a guitar, some voices, and some clapping. Some of the happiest moments of my life had been spent with Frank, the family, and some of the locals who came over for venison or pork and spent Friday nights making music and drinking a few beers. I was going to lose that, I was going to lose him, the family, and I was going to miss it all. I had fucked up again. Why couldn't I be a normal girl? Why did I have this need to be so destructive?

"Yes, I understand. I am sorry." What else could I say? Anything else would have been too much, and we both knew it. I did not think they could contract the herpes if I was careful but it did not matter.

"It is too late for sorry, Kay. You best be getting a hold of yerself. Actions speak, words don't mean anything."

I never turned to look at him. We spoke as I kept my back to him. My face had contorted of its own accord. I did not want him to see me cry. I did not want him to know how much I hurt from hurting him. I never intended to hurt people but I had done it again.

I held my emotions in check and went upstairs to pack my stuff. I did not own that much, and within an hour, I was ready to go. I called my parents and told my mother what had happened. My father came and picked me up at Frank's house. I was finally going home. I had been sober almost four months now, and my parents were going to give me another chance.

Chapter Forty-Three

Senior Prom (May 1983)

My sponsor Gail went to New York to learn how to design clothes. As a graduation present, she told me she would design my prom dress. I refused to wear a store bought gown with frumpy sleeves and cleavage enhancing bust lines. It was the 1980s and Fleetwood Mac was popular. I told her I wanted a dress like the one Stevie Nicks would wear, adorned with leather and lace. Alex was into dressing up, and told me he would wear a leather vest, tie, and chaps, and a white shirt with black cuff links to match. We looked hot.

When we got to the prom, I was happy we were there. But as the night wore on, we were bored and decided to leave. I think we ended up at an AA dance that night after we hit a meeting. Commitment was still a no-no for both of us although we had been playing around for a few months now and since the porn movie incident, we were trying to be less promiscuous.

We did not want strings, but as relationships go, you start caring about each other whether you want to or not. We were both sluts and that was our commonality. It is not easy to build a relationship on that alone but we rode the wave for as long as we could make it last.

Being back home at my parents' house was tough. I had been accustomed to being a free spirit but they did not believe in premarital sex and they discouraged my relationship with Alex. One time I called them from his house to tell them where I was, and they came and picked me up. They did not want me to spend the night and I had agreed that as long as I lived under their roof I would abide by their rules.

Chapter Forty-Four

Another Lost Child (June 7, 1983)

A few weeks before I graduated high school, my mom gave birth to my brother, a stillborn baby named Peter.

Dad and Mom went to the hospital to have the baby, but when they got there, Peter's heart showed signs of distress. He died, and then after he was deceased, Mom still had to go through the painful labor knowing her son was already dead. She and Dad held him for a long while before they said goodbye.

Dad came home without Mom and I could see in his eyes the pain he felt, but he refused to share it with us. Dad held it together, staying calm and strong, "Mom's okay but we lost the baby."

How could that be? Why had it happened? We had so many questions and he had no answers. It had been a perfect pregnancy. She had been happy as a newspaper carrier, getting her daily exercise, with her customers commenting on how great she looked during her pregnancy. She was supposed to come home with a baby. She was not supposed to be stuck in the hospital alone.

Suddenly the future was black. There was going to be no baby, no new family member. All the healthy living on my mother's part was wasted. There are no guarantees in life or in pregnancy. Peter had been an active baby and the umbilical cord had twisted over forty times.

Mom and Dad took it hard. I had been optimistic for my newest baby brother too. I was going to be the big sister that I had failed to be for my other siblings. I was sober now and had been planning to spoil him as much as possible, but now I would never get that chance.

Graduation day was approaching and I felt guilty. Mom was devastated and had been depressed over the loss of her baby.

I felt guilty because I felt happy. I was sad for the loss of my brother but at the same time, my life was much better than it had been in a while.

The week after my mom lost Peter, I moved out. The house filled with pain and I could not bear it.

Alex's mother knew a woman who would rent me a room for $50 a week. The last few weeks of high school, I worked third shift as a nurse's aide and rented a room in Windsor. I was not supposed to be able to do that but the school principal let my residency requirement slide because of the circumstances and the fact that I would graduate shortly.

We only had a few weeks left and I think he was impressed that I was still trying to complete my high school education while supporting myself. He knew I was in Alcoholics Anonymous and trying to get control of my life. For the year and a half I had been out on my own, he had talked to me often about why I couldn't conform to my parents' rules and I could not give him a straight answer. I just couldn't do it.

Even though I was stubborn and reckless, he took the time to talk to me almost every day to make sure that I was doing okay and was going to make it. He was just as excited as I was the day I turned eighteen because I could finally legally sign permission slips for myself.

For the last few weeks of school, I worked the 11:00-7:00 shift and went to school after a quick shower in the morning. At 2:00, I would go home and sleep until about 6:00 or 7:00 and grab a snack, hit a meeting, and eat dinner right before I went into work around 10:00 p.m.

The night I graduated, my mom had to fight with me to get dressed and go to school. I did not want to go. I had finished high school and that had been my focus for a long time but now I was petrified about my future. I wanted to drink and celebrate, as I knew my classmates would, but I knew I should not. Since my grandfather had made the trip down from Littleton, Massachusetts, I let my mother guilt me into attending the ceremony.

I hated every minute of graduation. I did not feel prepared to be an adult in so many ways, and yet in some areas I felt like I was already grown up. My classmates and I had little in common. I had disassociated myself from many of them in my final year. I had a few friends that knew precisely what they wanted to do with their lives. They talked of fancy cars, prestigious colleges, and professional careers as lawyers, doctors, and professors. I was not going anywhere specific and I was beginning to panic.

Our graduation song was "We may never pass this way again" by Seals and Crofts. The lyrics were significant to me, the secrets of the universe, fear of change, a dreamer playing a game, and the fact that I did not know where I was going. Though the song suggested I gather my courage, I was so used to finding refuge in a bottle, getting stoned, or having sex that I did not know how long I could stay on the path of sobriety. I knew if I did not change more, my life would be over. Maybe not immediately, but quickly enough, because I had not yet quelled the rage.

As soon as the ceremony was over, I said goodbye to my parents, and went to an AA meeting. While the rest of my class went to the beach that night, I went to the movies to see Flash Dance with Meg, Danny, Steve, and Pam, a few of my older friends from AA.

Danny was a drug and alcohol counselor and had about ten years of sobriety. He knew I was in a bad place that night, torn between the old me and the new me, scared shitless. He was the one who suggested we go to the movies when he heard I ditched the graduation partying.

I had made the right choice, and he and the others supported me. Afterward, we went to the Filling Station, a truck stop that was a frequent hang out of the Springfield, Massachusetts friends of Bill.

Irene Cara and the songs "Maniac," "What a Feeling," and "Gloria" were my favorite songs from the movie and they hit the charts when the film released. I felt like Alex Owens, the eighteen-year-old in the movie who had a lot of determination but no formal training. I too had big dreams. I loved the arts, especially music and dancing. Musicals were my absolute favorites, but I would never be a star. I was destined to be behind the scenes, just as if I had been in high school during my junior year in the drama club productions.

I did make-up, sat on stage behind props during performances, prompting actors if they forgot their lines, helped with moving props and dressing behind the curtains. I listened to my peers, these teenaged actors and actresses, envious of the skill that they had that I lacked. I called it all kinds of things but it was, in its purest form, confidence. I lacked confidence.

One time, I told Alex I wanted to be his whore, and he told me he would treat me that way if I showed up at his apartment in a skimpy teddy. I showed up at his front door dressed in a skimpy teddy, and he would not let me in until I handed him my coat. After I handed him my coat, he slammed the door in my face and I had to beg him to let me in.

It was broad daylight on Worthington Street in Springfield and cars were going by, tooting their horns. It was not usual to see a girl in my condition banging on the front door of an apartment building. Alex finally let me in, but when he did, he handcuffed my hands behind my back.

"Why are you here?"

"I heard you wanted a whore, and I need the money."

"How much do you cost?"

"I guess it depends upon how good I am."

"Yes, I suppose it does. As my whore, since I am paying you, you will do whatever I want. Is that correct?"

"Absolutely." I was curious about how whores were treated. It was something I was seriously considering doing after high school as it was one of the skills I had picked up.

He walked me to his room and then bent me over the bed, fucked me a bit, and then sat me on the floor at his feet while he watched a movie, making me suck him with no hands. His best friend Ray called and told him he was going to come over. Alex cuffed me to the bed, and when Ray knocked on the door, he let him in.

I heard Alex tell him that he had a whore tied to the bed, and when he led him in, he said, "See?"

I had met Raymond a few times before that and I knew he was gay. In fact, the three of us had gone to the gay clubs in Springfield together to dance. Ray got silly and turned red when he saw me and said, "Looks like you are all tied up."

Alex told him to sit down in the chair and watch TV with us, and then after a while Alex said he was going to cook us some dinner and told Ray to keep an eye on me. Ray and I sat in Alex's room, uncomfortable at first, but then he came over, sat on the bed, and asked me why the handcuffs.

I told him I had been a bad girl and had told Alex I was going to hide or change when Ray got there and that made him want to show me off even more. Ray thought the whole situation was funny, saying he wished he had a lover who would tie him up and put him on display.

"I have to go to the bathroom. Will you go into the kitchen and see if Alex will give you the key to the handcuff?"

Instead of the key, Raymond came back with a coffee and a promise that Alex would let me go to the bathroom when I was done drinking my coffee. I drank it and Ray was able to get the key, provided I used the toilet while I was standing up and that I did not close the door. As soon as Ray went into the kitchen to return the key to Alex, I shut the door and peed sitting down in privacy. Then I went back in the room and sat down on the bed, glad to be un-cuffed.

Alex came back in the room and it was then I noticed he had already set some of the food down. He must have done that when I had the bathroom door closed. "Get back on the bed. I want to cuff you back up," he said.

It was only after they both had settled down that he spoke about me closing the bathroom door. He ended up smacking my pussy with Ray's shoe for a while until I promised I would not disobey him or Ray again. I ate with my one hand, trying to balance the plate of Hamburger Helper on my lap. He told me he did not think I was worthy of using silverware. After Ray left, Alex found a roll of quarters and stuck it in my snatch.

"There you go, whore. Thanks for the good time."

What I had envisioned and what had actually happened had been two different things but it had been exciting and humiliating at the same time. I wanted to stay longer but Alex had another date. It was time for me to leave. I was not going to pursue this as a profession. My heart would never be in it.

I was jealous and wanted all of his attention. I was insatiable and he was getting restless. We both needed more.

Chapter Forty-Five

A Promise to Marie (July 1983)

Not long after that, I quit the nursing home job after I lost my favorite patient.

Marie was a walker and spread her smiling face throughout the ward. Sometimes she would help other residents get to their rooms, or she would go to their room to fetch them a sweater if they were cold in the dining hall. She always had a kind word to say.

I started my training on the day shift, but when I went to nights, I still got a chance to see Marie in the morning as I was setting up breakfast for the patients. Sometimes, she would follow me on my rounds and we would chat about the weather or the news. I had two men who roomed together that I had to wash up twice a week in the morning, and they were always excited to see me.

Marie kept them in line from the hall as she told them to behave and not to give me a hard time.

Of course, they cracked up at that, and I caught one of them stroking his penis when I went to the bathroom to fill up the basin. Later, when I told Marie about it, she told me she heard them talking about me in the cafeteria and warned me to be extra careful. They were just old men getting their jollies jerking off to bathing techniques. It did not bother me. Heck they were entitled to have an orgasm here and there.

During my third month working there, scabies broke out in the nursing home. Everyone had it, the patients, nurses, and the aides. Marie was itching so bad she had to be medicated because her skin became infected. The medication caused her to be loopy, which caused her to fall. When she became bed ridden, they moved her from the ambulatory wing to the long-term care wing and she was depressed.

One night as I was doing rounds, I went by her room and was surprised to find her awake. I was not working that wing that night but something told me to run by her room to check on her. When I went in and asked her how she was doing, she asked me to sit on her bed. I put the side of her bed down, and put the head of the bed up. She patted the bed right next to her, indicating she wanted me to sit there.

After I sat on her bed, she leaned against me and told me that she was tired of fighting and that it was time for her to go. I argued with her but she was adamant, saying, "It is my time."

She explained that she did not want to die alone and asked me if I would be kind enough to sit with her. I hugged her and I told her she was not going to die, but she insisted she was ready.

She did not want to live anymore. She explained that when her kids put her in the nursing home it had been bad enough, but now that she was bed bound, there was no more reason to live. In her youth, she had chosen to walk away from her family; and in her old age, they had abandoned her, selling her home and her possessions, and stuck her in a nursing home when she could no longer cook or care for herself.

I wrapped my arm around her and I listened as she talked. "I deserved what they did, but I do not regret what I did either. I am not angry with them, dear. They did what they had to do and I did what I had to do, and you must too, Kay. Do not let other people tell you cannot do something. You are growing up in a time when women will be able to accomplish so much. You have to try to live your life to the fullest. Promise me you will live your life with no regrets?"

"I promise, Marie." There was very little to her anymore, she was just skin and bones, and yet there was a glow to her face. I thought for a minute this cannot be happening.

She smiled at me when I responded, and squeezed my hand. As quickly as she was there, she was gone. Her body got heavy and her breathing ceased. I did not even realize she was dead until I went to remove myself from her weight, and realized she was not breathing.

I ran to get the head nurse and told her what had happened, and she just told me to calm down. She would be there in a minute.

The nurse took a half hour and I was pissed at her but she explained to me that it had been Marie's time. I did not think people could just will themselves to death but she assured me, some patients did.

She walked down the hall with me and confirmed my suspicions. She had to call the doctor to make it official. Fortunately, I was not on that wing that night and I did not have to clean Marie up for the medical doctor to pronounce her dead; but if I had, it would have broken my heart.

I had already touched a dead person once before. Agnes was old and could not speak, though I believed she could hear because her eyes moved appropriately when I entered her room. Paralysis kept her immobile. The nurse's aides were supposed to move her to prevent bedsores but because she could not speak and many of the staff thought her retarded, when chores needed to be short cut, Agnes would be one of the ones the aides skipped. As a result, she had bedsores that turned into gangrene.

Even after they removed her legs, she stank like rotting meat. She did not last long after that, and the night she died, I happened to be working her wing. It was my first month on the job, and even though one of the other aides discovered her, the head nurse told me I had to go clean her up before the medical doctor would come and sign a death certificate.

The stench in the room was horrific, a combination of urine and rotten flesh that had accumulated for months. I got out a washbasin and went into the rest room to fill it with hot soapy water. I laughed at the lunacy of that, and then justified it by thinking that just because the patient was dead, I was not, and I did not want cold hands. Everything went smoothly for the first few minutes.

Her eyes were open. I knew they might be from my training. I had hoped the nurse had closed them when she checked on her, but I had a hunch she had left them open on purpose because I was green. Some of the other nurses' aides called me a troublemaker, saying I was making them look bad with my working too hard.

I washed Agnes's front side and thought it was a blessing she was dead. There is a point in time where euthanasia for people seems kind. It did not seem fair that we put our animals down humanely but we made our people suffer so.

I rolled Agnes's sheets up to her back and lay down a fresh sheet. My training had included education on the fact that when people die, their bodies emit all body fluids. Although she had not eaten anything much in months and was pure skin and bones, she had released some bodily liquids and I needed to change her before the doctor got there.

I bent my legs to protect my back and then I gently rolled Agnes. I felt foolish at my gentleness with a dead person, when all of a sudden, Agnes let out a howl. She was still alive!

I dropped her back down and ran to get the nurse. The nurse heard my scream and had come running, but she quickly laughed when I told her what had happened. There is often a pocket of air in the lungs that escapes when a person is moved after they die. I was scared to go back in to clean Agnes up but the nurse's ridicule shamed me and I went back in to complete the job.

There was a lot of animosity between the union and the administration. Watching people die began to depress me. I decided that I was not going to go into nursing or become a doctor, and I quit my job. The next day, I went to Kelly Girl and they were amazed with my typing skills. They began placing me into a different job location every day. I got an apartment on Bay Street in Springfield, Massachusetts.

I worked as a Kelly Girl until I found a permanent position at an Office Furniture Store. I was an order entry clerk, inputting orders into the company computer. My boss Susan loved my work ethic; I was always asking her what else I could do. Soon she was giving me more responsibilities, like calling suppliers, contacting customers, and placing orders.

Diane sold me her Pinto after our trip to Philadelphia. We had gone down to see a friend of hers from college. We stayed with her friend in this small apartment in Philly. We had gone to an AA meeting, as was our custom. We picked up some local guys to show us the town. Then we ended up in the bad side of town but Diane heard music coming from a bar and wanted to dance.

We walked into this all-black bar, sat down, and ordered Cokes. The loud music was coming from a jukebox that was playing "Philadelphia Freedom" by Elton John. There was nobody on the dance floor but there were people sitting at the bar or on chairs at tables. The other patrons did not intimidate Diane or me.

We got up and started to boogie together, and the next thing you know, a couple of other girls joined us. Then men were on the dance floor and the place was rocking. We plugged some quarters in and chose "Car Wash" next, and then I had dancers surrounding me as I did a solo dance in the center. Diane was leading them around in a circle. We had so much fun, I was happy to be alive.

We chatted with the bartender and he asked us what we were doing in a black bar. We told him we liked the music and the people and he just laughed and told us we were all right. Nobody hassled with us, though we knew if we had been two white men it would have been a different story. The year before, in Springfield, a racially induced riot resulted in a man being stabbed about a mile from where I now lived.

Martin Luther King's speeches and infamy gained visibility and the civil Rights Act of 1968 banned discrimination because of race, but there were pockets of rage and some people were still prejudiced.

Had I been at home, I would have been looking over my shoulder; but for some reason, in Philly, with Diane by my side, it was an adventure. She picked up a black guy and brought him back to our room. I listened to her fuck him and make all kinds of promises I knew she would not keep. I marveled at her ability to get rid of him quickly the next morning.

On the way home from that trip, while I was driving the car engine blew. Diane had been holding my hand as she always did, or sometimes she would ride with her hand on my knee. That day she had been talking about fucking and I had gotten aroused, pushing the accelerator faster than it wanted to go.

We blew the timing chain and valves and got as far as we could before the car just stopped. Fortunately, we had gotten off an exit and there was a gas station not too far up the street. We walked over and arranged for a tow truck driver to tow us back to Windsor, Connecticut. We stopped at the house so we could get my ATM card because we did not have cash and that was all he would take.

He took us to the ATM and then we paid him when he dropped us off at the Mobile station at the end of my street. Diane called her brother and he came and got her. She was not mad at me for blowing the engine but she was not sure if she could afford to fix it or if she even wanted to. At least, towing it home had gotten us into the local area.

I convinced her to replace the motor, paying for the entire bill since I felt guilty, as I had been driving. While we had the car fixed, Diane bought a new car, and sold me the Pinto for fifty dollars.

I was not close to my family at all during this time. I felt I had burned my bridges and there was no going back.

I had guys coming and going almost on a daily basis for about a year once I had my own place. Alex had a key and sometimes he would surprise me in the middle of the night.

Then, one day Alex and I were at a party together. We knew Danny and Meg from AA; they had gotten married over the summer. It was the first time I had been to their home up in Wilbraham. It was right on Route 20, and now that they had a daughter, they were thinking they should probably move to a safer location because of the traffic on the highway.

I walked into the living room and saw the television on. Not being much of a television watcher, I did not expect to recognize the show anyway but I was surprised to see some people that I recognized. There were about ten of them sitting around on a couch watching TV. The couch was faintly familiar. As I walked across the living room to get closer to the television, my stomach lurched. Those people were sitting in Jimmy's living room, watching my porn tape, rating it, and degrading it. He had apparently taped them as they were watching it, and they thought it was hilarious. I bolted from the room, and as I went through the kitchen, I saw Alex.

"Do you know what are they watching in there?" I asked him.

I had not foreseen this consequence. One that made me angry with myself for not realizing in advance how I might feel if I saw myself in public like that. Alex and I had watched the movie in private several times and it always made me hot but vulnerable, but this time I felt used, degraded, and explosively pissed off. How could Jimmy do that to me? How dare he? He did not have my permission to show the film and certainly not to tape others watching it.

I ran out of the house and I ran as hard as I could along the highway. I am not a runner and I did not make it very far but I had to do something with that energy. I felt like I was going to have a heart attack, my heart was beating so fast and I was crying so hard. I wanted to run in front of the cars that were flying along the highway doing sixty mph or even faster. I imagined it would only take a second, but what if I were only badly hurt and became crippled. That would be worse.

Eventually I turned around and went back. Alex said he was so sorry. He had gone into the living room and taken the film from the host, and then he had called Jimmy and demanded all copies of the film, which eventually did make me feel better, but I always wondered if there were films left undestroyed and whether or not they would resurface someday. Thank god, I could not have kids. At least that was something to be grateful for, I would have been mortified to know a child of mine had seen that video.

Alex and I tried to be monogamous and sane after that, but neither of us could make that commitment. Finally, we agreed to end it.

After we broke up, Diane suggested she and I get a place together. We found a nice apartment on the street floor of Van Deane Manor in West Springfield and I gave up the apartment on Bay Street. Diane and I went to tag sales and acquired pieces of furniture that we refurbished on our back step. We shared chores, groceries and enjoyed living together.

Chapter Forty-Six

A Girlfriend (1984)

Diane filled a void in my life as no one ever had. If I called her and said I needed her, she would come running. Sometimes when she did, I did not know what I wanted and she would just sit with me. Alternatively, we would go to the park and I would bring my guitar. I would sing to her, she would sing to me, and we would laugh and watch the children. She did not want kids and I could not have any. We were just close friends. When we were home, sometimes we would lie on the couch. I would lie with my head in her lap and she would run her fingers through my hair.

Sometimes she was lonely and she would ask if she could sleep in my bed. We often held hands and sometimes she would kiss mine and I never once thought I was in a lesbian relationship, but I suppose that is what it was, or at least on the road to being that. We loved each other and were happy in each other's company. One time she got a little too amorous and I pushed her away. I chalked it up to her being in a silly mood. She apologized the next day and I brushed it off. College kids do things like this all the time. She did not repulse me but I was not attracted to her sexually. I thought of her as a wonderful friend.

We had a conversation about gay relationships one time and I told her that I would never put myself in that position. Even if I loved a woman with all my heart, society was too cruel. I would live with a man, and have my female lover on the side. I knew many gay people and their lives were tough. They could not get married, share medical benefits, reap tax benefits because of their union, or be automatically recognized as next of kin. It was not right that they were discriminated against but that was how things were.

Diane and I decided to go to New York City for my birthday. We were going to see *A Chorus Line* on Broadway. We wanted to do it cheap, so we took the bus down and stayed at the Y. It was a coed facility, the females had some of the floors, and the males had others. Diane and I had a small room with two twin beds and shared the communal shower and toilets with the rest of the floor.

On the trip down, Diane started to feel sick. We managed to walk from the bus station to the Y. We grabbed hot dogs from a street vendor and made our way to our room. By midnight, Diane could not talk and was running a very high fever. We had no idea what was wrong with her but she asked me to take her to the hospital.

The cabby must have taken one look at us country bumpkins and laughed his balls off. He took us to Bellevue Hospital. It was about 1:00 a.m. when we got there; the ER was very busy and we had to wait our turn. Although Diane's face was puffy and her lips swollen, they did not believe her condition was life threatening.

While we were waiting, a six-foot-four-inch tall transvestite walked in of her own accord. Her metallic gold lamé jumpsuit was complete with bloodstains and a knife sticking in her chest. Fortunately, it was not on the heart side of the body so the ER nurse asked her to sit and wait next to us. They took her next, and then Diane went in. The nurse came out in a few minutes because she could not understand what Diane was saying. I was able to figure it out. Apparently, she had slept with someone who had given her herpes.

I had never told her about my herpes situation because I was too embarrassed. Fortunately, for me, I had contracted herpes vaginally. Unfortunately for her, she had it on her hands, in her eyes, and in her mouth. I wanted to go home because I knew where she had contracted it but I did not want to confront her and find out the truth. I hemmed and hawed but did not say a word as we made it back to the room.

The prednisone the hospital gave her did not do much for the swelling but it made her happier. I tried to convince her that we should just go home but she insisted that she wanted to stay. We tried to get some rest before the show, but the Y was very noisy during the day. We grabbed a sandwich on the way over to Broadway, but Diane could not eat hers. She still was not feeling very good, though her fever had broken.

The Saturday matinee performance began promptly at 2:00, and even though I was upset with her, I enjoyed every minute of the musical performance. I had not seen a show on Broadway since the time I was sixteen and my aunt had taken me for my birthday. I loved New York City, the hustle, the bustle, and constant movement.

After the show, we caught a cab back to the bus station and waited for our bus to arrive. We had barely spoken all day. She could not talk and I did not feel like talking. Instead of sitting next to her on the bus as I had on the way down, I sat behind her. I needed some space and I refused to feel sorry for her.

The following Friday, Diane and Alex were at the Friday night Young Peoples' meeting. It was where we usually hung out on Friday nights but I was not happy to see either one of them. They caught up to me when I went outside to have a cigarette. They both apologized to me for sleeping together, and I forgave them. I hated the situation, but I could do nothing about it, the damage was done.

It was crazy. There was no sense making promises you could not keep. I dated a few other men here and there but nothing serious came out of it. Occasionally, Alex would resurface, but those times became less and less. I was restless, wanting to settle down and get on with my life.

After seeing what had happened to Diane, the herpes situation put a damper on my devil-may-care attitude toward unprotected sex. If there was even a remote chance I might end up in bed with someone, I told him I had herpes. I did not want to put anyone else in a situation where he had no choice. It was not right.

Most of the men I dated were grateful for my honesty. Some chose to move on, others chose to use a condom, and others chose to be with me unprotected. I did not care what they chose to do as long as I had given them a choice. I did not want anyone to come after me and accuse me of giving him a disease that was incurable.

I was glad I had not contracted AIDS. It could have just as easily been AIDS, considering my life style. I started thinking about working on myself again using the AA steps. After all the sex I had, I still did not feel complete. I still felt like I had something to prove. Maybe chilling out on the casual sex would give me time for other things.

My friend Danny asked me if I would like to get involved in a Young People's conference. He had contacted Westfield State College and they were willing to host the event if we did it in the summer after school let out. I decided I would get involved, and before I realized it, I was voted co-chairman.

I had no idea what I was doing, but Danny told me to keep showing up and I would figure it out. Literally, that is what happened. I was starting to say yes instead of no and good things were happening. The loneliness that I had once felt was dissipating. I still got depressed, but working on projects with others helped me to focus my energies and get out of myself.

Chapter Forty-Seven

Young People's Convention (1985)

Hosting a conference for 2500 AA people requires a lot of planning. We had to come up with a schedule for three days and include guest speakers, topical discussions, and activities. We had to deal with reservations, allergies, and handicaps. We contracted the food out to the school's cafeteria service but we had to make sure our costs stayed under the ticket prices. Friday night we had one band, and Saturday night we had two. Although we were holding a conference for sober people, we knew that when fellow drunks got together things could get passionate or heated. We arranged for security and began selling tickets. Six months later, it was time for the event.

I spent very little time sleeping that weekend. We had people on the reservation desk and people stationed throughout the campus to help those attending get around. Our guest speakers arrived and we split up the job of introducing them. We went from conference room to conference room making sure our guests were happy and having a good time, fielding questions, providing directions, and providing contacts for this or that.

Every few hours I would go back to my room and grab a shower. Sometimes I would take somebody with me, and other times I went alone. I was running on adrenalin, hot showers, and sex.

Paul really cared about me, he told me that weekend, but he was afraid I was going to crash and burn. I was not taking care of myself and he thought that if I continued this kind of pace—including my penchant for anonymous sex—that I would drink again. He suggested I stop hanging out with the guys and start working on myself instead. In addition, maybe get some help for my sexual disorder.

How could I tell him that I did not know where to start? I had started doing my fourth and fifth steps, but had been stuck. Facing my past was no easy feat. I had a few people I was sponsoring. I was doing radio broadcasts on Sunday mornings. At night and on weekends, I was going to schools, detoxification centers, and prisons, sharing my alcoholic recovery story.

After learning the lingo of AA, I began to feel comfortable sharing some of my secrets, and surprisingly enough, some people found that inspirational. I was trying to give back but Paul told me I was trying to give back in the wrong ways.

"Work on yourself first, Kay. Try to understand why you keep sabotaging your relationships. Why do you keep choosing men that do not have your best interest at heart? You have to learn to love yourself first before you can help anyone else."

That was the last time I saw Paul. We obviously were not on the same page.

Promoted to Internal Sales Rep at my job, I was working hard but not performing as my boss had hoped. I was not selling enough, and although he did not want to do it, he said, he let me go. I began temping for Kelly services again and landed a job as a mortgage assistant. I had never worked in a bank before although my mother had for years. Numbers were not my strength but dealing with abusive and rude people was.

I did not like the stuffy pompous attitudes of the people I worked with nor did I like having to give customers bad news as their closing date was cancelled or delayed. It bothered me that this happened most frequently on Fridays and Mondays when certain key bank executives were on the golf course. The bank had the power to make people's lives miserable and they did not seem to care. I sided with the little people and moved on. Kelly Girl placed me at Holyoke Hospital next.

Besides sex, I had taken from high school basic business skills. I knew how to file and type, and do data entry with speed and accuracy. The head nurse at Holyoke Hospital asked me to take their records department and automate it.

I knew nothing about computers but she had had someone build her a database and the contract did not include maintenance or data entry. She gave me a book about how the system worked, and I set out learning the program, and transferring her hard copy nursing information into the database. It took me about three months to convert everything.

The head nurse was very happy with my work ethic and decided she did not want to let me go. The community had not been happy with the time it took to get service in the hospital's ER, so she asked me to work with the physicians and ER staff to see what we could do about making the hospital emergency room more responsive.

Together, the team instituted a triage area that helped prioritize patients and organize the subsequent treatments in stages. We used erasable white boards to communicate nurse coverage and remodeled the waiting area to be friendlier. The staff and community were happy with the results, and before the ribbon-cutting ceremony ended, they asked me to stay on and work in the administrator's office.

The administrator, Henry was a bull of a man. He was six foot six and broad from the top of his shoulders to his feet. From a distance, he looked like Superman. He had been a green beret, and when he walked by you, you would feel the wind from his movement.

His assistant Nancy would be trailing behind him quickly, almost running in her heels to catch up with him as they planned his daily schedule for the hospital and she accompanied him to meetings. She looked like a prima donna but she knew how to keep him on schedule and I think he liked the fact that a pretty girl in heels and feminine dresses chased him all day. On days she was out sick, I would cover for her but I wore flats and business suits. I was not looking for extra points or a bonus, although I would not mind a full-time job.

Henry told me there was a project in the works but it was not quite ready yet, so I organized the administrative files and then began creating lists of doctors' names according to their affiliation with Blue Cross and Blue Shield in anticipation of my new job.

After a meeting he had with Jim and Kelly, CEO and marketing director of a new health maintenance organization, he invited me into his office and introduced me. They offered me the job of signing up the doctors to the new hospital and HMO affiliation.

It took me several months to meet with each doctor, explain the contract, and get him or her to sign. Some refused, others requested follow-up meetings, and others dodged me until momentum picked up. The buzz generated curiosity and then acceptance of the new HMO model that talked of primary care physicians, co-payments and managed health care.

Jim and Kelly asked me to join them at the HMO and I jumped at the idea of a permanent position. My job duties would be largely undefined.

I would help with marketing, advertising, membership materials, and enrollments, whatever they needed. It was a start-up and they wanted to take it public in the next six months. They needed a few customers to join to get people talking about investing and that meant they needed to get a lot done.

The services and per diem rates were still in the final negotiation stages when I started. I watched as the office grew from five of us to twenty-five in a matter of six months. It felt like we were building a family. Exposed to many things in business that only happen in a new company, such as the development of the marketing materials, including the logo; the building of contact lists; the hiring of sales people; and the development of member services brochures, I was thrilled at learning many different aspects of business.

I met Phil at an AA meeting after the Young Peoples' conference and he asked me out for coffee. We went out and then went back to his place. I thought he would make a move on me, but he did not. By the third date, I was beginning to think he was gay, but when I asked him why he had not hit on me, he said he wanted to but he wanted to show me respect. That was a first, and it made me somewhat uncomfortable.

I thought Phil was sweet and we began spending time together, going to different meetings. On the weekends, we would go to his mother's house and he would spend time with his son.

Chapter Forty-Eight

An Attempted Suicide (1985)

About a year later, Phil asked me to marry him. When I broke the news to Diane, she seemed fine. At least I did not notice any difference. Then one night Phil and I went back to my apartment and we found Diane hanging by her neck in the bathroom.

Phil cut her down as I dialed 911. I waited in the bathroom with her until the paramedics got there. She was still alive and they rushed her to the emergency room. They said it was an attempted suicide. Diane's aunt was an administrator in the hospital, which enabled Diane to bypass the psych ward and come home in three days.

I asked her what was wrong. She could not tell me. Her doctor prescribed Antabuse, a drug that would make her sick if she drank. She seemed like she was getting it together for a while and then one night we took a ride and she admitted to me that she wanted to die. I tried to talk her into seeing the good things in life but she was hell-bent on the bad. Maybe there was another presence with us that night because something that I finally said turned her around for a few days and she seemed happy again.

It was not long after that that I came home to find her deathly ill. She had decided to drink and take sleeping pills while still taking the Antabuse. I called the ambulance and they took her away again. That time she did not come back to the apartment when she got out of the hospital. She had decided to move home with her mother and that left me with a lease and rent that I could not afford.

Phil was going through problems with his landlord, with him wanting to jack up his rent. We decided that he would move in with me and we would have the spare room for his son Collin when he stayed with us every other weekend.

Collin had an olive complexion like his dad, with dark brown eyes and dirty blond hair that became blonder as he stayed in the sun. Collin was five the first time I met him and he was just learning how to read. I spent that afternoon sitting next to him on the couch in his grandmother's living room, alternating taking turns reading a story with him. He was so cute; I just wanted to hug him.

I realized that being a mother or a mother figure did not always mean that one was a role model through birth. My doctor had told me at age thirteen that I might someday consider adoption. I began to entertain thoughts of being a stepmother. I was fourteen years older than Collin was and seven years younger than Phil was. I hoped the age differences would not matter.

Phil and I got along fairly well and I started to envision a happy family, eating meals together, watching television together, going places, and doing things. I never imagined that Collin's young life would be so messed up already and that my husband's reaction to his son's situation would negatively influence our marriage.

In the beginning, Collin and I got along very well. Phil worked second shift so often I would go to collect Collin from his mom's house and bring him back to our house for the weekend. Collin's mother was with a man she had been dating for about five years at that time. She had three children, each from a different father. She was a petite pretty girl with big dreams but she had had a rough life and I got the sense that she was not very happy with her current man.

Phil told me that she had lied to him to get him to marry her the first time by telling him she was pregnant. After they got married, she did become pregnant and he gave his best effort at the marriage. But when he came home and found her entertaining one of her johns in his bed, he decided he had had enough and filed for the divorce.

During the first few years of Collin's life, Phil had been drinking and did not spend much time with him when he had his son. In fact, he left his son with his Mom a lot while he went out to the bars. I felt sorry for Collin and thought I had something to offer him. I set out to make the guest room his so that when he stayed with us, he would feel at home.

Then one night I woke up in the middle of the night to find Collin lifting up the covers on my blanket so he could see my boobies. It made me very uncomfortable but Phil and I laughed it off, joking that kids would be kids.

Phil and I wanted to buy a house and my parents were willing to help pay for our wedding. We decided to keep the expenses for the wedding minimal so that we could use the leftover money toward a down payment on a house.

Chapter Forty-Nine

Marriage #1 (1986)

Although we had a large invitation list of 250 people, we opted for an inexpensive buffet at the Knights of Columbus Hall. We had a church wedding and hired a DJ for the reception. I used a friend in AA to do our flowers, another friend to do our photographs, and my grandmother made my wedding dress; the material cost $99.

One of my co-workers offered to make and decorate the wedding cake. I collected coupons for the cake mix and she made the cake for $20. The entire wedding bill cost us around $1500, and with gifts we received, including the left over cash we had from my parents, we had a little money to put down on some property.

In Westfield, Massachusetts, we found an owner of a two-family house who wanted to convert it into two separate condominiums, allowing both sides of the house to be sold individually, with a clause for both owners to share the costs of maintenance. The ad read, "Rent with option to buy."

The apartment was small, about nine hundred square feet, but it had a decent yard on what we thought was a quiet street. We made plans to buy the place and signed the agreement to rent for six months, and then we planned to start putting more money down with the option to buy. It was a two-bedroom unit with an upstairs bathroom and a kitchen and living room on the main floor. The back of the house faced the Mass Pike; we could hear the cars going by, but it did not bother us.

Phil and I were married in September of 1986 and moved into the condominium. I wanted to make more money and I was bored with my HMO responsibilities. I changed jobs in December and began commuting to Windsor, Connecticut to a manufacturing facility that made turbines.

Two months into the job, the executives announced that the facility would be closing because of an acquisition. I was not sure what I was going to do and began looking for another job, although they told me my job working for the purchasing and production managers would be one of the last ones to go.

Then a few weeks later, I started feeling sick in the morning when I awoke and my breasts hurt. I thought maybe I had cancer but then I realized the symptoms also could mean I was pregnant. It was not possible, I thought, but just to be sure, I went to a clinic and had a pregnancy test.

Chapter Fifty

A Miracle Baby (1987)

Around 10:00 a.m., my desk phone rang. I was standing on the other side of the desk when the phone rang, but as I heard the technician telling me the results of the pregnancy test over the telephone line, I almost fainted and had to sit down. The test was 100 percent accurate, she told me, and I was going to be having a baby. It was not possible, I told her, but she told me it had to be, there was no disputing the test.

Phil, who worked second shift, was still sleeping when I called the house.

"I am pregnant."

"What? I thought you said you could not get pregnant?"

"I did not think I could. Look, you know my history. I was not lying to you. This was not supposed to happen. I am sorry."

"I am just having trouble understanding how this could happen. With my car accident and your surgery, it should not have been possible."

"I cannot explain it, Phil. It happened. I am not sure what we can do about it now."

"How far along are you?"

"I do not know. I need a check-up to tell me when I am due. We will talk about this when we have more time, like this weekend." We did not see each other much during the week because of our different schedules. We were both in shock.

I hung up the phone and bawled. My world was crumbling down around me. I was losing my job, my husband and I were not connecting emotionally on any level and I had been contemplating filing for divorce, and now I was pregnant.

My boss saw me crying and he wanted to know what was wrong. I told him I was pregnant and he congratulated me. I did not feel like it was a joyous occasion at all. He did not understand my reaction.

"You are married, right? That is what married people do; I mean, they have kids and raise them, right? It was not like this was an out-of-wedlock pregnancy."

He clearly did not understand. I excused myself and went into the ladies' room. I did not know what to do. I wanted to run away but there was no running away from myself. The baby was inside of me and it was going to be there for a while.

It was a miracle I was pregnant, in so many ways. I knew the moment I walked down the aisle that I had made a mistake getting married but it had been too late. At the time, I crossed my fingers and hoped that life would get better with Phil, but in fact, it got worse almost immediately.

Phil was quiet and I was loud. I wanted to go dancing, he wanted to stay in and watch TV. I wanted to have sex and he did not. Before we had gotten married, I had had to cajole, trick, or beg for sex. I thought he was being a gentleman and was trying to protect my honor, but I learned after we married that he just had no interest in sex or maybe my interest in sex intimidated him. Whatever the problem was, we never got over it. I was a daily girl and he was a once-a-quarter man.

I have never used birth control, well maybe once or twice, but never on a regular basis. Phil had been in a car accident that left him with a low sperm count. He was not supposed to be able to father again. This should not be happening, this cannot be happening, I am freaking out, but it is.

Immaculate Conception, I laugh to myself. It has happened before, they say. What the fuck am I going to do now?

Everybody around me is excited and I am scared shitless. For almost a decade, I have believed having children was not ever going to happen for me. I had thought about adoption on and off, and decided I would not adopt.

Instead of being a mother, I had decided I wanted a career. I wanted to travel and see the world, just as my father had done. I was a dreamer. I was a dancer. I was a singer. I was a crazy lady, but I was not a mother. A step mother maybe, but a mother, never.

I went to the doctor right away to check for genetic problems. I explained my birth defects to the technician and told her I was not supposed to be able to get pregnant.

"What if my child is deformed? I need to know before I can make a decision. If there is something wrong with the fetus, I want an abortion. I am not ready to be a mother, let alone be a mother of a child that has to go through life as I did. I would not bring a child like that into this world. Life is hard enough when everything goes right. Can you check to see if the baby is a girl, and if so, will she be normal?"

The technician came back after running all kinds of tests on my blood. The genetic testing on my baby found that a) it is a girl, and b) she is perfectly normal.

I was on the fence, and on either side, there were spiders and snakes and alligators. I felt alone. I was afraid. I wanted this baby, but I wanted it to be happy and have a good life. My husband was distant and we were living more like brother and sister than lovers.

Before this, I never thought of him as a father to my child, and with what I have seen with the way he neglected his son, I could not, in good faith, believe that I would stay here long.

My best friend and her husband had a baby and I spent most of my time with them. They loved me as my breasts began to fill with milk and soak my dress. They let me sit in their baby pool and cry as I tried to reconcile with where my life was headed. I should feel excited, but all I felt was despair.

I told my sister about my fears of becoming a mom, and she told me I should be grateful for my miracle baby. I was three years older and married, and the year before I got married, my parents forced her to give her baby up for adoption. She had not wanted to do it but they told her they would not help her and that she was not capable of raising a child, as she was just a child herself.

She was angered that I even contemplated abortion, and I could not explain how incompetent and unworthy I felt. It was not fair. It just was not fair. I cried, feeling guilty for being alive. I was not even sure how I got pregnant, and now that I was, my husband would not touch me at all. Pregnant women grossed him out. I just wanted to be held and told that everything would be all right, but there are no guarantees.

I told my mother I was afraid. She told me it would be fine. I told her I do not think I could handle being a mother and that it would be better if I aborted the pregnancy. She was enraged. She did not believe in abortion; to take another's life is a sin in her eyes. "How can you say that? This is a miracle, a gift from God, K. C."

"I do not believe in God, Mom."

I knew she was exasperated with me. My brother's son had been born on my second-year AA anniversary and he could not see his son because of his alcoholism, his non-payment of child support, and his temper. My sister gave up her first-born baby to adoption the following year and she was now utterly depressed. Mom lost Peter three years prior to that with a stillbirth. Keeping babies in our family had not been easy.

She knew what it was to grieve for a lost baby. I, on the other hand, could only think about the possibility of fucking up another human being.

Mom did not know how promiscuous I have been, she did not know the angst I felt over being responsible for another human being. I had not done well with my own life. I had messed up my brother and sister's teenage years. How could I possibly be a positive influence on a child, my child?

Chapter Fifty-One

Lynne (September 1987)

The night before my planned cesarean, Phil and I went to the Big E, a local fair in West Springfield that serves the Tri-County area. I was huge, having gained fifty-four pounds during the pregnancy. I ate food until 11:49, enjoying a sausage, peppers and onion grinder, some fried dough, and some coffee.

The morning sickness that I had had the first six months had gone away. Lynne was an active baby who kicked me constantly. The only time she was still was when I was dancing or sitting on the bow of my father's boat and we were riding the waves. I sang to her and her dad talked to her while she was in my belly.

I have resigned myself to becoming a mother, although I am still petrified. I sign the waivers that say I might end up crippled right before they gave me the spinal and wheeled me into the operating room. I told the anesthesiologist that I felt sick during the beginning of the surgery and he told me that I could not possibly feel anything. I threw up all over him and he instantly became a believer.

The doctor banished my husband from the room but I called for him anyway. I wanted him there but they kept him out until she was born. Why did I have to go through this alone? There were people at the other end of the table but I did not know them. A green sheet draped over my knees sagged in the middle. I could see their faces concentrating on whatever it was they were doing to me.

I did not feel the birth as they made the incision across my groin and pulled her out, but I heard them say it was a girl. My legs were strapped in the foot stirrups and my torso was strapped to the table so I could not sit up. Sitting up within six hours of having a spinal could cause headaches and possible paralysis.

As I watched them take her to the sink, Phil came in, and soon they laid our new baby on my chest. I loved her instantly. She was perfect in every way, and everything I hoped for, and more.

She had dark hair like Phil and she had my mother's eyebrows. Maybe she had my nose and lips. I hoped that she would have bigger breasts than mine, and hoped that she would inherit Phil's height. She was twenty-one inches long, 6.8 lbs. We named her for nobody. We had no previous connotations or expectations with her name and that was what we were looking for. We wanted her to become whoever she was going to be without trying to be like someone else.

The calamities of motherhood hit me quickly. I spilled a cup of coffee on her while I was nursing for the first time. Right away, I knew I was destined to fail. How could I have been so stupid? Drinking fluids was a good thing, drinking hot fluids while nursing was not. The coffee had only been lukewarm but it awakened me to the possibility that it could have been much worse.

Lynne cried a lot when she was a baby, so I held her, sang to her, danced with her, and she calmed down. After the cesarean, I was not supposed to lift anything, but we had already been planning a move. The day of the move, I walked around with her at my breast as my husband and our friends loaded the truck.

We moved in with my parents for a few months until we saved enough money to buy a house. The condominium deal had not seemed so appealing after all. We were able to get out of the deal without penalties and began saving in earnest.

One of the issues between my parents and I had always been religion. They wanted me to baptize Lynne and take her to church, but I did not believe in the concepts of original sin, heaven, or hell. When I was a young child living under their roof, I did not have a choice. I had to follow their rules and respect their wishes. As an adult, living under their roof, I still had to follow their rules and respect their wishes but their responsibility and control over certain aspects of my life, like religion, had changed.

Now, I was responsible for another person and I had to think carefully about how I wanted to influence Lynne about God, spirituality, and or/ faith.

Chapter Fifty-Two

Family Life (1988)

I nursed Lynne until she was about five months old but she was not getting enough milk. I was exhausted from being the primary food source and I think my moodiness was starting to get to her too.

The day my mother fed her a little cereal, I finally got more than two hours of sleep at a time. Then she took to the bottle. It granted me a bit of freedom, which I relished. I ran to the local AA meeting and was just happy to be by myself for a change. I loved being a mom but I missed my independence too. Then, I felt guilty for being gone from her and rushed home to find her in my mother's capable care, sleeping.

After ten months, my husband and I finally had saved enough money. We bought a house in Springfield, Massachusetts.

The house was dilapidated after being used as a rental property for fifteen years. We spent almost two months cleaning, fixing, and painting the house before we moved in. During that time, Lynne exhibited behavior that scared the crap out of me.

We were outside playing but I had work to do inside, so I had picked her up off the back step to bring her into the kitchen. She did not want to go inside and she started crying. She cried so hard she just passed out on the kitchen floor with no warning. I watched as her eyes rolled back in her head and her lips turned blue. I could find no pulse, and I looked, but her chest was not moving. I did not think she was breathing and I thought she was dying at my feet.

I tore across the driveway and ran to the neighbor's house with her in my arms. I thought she was near death. By the time, I got to the neighbor's, banged on her door, and she let me in, Lynne was limp and unresponsive. I placed her on the neighbor's kitchen table, and as soon as I did that, her head started moving and she started breathing again.

It had been no more than three minutes, but in that space of time, I saw her short life pass before my eyes. I remembered the agony I had been in when I found out was pregnant. Then I remembered the day I had made the final decision to go through with the pregnancy and accept fate and all it had to offer. I was not in control. The Group of Drunks (GOD) was. What were they doing to me? Trying to drive me mad after I had gone through so much to get this far?

I regretted all the bad things I had ever done in my life and wished that somehow I could undo them if it would change the current situation. It is funny how perspective changes things. For so long, I lived with a death wish hanging over my head. I didn't care whether I lived or died, even after getting sober. Now that I had her in my life, I had someone else to think about and my life seemed worthwhile.

Lynne came around and eventually I brought her back home. My neighbor suggested I take her to see a specialist to see if she might have epilepsy or some other neurological issue. I did just that after talking to my husband and learning she had done something similar when he was taking care of her.

Fortunately, after several tests, the doctor advised me that everything was fine and that unconsciously she was going into this non-breathing mode to get her own way. I had a hard time believing it but the doctor recommended that I just pay no attention to her when she went into these fits and soon she would realize that the process was not working for her.

Let me tell you it is emotionally wrenching to let your kid pass out. I feared she would never come back, but he had assured me that her body would not let that happen. After just ignoring her once after another episode, it worked and she stopped.

Lynne spoke her first words at my mother's house. We were outside next to the farmer's fence, looking at the cows. I said, "Moo." The cows said, "Moo." And then she said, "Moo." I was thrilled.

After that, she went through a period where she would just wave to everyone and say hi repeatedly. It was cute. I took her to AA meetings often when she was young. She would jump up into the arms of just about anybody, and although she was friendly, I was always afraid she might just jump into the wrong arms.

I was lonely. I worked first shift and Phil worked second. We did it to manage childcare costs but whatever closeness we had once felt had evaporated. The only time we enjoyed each other's company was when it involved Lynne and even during those times, we disagreed on how to parent her sometimes.

Chapter Fifty-Three

Collin (1988)

Collin had moved to North Carolina with his mother. Phil talked to him over the telephone on weekends. He was seven by then and had been in school in Niantic when his mom pulled him out right before the holidays. They were living in a Muslim commune, and she shared her husband with other wives. She asked us to call her Yasmeen instead of Mary. Yasmeen warned us that Collin, now indoctrinated into the Muslim community, would pray seven times a day when he came to visit us.

The plan was for Collin to stay with us for the summer that year. The evening his flight arrived, Phil was working, so I went to the airport to get Collin with Lynne. They got along on the ride home from the airport, giggling in the back seat the whole way. It looked like it was going to be a great summer.

While I was cooking dinner, Collin hooked up his Nintendo to the living room television. As suppertime drew closer, I asked him to set the table and he ignored me. He was obviously into his game, and thinking he did not hear me, I yelled.

"Collin, please set the table. Supper is almost ready."

"That is not my job. It is women's work." He had heard me and he was being deliberately disrespectful.

"Collin, turn the TV off and set the table. I have cooked and you can set the table. We work together in this house, everyone participates."

He got up from the floor, shut the television off, and stormed to his room, slamming the door.

I counted to ten backward and walked down the hall. Lynne was in her high chair, ready to eat.

I knocked on his bedroom door and he yelled for me to leave him alone. Maybe I should have let him be but I was angry that he was not listening to me, particularly as it was his first night with us. "Collin, I am coming in."

"Leave me alone, you are not my mother."

When I walked into his room, I did not see him. I looked under the bed and behind it, and finally, I checked the closet. He was sitting on the floor of his closet, rocking back and forth, with his arms wrapped around his knees and his eyes closed. He was mumbling words that I did not understand.

"What are you doing?" I asked him.

"I am praying, leave me alone. You are not my mother. You cannot tell me what to do. Men do not do kitchen work, and I am a man." He was sobbing now.

"Calm down, Collin. I am sorry I yelled at you. I did not mean to yell, it is just that you did not do what I asked you to do. I did not think you could hear me." His eyes were blinking non-stop and he was shaking. I had not screamed at him, and had only raised my voice a little. He was hyperventilating. I got him a paper lunch bag and had him breathe into it. He finally calmed down.

"Look, I will set the table. Go wash your hands and meet me in the kitchen. You are probably hungry. It is getting late. When was the last time you ate?" Changing the subject helped me get him out of the closet. I went into the kitchen and set the table, thinking this is not what I should be doing but not knowing how to establish authority without alienating him further.

When Collin came into the kitchen, he was instantly upset with me again when he realized I had set places for the both of us at the table.

"That is not how it is supposed to be done. You sit in the living room and wait for me to eat. Then, when I am done, you can come to the table."

"Collin, there is no way in hell that I am going to serve you and go sit on my living room floor while you eat." It turned out his life had changed drastically with the new Muslim culture. He must have watched his mother sit with the rest of the women in the commune while he and the men ate together. I really had no idea what to do. I wanted to respect his new culture but I also wanted him to respect my authority.

He was ready to storm to his room again when I caught him by the arm. "Just sit here and eat, Collin. We used to do this all the time before you moved to North Carolina. Remember when we ate together as a family? It was less than a year ago."

He was angry but he was hungry too. He ate in silence, refusing to look at me. I was exhausted from the evening's events and let it go. I was glad when he went back to his room after dinner. This was more than I could handle.

Later that week when I did the laundry, I discovered Collin had unlearned how to wipe himself when he went to the bathroom. His underwear was full of shit. He had been potty-trained years ago, but he was regressing. It was obvious to me that something had happened to him, and that he was having emotional problems because of it.

I talked to Phil about getting him into some form of counseling. He did not think there was anything wrong with Collin until one of the neighbors came over and complained that Collin was sexually abusing his son. Then we had repeated events where he stole things from our friends and from stores. We got to the point where we had to warn people that he was prone to taking things that did not belong to him. He was seven and he was already messed up.

Phil finally relented. We found a counselor, and gradually, Collin stopped the rapid eye blinking and began wiping himself again. We talked to Yasneem about Collin's problems. She said she did not know anything about anything. Then she said she was struggling financially with the two girls and was wondering if Phil could send her money. Then she called and wanted to know if we could keep Collin for the school year. I thought it would be best for Collin, so we agreed.

I was beginning to worry about Collin's influence on Lynne. I did not think he would sexually molest her but I was not 100 percent sure either. I did not know what he had been through in the last few years, but I had a feeling he had been abused and molested. He would not talk about his life with his mother to me, and his father did not ask.

One day I was in the kitchen and heard the outside faucet turn on. I ran outside expecting to see Collin and Lynne playing in the backyard. He had positioned the garden hose in her mouth and had turned the water on full force. He was holding the hose in her mouth and she was choking, gasping for air, and he was laughing.

I picked her up and banged on her back, and she eventually coughed and caught her breath. I was so scared, I was shaking. I wanted to scream at him but I did not know if he had tried to kill her on purpose or if the incident was a stupid kid's prank, with him not realizing the possible dire effects. I wanted to believe it was the latter, but I was not entirely positive.

The situation scared me. Things were not going how I had envisioned them. Phil had an older brother who lived at home because of mental illness. His family had tried to get him help but he had checked himself out of the hospital when he was eighteen and had refused all medications. Instead of living a normal life, he was living in his bedroom, afraid of germs at the age of thirty-eight. His mother spent her entire life taking care of him and Phil's father.

Norman, Phil's dad, never had a nice word to say about his wife, and his kids hated him for it. He was an alcoholic, a retired carpenter, and a veteran. He would sit at the table, drink, and call his wife Janet when her name was Jeannette just to piss her off. She was a timid woman and put up with his crap because of the children, and because she was a devout Catholic and thought divorce was a sin.

They bickered day and night and I hated visiting. When I looked to the future, I could not see anything different for me if I stayed married to Phil. I changed from part-time to full-time work as I began to prepare for a divorce. I built up my credit by opening a checking account. It would take me a year to establish a presence. I bided my time. We found a new day care that took both Lynne and Collin and he was enrolled in school.

September 17, on Lynne's second birthday, right before our guests arrived for her party; I told Phil that I was thinking of ending our marriage. He was surprised and thought all was well. I knew then that if he was not feeling the emotional loneliness that I was, we were doomed. I had been crying myself to sleep for months by that point.

By Christmas, Collin was doing better in school, and although I did not think our marriage had any chance of making it, I wanted Phil to file for custody of his son and told him I would stick by him and help. Phil loved Collin but he did not want to file for custody and then find out we were getting divorced and end up being a single dad. Yasmeen wanted Collin to go home, saying she missed him. We told her we thought it would be better for Collin to stay with us. In fact, we told her we were thinking about fighting for custody.

Once she heard that, she demanded we send him home right away. The only way we could fight it would be to get a lawyer and claim her as an unfit parent. Phil did not want to make the claims or fight the fight.

Chapter Fifty-Four

Divorce #1 (1989)

As was usual, I was the one to put Collin on the plane to go home. I felt like I was sending him to the guillotine. I knew in my heart that I probably would never see him again. I could not respect a man who did not fight for his kid, and in my eyes, Phil had failed his son. I would not give him a chance to fail his daughter too.

I wanted out of the marriage. I had gained enough confidence in myself to feel like I could be a good mother. I had gained enough financial credit where I could get a phone in my own name. I had stashed a little cash and felt confident that, even if we ended up living on food stamps or in a cardboard box, things would be better than the way we were living and at least I would be teaching my daughter through osmosis how to stick up for herself.

I took Lynne's crib apart and tied it to the roof of my car. I packed up our clothes and toiletries, and lugged the plastic garbage bags to the backseat and trunk. I went through the house one last time. Nope, there was nothing there that I wanted. Besides, the more stuff I owned, the harder it would be to react to change. I told Phil that I was leaving the night before and while he was at work that afternoon, I made it happen.

With one car trip, I managed to grab our clothes and the crib, and we left. It was not much different from the time my dad had kicked me out after finding me in bed with Stephen. Except this time, I was leaving of my own accord and ready to start a new life.

We moved in with my best friend, Becky, who was also going through a separation with her husband. Her daughter was a year older than Lynne was and we were like family. Becky had been the one to convince me to go through with my pregnancy and she had been there, listening to me wishing that I were not married to Phil on a daily basis.

Becky was going through a difficult time too. She was remembering instances of her mother sexually abusing her when she was her daughter's age. She was having trust issues with her husband and she was now dating a woman. To my surprise, one of the women that came over her house as a lesbian friend was my old friend Diane. She had finally made the move and was dating a woman. I was surprised that they both had "turned" gay or more likely, they always were but it had taken working on themselves and being sober long enough for them to come out of the closet. I was happy that they had reached new plateaus in their lives, and I wanted to do the same.

During the final months of my marriage, I realized my anger toward my husband and our life together was spilling over on how I was raising my daughter. She started fussing when he was around and I realized I was doing her more harm than good by keeping her in that environment. She was feeding off my angry feelings and that was not healthy.

When I suggested to Phil that maybe we had made a mistake in getting married and that I was not happy, I also told him I had had an affair. He acknowledged that we were on different paths sexually and he even went so far as to suggest that I could have a discreet affair and it would be okay with him.

I could not agree to that for the simple reason that it was not part of our original marriage contract. If it had been our original agreement, maybe; but I could not, in good faith, go out, sleep with other people, and expect to have any emotional connection with him after that.

Phil suggested we try counseling. He did not want the marriage to end and I was sure he was afraid of losing another child. It was not the first time I had been in therapy. I had been when I was a kid for my alcoholism and drug addictions, as well as family counseling and for my bout with anorexia. I was not afraid of counseling, but it did not go very well at first because Phil wanted the session to be about us maintaining or improving our relationship and I had already decided that he was not capable of giving me what I wanted no matter how hard he tried. I knew he loved me but love was not enough.

Our divorce was finalized after we spent about ninety days in therapy. During that time, we focused on how we would deal with custody concerns, face critical decisions, and provide financial support to our daughter, separately but together. We did not want to use her as a pawn. Going to counseling with Phil was one of the best things I had ever done because it allowed me to see that I still had some growing up to do. I knew I had better do it before I tried raising my daughter alone.

After completing couple's counseling, I found a new psychologist, Arlene, who specialized in relationships and sexual disorders. She helped me see things I had not seen before.

Chapter Fifty-Five

SAD Awareness (1989)

It was the first time that I had actually felt a connection with a therapist and I was able to verbalize that I was scared shitless to be a mother, never mind taking on the added responsibility of being a single mother.

"I do not want to fuck her up."

"What? You mean you do not want her to have to see a shrink. Should I take offense?" I was sitting on the gold and orange striped couch in her office. It accented the orange walls and golden carpeting. Her comment broke the ice and I laughed.

"So why are you here?" Arlene asked me.

I told her I felt terrible about the way I had abandoned Collin. It was the biggest regret I had over the whole divorce. It was something I could not vocalize in my couple session with Phil because I did not want to make him feel bad. I had let Collin go even when I knew whatever he was going back to was going to be worse than the life we were providing for him. However, it had not been my fight because he was not my son.

If I had had the option, I would have taken him with me but I had no rights as his father's wife. It was not fair that he was with two parents that seemed to care more about themselves than him. I knew what it was like and it sucked.

That explanation brought unexpected tears and she handed me a box of tissues and calmly waited for me to get a hold of myself.

"You know, becoming a parent changes our perspective on things. Fortunately, it is a gradual process. For most of us anyway, it is not as if we are instantly the parents of a seventeen-year-old. Normally, being a parent starts when they are babies. It is a learning thing that happens over a span of a lifetime. Nobody is a perfect child; nobody is a perfect parent. We can only hope that we become better with age." Arlene showed me her two kids, dog, and a picture of her husband in front of her home as proof that life can be good.

"So explain to me why you decided to get divorced?" Arlene began digging the way an archaeologist does, carefully at the surface.

"I do not know. The marriage was not right. It was too much work for not enough reward. We were not compatible. I started to hate him and I used money and my daughter as a way to get back at him for not being who I wanted him to be. It was awful. I could not stand what I was doing, buying things and sneaking them into the house and lying about my purchases. I wanted to feel like I had control." I paused for a minute as I laughed out loud, remembering how I would stage my purchases so Phil would not be aware of what I was buying.

"Then I was sneaking around his back to go on dates, taking a vacation day at work, or lying to him about where I was. One time, I brought my kid on a date. She was only a little baby, she could not talk yet and did not know what was going on, but I should not have been doing it and I knew it. It made me feel like an unfit mother."

"At first, I justified my behavior because my husband would not touch me, and I was lonely. Before the affair, I felt ugly, unlovable, and emotionally dead. After the affair, I felt alive and beautiful, but what I was doing was wrong and I felt guilty. It was not until after I witnessed another family member in an embrace with another woman that I realized that the effects of having an affair went beyond just the three or four people who were immediately intimately involved."

"I did not set out to be a liar and a cheat, but it happened and I did not like what I had become. I became full of hate, feeling trapped in a loveless marriage. I decided to get the hell out before I killed him. You know the whole 'until death do us part' thing? I was having those kinds of thoughts and I knew that was a sign, it was time to do something." Arlene laughed at my reference but I shook my head, indicating it was not funny.

"Honestly, I am not kidding; I got scared that I would kill him. One day, he was walking behind the car as it was parked on a hill. For a split moment, I thought about unlatching the emergency brake so that it would roll down the hill and run him over. I thought I could lie well enough to pretend it had been an accident. I read about women going to jail for that kind of thing. I scared myself with thoughts like that and I realized I was in trouble. There was no question in my mind; I needed to get out. Divorce was a dirty word in our family. I did not want a divorce. I just wanted to be free."

"Well, I think you certainly made the right choice if that was how you were feeling." Arlene's simple comment validated my feelings.

"Well, I think I did, but nobody else does." I explained to Arlene that my mother had tried to convince me not to get a divorce. My sister thought I was crazy to leave Phil. He did not beat me and he went to work every day, what more did I want? My grandmother did not understand me either, but she told me she respected the fact that it was my choice. That was enough for me.

"So explain to me why you got married." Arlene was digging again.

"That is a really good question. At the time, I thought I was ready. I was twenty-one and had lived an adventuresome life. I had caught herpes from a boyfriend and I wanted to get out of the meat market. I thought getting married would give me steady sex, which was my primary goal. Secondary to that, I wanted a house, a partner, and a life filled with memories of doing things and going places."

"Phil was a good man, he was a good provider, he could read and write, and he was consistent. Collin was the kicker; I fell in love with him. I thought having him in my life would be a good substitute for me having kids, as I did not think I could get pregnant. I was unhappy before I got pregnant, but after I decided to keep Lynne, I started looking at my husband in a different way. When I looked at him as a father, I did not like what I saw."

"Why did you think you had to settle down at twenty-one? That is young to get married."

"No, it is not. My mom got married at twenty-one and I think her mom was married even earlier. I was no different. Of course, I was different from my mom in other respects. She married the second person she fell in love with, and she has never had sex with any other man besides my dad. I cannot imagine that. I moved out of my parents' house when I was sixteen and a half. I'd been taking care of myself for five years by then and it just seemed like the next logical step."

"Why did you move out so young?" Arlene had her hands in her lap.

"Well, I did not move out really, I was thrown out but it was probably the best thing my parents could have done. I was out of control and they did not know what to do with me. I would not listen or follow their rules, so I was out. Tough love, I am sure you have heard of it. They have meetings just like AA and Alanon."

"Wow that seems drastic. How did it make you feel?" Arlene was asking about my feelings again.

"Well, I am here, and that might not have happened if I had not been in counseling before. At least I know the value of getting help. I did okay. I stayed out of trouble for the most part. I did some crazy things but I could have been a lot worse. I am here to talk about it so it could not have been that bad, right?"

"Right, unfortunately, we are out of time. Let's pick up next week where we left off." Arlene was professional, but she was doing what I was paying her to do and that was to help me understand myself. I liked her.

The following week I was back in her office again.

While she glanced at her notes, I noticed that she was heavier than I thought the first week. She was Jewish with her dark hair, olive skin, distinct nose; but what gave her away was her last name, Weinbaum. She had married her man out of college. I could have had a similar life but I threw it all away.

During one chat with my probation officer when I was 16, he offered me a full paid scholarship to college if I stayed sober. I told him I didn't want any handouts. As a result, now I would have to work several jobs to survive.

Her voice drew me back in. The art in the room was eclectic. She had her degree posted over her desk in a delightful frame that exactly matched the ticking in the upholstery and draperies.

She says to me, "Okay, remind me again how you felt when you were kicked out of your parents' house."

I shrug. "Okay, I guess. What was I going to do about it? I did not follow the rules. I knew it. I was caught. My parents held me accountable. I would not expect anything less. What more is there to say? That is life, you play, and you pay."

"Let me ask you again. How did you *feel* when your parents kicked you out?"

"I did not feel anything. I had been drinking the night before, still buzzed, and my main concern was where I was going to live. I did not really know where to go or how I was going to manage, but I reasoned that I would figure it out. I was not stupid. Well, let me rephrase that. I was stupid. I had been caught being stupid. I put my clothes, books, and stereo system in large plastic trash bags and my dad hauled them to the back step. When the last bag came down, Dad heaved it on the back step and said, 'I am sorry, K. C. Your actions have not given me any other choice. Good luck.' He proceeded to shut the door and turn away down the hall.

"I was alone, and probably more surprised than anything else. I might have cried out of frustration, anger at myself for being caught. It certainly was not what I had expected to be doing that morning."

I was recalling the day in my mind. "There was an abandoned hunter's cabin in the woods that I thought I might live in, at least until school was out. I did not want to stop going to school. I knew I needed my high school education if I was going to make something out of myself. I had wanted my freedom, and now I had it. The question was what was I going to do with it?"

She had uncrossed her legs and re-crossed them the other way. "Weren't you angry with your parents?

"How could I be angry with them? I was the one who had fucked up. They had given me choices and I had made the wrong ones. They were just doing their jobs. Besides, they had two other kids to think about, and my influence on them was not good."

"Do you always take the blame for everything?" Arlene was leaning forward in her chair and coming closer to my personal space.

"What do you mean?" Her question had caught me off-guard.

"I hear you rationalizing and justifying behaviors but I do not hear you expressing your own feelings. Emotions are things like joy, sadness, trust, disgust, fear, anger, surprise, anticipation, anxiety, embarrassment, helplessness, powerlessness, frustration, guilt, shame, envy, doubt, hurt, or stress. Did you feel any of those, because I did not hear you use any of those words except maybe frustration?"

"Well sure, I was worried I would not be able to make it on my own financially. I was surprised that I was out on the back steps with all my stuff in bags. I was embarrassed that I had been caught doing something wrong. I was angry with myself for screwing up again."

"Right," she said to me as she said slowly, "what about how you felt about your parents?"

"I did not feel anything."

She pressed me. "C'mon, tell me how you felt as your father closed that door."

As I thought about it, I could feel the tears coming. "I guess I felt angry."

"Why did you feel angry?" She was pushing me into a place I did not really want to go.

"I was pissed that they were kicking me out. Parents are supposed to love you and support you no matter what. They had given up on me. All they offered was conditional love. As long as I followed their rules and believed what they believed, I was fine. As soon as I had my own opinion or acted in a way that they felt was unacceptable, they stopped loving me. It hurt, okay. It hurt and I felt abandoned!" The tears had come again.

"You know that not all parents are capable of giving unconditional love."

"I guess."

"It is true. Some parents try to but fail. Others do not even try. Parenting is not black and white, you know, there are many gray areas."

"Well, my mother is a black-and-white person. There is no gray with her. It is either good or bad, and I hate that about her. I think my father sees the gray but he chooses to hold back his emotion and sides with my mom because it is just easier."

"Why is that?" Arlene is digging again.

"I do not know. Marriage encounter changed their relationship. Before that, they were somewhat normal but then they started spending time together and dialoguing. They made it obvious to us kids that their relationship took precedence over us. I can see why, kids grow up and move out and you are stuck with your partner for life; but somehow, it did not make it any easier to deal with. We kids ended up finding other ways to find love. Our house was volatile and passionate but dysfunctional."

I think about it for a bit. "I guess that was the point when I had felt abandoned by them, even though they did whatever they could for me when I was a kid."

Arlene writes something down on her pad and then says, "Tell me about your marriage."

"Phil was steady, dependable, and honest. He was looking for a wife, someone to take care of him and his son. Because I thought I could not have children, it seemed to be a good match. It was before the wedding day when I realized I was making a mistake. But we were making plans and I didn't feel like I could stop the train once it started. I didn't have a lot of self-respect. Then I found out I was pregnant. I thought maybe I could be a mom and a step mom until Phil decided to send his son back to his mother. We had surmised through help with therapy that he had been in a sexually abusive relationship during the time he had previously spent with his mother. He needed help but my husband seemed oblivious."

"My head was screaming NO, NO, NO. I cannot take this anymore, and yet I was going through the motions. Trying to be a good wife, a good mother, a good stepmother, a good daughter, a good daughter-in-law; and yet every day I felt this big dark cloud over my head getting bigger and bigger. My emotions were stifled because I was pretending. I could not laugh, I could not cry, I could not show much of anything but contempt and anger. I started spending money, more than we had to spend, just to show some control in my relationship. I did not want to raise our daughter in this kind of environment.

"I had a few affairs during the marriage, one with my previous boyfriend, Alex. I brought my daughter to see him once, and another time I went alone. I also had affairs with a few of the men I worked with. One was my indirect boss, and another was the union negotiator. My boss, Bob, was a very nice man. He taught me a lot about sales, personality, and listening."

"We had crossed the boundaries of professional talk on occasion in the office and I really did not think much of it, until one day when his birthday was coming up, I asked him what he wanted and he said a blowjob. I told him I thought I could accommodate that and we arranged for me to meet him at his apartment for lunch. When I got there, we kissed a little and then he led me to the bedroom and he lay on the bed. I started taking some of my clothes off, and when I went to kneel on the bed, he came. I did not touch him; he apparently had been excited about our talks, he explained as he cleaned up. I did not bother to stay for lunch; he had gotten his gift from me."

"The other man intriguing me was Pierce. He came in to where I worked in Human Resources to interview for a job and my jaw dropped. He was well dressed, had dark eyebrows, an olive complexion, and was Kojak bald. I had never been with a bald guy before, but if I were going to be, he would be the one. At the time, I was twenty-three and he was forty-five."

Arlene shook her head for me to continue.

"I told him I wanted him to fuck me at our company picnic, and not long after that, we hooked up. The first time, we arranged to meet in a parking lot. I ended up blowing him in his car while he washed and dried his laundry at the Laundromat. Another time, I took a vacation day and met him down at his house at the beach. He lived in a small apartment and we fucked on his bed until his daughter barged in. She was a year younger than I was, and I hid in the closet the whole time. I was embarrassed about our ages and I knew I should not be there—I was, after all, still married and sporting my wedding ring for goodness sake. Pierce made me feel great because he was dangerous, dominant, and sadistic. I suspected he had issues, as he had been married a few times already and going through a nasty divorce. After his daughter left, we took a walk out to the beach and he started drinking. I lost him somewhere in the crowd and made my way home. The last time we hooked up was the day of the union negotiations."

"I had worked for him and the owners of our company, typing the stipulations and contracts up. I had endured their many edits and I could almost recite word for word the contract terms. I also knew the unwritten contract terms. The ones that they had discussed in front of me, the things they would give up or provide more of if pressed."

"The union negotiations held at a hotel in Enfield were not far from our plant in Suffield, Connecticut. Pierce had arranged to get a room for the night as he lived a few hours from the office. He was not sure if the negotiations were going to go all night long. He invited me along, I lied to my husband about what I was doing, and I went."

"I waited naked in his room while he went back and forth between the labor rooms where he was negotiating the terms of the contract. Three years prior, the company had had a strike. The company did not want to have to endure another one so soon. It had taken them six months to get back what they had lost during the three-week negotiation."

"Every once in a while Pierce would come in to the room and we would fool around. At 10:00 p.m., he ordered room service and was lucky enough to stay to eat almost all of it before the phone rang. 'Sorry, doll, I must go.' Buttoning his shirt and tucking it into his pants, he threw his suit coat on and was out the door, back at the negotiation table."

"It was the scent of a woman, he said, that had helped him close the deal in under six hours. It had made them want to go home for some sex." Boy, did we laugh over that one. He said, 'They underestimated me. The company president, Jeremy will be happy, and it looks like I just worked myself out of a job.' We fucked and went home in the morning. It was true. Pierce was gone within a few weeks as the company had no need for a union negotiator for a few years."

Arlene had been silent this whole time, and remained so as I finished my monologue.

"I justified my behavior because my husband would not touch me. We rarely had sex, and when we did, it was awful. There was no intimacy or emotion. It was one of two positions, and I always had the feeling he felt obligated instead of interested. I cried myself to sleep frequently and I began to take matters into my own hands. But having affairs was not enough. I needed emotional connection, I needed passion, and I needed a sense of excitement; and sadly, I realized what I wanted could never be with him. I could no longer justify my behavior, nor did I want to live this way; living a lie, feeling alone in a relationship, wanting my husband to just disappear so I would not have to deal with a divorce."

"It got to the point where I was afraid to be alone, but I was more afraid of bringing my daughter up in a house full of anger and passive-aggressive behavior. I just had to get out of there, and that is what I did."

I spent six months visiting Arlene on a weekly basis. She helped me see how detached I had become from my emotions. She made me realize that my sexual promiscuity was a cover up for my feelings of inadequacy of being a woman. She helped me understand that my desire for sex is not the same as a desire for intimacy. She explained that humans need both. She explained that we could not expect one single person to meet all of our emotional needs but that we have to trust that some people will meet some of our needs.

She noticed that throughout my life I had had bouts of depression as well as bouts of hyperactivity. She suggested that the sun might have more to do with my mood swings than I realized. She thought I had Seasonal Affective Disorder or S.A.D. I would start getting depressed in September, often ending many of my relationships during that time of year. In the spring, around March or April, I would get a burst of energy, and depending upon whether I was feeling good or bad about myself at the time, I would either take on great projects or become extremely self destructive. Knowing this about myself gave me ammunition I felt I never had before. I could manage something if I knew what was causing it.

She also helped me identify feelings I had not acknowledged for many years. As a teenager, I hated my parents; but as an adult, I found that I understand better why they did what they did, and that they did love me. I had struggled with verbalizing how I felt but as a parent, I felt like I had to try and I achieved some major successes. I ended the sessions feeling much better than I did when I started. Arlene's final words to me were, "You know, Kay, you are a beautiful woman with a lot to offer. You need to learn to love yourself more and not be so hard on yourself."

With Arlene's help, I had realized the word "woman" had been a trigger for me for a long time. I was trying desperately to find myself and to become a real woman but I was going about it all wrong. It was only in Arlene's office that I realized being a real woman started from the inside, emotionally. It had nothing to do with the physicality of a body or how it was used.

Chapter Fifty-Six

Learning to Become a Mother (1989)

What is important to you as a mother?

To me, a big part of it was learning to say yes.

One of the articles I read on rearing children was about learning how to say yes instead of saying no. It was in a Reader's Digest monthly issue back in 1988. The article said that when your kids approached you for something and your instinct was to say no, examine why you were saying no first. If it was because you were afraid for their safety, think no further.

However, the author suggested that, in many ways, parents stifle their kids by providing boundaries that are too constraining. The other thing the author spoke of was to provide an environment where kids can learn how to make the right decisions. By allowing them more freedoms on the little things in life, we can ensure that when it comes to making bigger decisions, they have more experience under their belt; they can be logical in their approach to serious situations.

Lynne was deciding what she would wear by the time she was ten months old. Sometimes, she looked silly but she got a chance to explore her own style early and get used to making decisions.

The Generation of Mothers

Both my great-grandmothers in my family had come to this country in the late 1800s. They had been little girls to first-generation immigrants. My mom's mom was one of the first women in the family to get a college degree, though she became a homemaker. My dad's mom owned a grocery store with my grandfather. Neither of these women contemplated divorce. It was not an option because their livelihood depended upon their husbands.

I was grateful to have been born in a time where I could have a career and afford to support my child with or without a husband.

My mother chose to live her life primarily taking care of our home and my father, and that seemed to suit her, but I could not trust a man enough to rely on him to take care of me. I wanted to do it myself.

I wanted to give my daughter an environment where she could choose her life partner based upon what she wanted, rather than what she felt she needed. I would teach her how to be independent.

Chapter Fifty-Seven

Traditions and Memories (1990)

Girls in white dresses with blue satin sashes,
snowflakes that stay on my nose and eyelashes,
silver white winters that melt into springs,
these are a few of my favorite things.

When the dog bites, when the bee stings,
when I am feeling sad,
I simply remember my favorite things,
and then I don't feel so bad.

The Sound of Music

As I have told you, music has always been a big part of my life. Lynne was now two and I was adjusting to my responsibilities of being a single mom. Looking at the choices I have made has not been a pretty sight to see. I had been irresponsible as a child in some ways and overly responsible in others. I felt bad for pursuing the divorce but I knew it was the right thing to do. I felt like I missed part of my childhood because I grew up so quickly.

My anger towards my parents was diminishing. They had resorted to the tough love approach when they could not control me anymore and I had resented it. The fact of the matter was they probably saved my life by kicking me out and forcing me to grow up. I knew they loved me and I always had.

I was an adult and felt that I was starting to fly. I was doing well at work, and have started to date a new man named Dick. He had different ideas of how to discipline my daughter than I did. He grew up with his mother giving him a backhand, and once, she even hit him with a frying pan.

I had slapped my daughter only once, and it was a gut reaction. She was about eight months old, still breast-feeding, and in my arms. I was talking to an owner about renting his house with my husband and she wanted my attention. After I ignored her for a minute, she decided to get my attention by biting my breast. I slapped her softly but quickly and we both started crying. When she was born, I had vowed to try to control her through my wisdom rather than my voice or physical strength but I had failed miserably. It was a good lesson for the both of us.

I never hit her again. I did not have to. She was hypersensitive, all I had to do was look at her, and she knew she had erred. There were a few timeouts when she was little, and a few experiences with losing privileges like her television and going to visit friends, but I used these techniques on a limited basis.

Perspective is a funny thing. As a parent now myself, I started to realize that as parents my folks had done a lot of things right for me. My dad had kept a decent job so that we had health insurance, steady income, and a steady home environment. My mom had made sure we had balanced meals, clothes, and a social connection to our families. Now, as a single mother, I realized how hard it is to provide these things to my child and to maintain a sense of self at the same time.

As children, my siblings and I had performed different chores over the years so that we knew how to garden, how to fish, how to wash windows, cook, clean, do laundry, change our oil, change a tire, budget, and even plan a menu. We were raised Catholic, and with that came social responsibility. My mom was quick to take care of people when they needed it, and often put her own needs last, even when maybe she should not have. We learned all that and more.

No matter what the bad might have been, we also learned a great deal of good. I wanted to pass on traditions that I had appreciated. Music as a part of living was one of them. My daughter and I watched *The Sound of Music* together and formed a special bond with some of the songs like "Doe a Deer" and "My Favorite Things." Sometime we sang while doing housework or working in the garden in the backyard or even playing catch. On the weekends she would go to her dad's, we would talk in the car. We were close and she knew I loved her.

Chapter Fifty-Eight

Dick (1990)

Dick was the baby in the family and the only male. His dad had taken off on his mother when he was young; his mom had babied him, as had his five sisters. As long as I took the same role, all was good. Occasionally, when my daughter took precedence in my life, it irritated him; he liked to be the center of attention.

I never thought I would be one to walk on eggshells; I mean, really, I was tough for a girl. I had been around the block a time or two, but as time went on, I gradually gave up my will to follow Dick's.

I kidded myself that it was just easier to go along with what he wanted than to argue with him, and I justified it by saying the small things were not worth conflict. I had been honest with him when I married him, telling him about my past relationships. I even told him about the affairs I had in my first marriage, thinking that if I were honest enough about how much sex meant to me it would help him understand me and keep us on the right path. That was a mistake on my part because he always suspected I was cheating on him although I never did.

People with addiction prone personalities tend to have multiple addictions and we were no different.

I met Dick at an AA meeting and we decided to go to a dance afterward. He did not want to dance; he wanted to get in my pants. After a few dances, he asked me if I would leave with him and go back to his house, and I did.

I called my girlfriend and she agreed to keep my daughter overnight. The next morning, I told her I had had the best sex of my life and had met my next husband, and she told me to chill out; but it was less than a month later when I moved in with him.

Chapter Fifty-Nine

The Signs (1991)

We had been living in Windsor Locks, Connecticut at his mother's second home. At Christmas time in 1991, we took a vacation down to where his mom now lived in Jupiter, Florida. I became enamored with the sea, the beaches, lifestyle, and we discussed possibly moving down there if we could find jobs. I arranged with some of my suppliers from work to do some impromptu interviews. One of the companies said that if I relocated to Florida, they would hire me on the spot, so we began making plans to move to Florida. I was excited but sad to leave my support system, all my friends, and family in the northeast.

Before we moved, I gave Phil the chance to be a full-time father. "I am moving so that I can support her," I told him. "I cannot make enough money up here working one job, but if I move, I will be making six figures within a year. If you want full-time custody, I will not fight you and I will pay child support if you want. I want to do what is right by her. If you think you can do better than I can, I will understand."

He was not happy about the choice he was given and his response was, "No, you take her. I will visit or she will visit me. I cannot be a full-time father

That settled it. We agreed that they would talk on the phone every weekend and in the summer; she would visit him for several weeks, but that she would live with me. She had become the center of my world and I was not sure what I would be doing without her in my life. She had given me a reason to live and another chance. She loved me unconditionally and I had never felt this before.

Dick, Lynne, and I left for Florida the following February with a truck and our car. We got to his mother's house two days later. We slept for four hours and then he and I took off for Plantation. We found an apartment that had a daycare on site. We rented the apartment and went back to his mother's to get the truck. We unloaded it and I started my new job the next day, exhausted but happy to be in Florida.

We did not have any money to spare and the only reason we had had enough money to make it that far was because I had lied to my employer and told them I was going into brokering stock on Wall Street, rather than staying in the food business, diverting groceries. I was breaching my non-compete but I did not think they would come after me. I knew the food business and they could not stop me from earning a living.

Dick had an entrepreneurial spirit and landed himself a job selling credit card machine processing straight commission. It was tough work because the competition in Florida was fierce and the businesses transient. At night, he studied and put himself through GED courses so that he could apply for a sales job at a big insurance company. He wanted to be an insurance sales representative, and to his credit, he worked hard day and night to get there.

We started to make plans for our wedding and then I found out I was pregnant. It was nerve-wracking. Because I had changed jobs, I had three days of non-coverage between insurance policies when I landed in the local emergency room.

Chapter Sixty

Ectopic Pregnancy (1992)

I was on the kitchen floor in my apartment and sobbing. My underwear was pink. My stomach had been cramping all day. Dick was at work but due home shortly. We were planning to entertain company from the north. Party Marty, Dick's high school friend is in town and we are supposed to go out for all-we-can-eat crab dinner, Marty's treat.

I called my mother. "Mom, I am spotting. Does that mean I am losing the baby?"

"Oh, K. C., it could be. How bad is the bleeding?"

"It is bad, Mom. I am scared."

"K. C., you need to get yourself to the hospital because you are built funny. You should be checked out to make sure there is nothing wrong."

Dick walked in and found me on the phone. He saw the tears, and I whispered to him that it is my mother. He told me to hang up and I did after telling her I love her. I would let her know what is going on as soon as I knew more.

I told him I was spotting and he yelled, "Jesus Christ, why didn't you call me? I am the father of your baby. You should not have called your mother."

I said, "I thought she might be able to help me since she has had nine miscarriages over the years." My sarcasm was lost on him. "She thinks I'm having a miscarriage. She told me to keep calm. You need to take me to the hospital. I have already sent Lynne over to Chrystal's apartment to play. Please call Colleen and ask her if she can watch Lynne for a bit longer while I get my purse and change my underwear." Colleen was a

Jamaican neighbor who had a daughter named Crystal. Crystal would come to our apartment to play, or Lynne would go to theirs. The girls played together well.

The phone rang and I heard him on the phone in the other room. "Hi, Marty, I am sorry but we are going to have to take a rain check on the all-you-can-eat crab dinner. Kay's having some problems and I need to take her to the emergency room." He was laughing and oblivious to my situation. They talked for another fifteen minutes and I was getting upset.

"Dick, I need to go now." I do not bother changing, what is the point? I put on a pad and resign myself to hell. "Did you call Colleen?"

He hung up with Marty and called Colleen on his cell phone as he brought the car around to pick me up. Fortunately, Dick was loud mouthed, and demanded medical attention for "his wife." While normally I would object to being referred to as someone's property, in this case, I am grateful because the head nurse comes to speak to us.

She told me I was having a miscarriage and wanted to send me home. Dick refused to take me until I had seen a doctor.

"Look, I would go under normal circumstances, but I am not normal. I have to be checked out. Passing a fetus could kill me. I was born without a vagina; I have no elasticity and I am tiny."

After four hours, the ER doctor finally made it in from the golf course after Dick threatened to call the media. Even though I did not have insurance, the doctor saw me and I explained my situation. He told me to calm down. He was going to run some tests to see how far along I had been.

Surprised to find that my white blood count was so high, he ordered an ultrasound. The baby was still alive and stuck in my fallopian tube. It was beginning to break and I was going to die if they did not get me into surgery immediately.

The surgeon called for the anesthesiologist on duty and the attendants wheeled me away. They had to operate now. Shaved, embarrassed, but still emotionally strong, I asked the doctor if he could save the baby.

He told me that they did not do that kind of procedure at this hospital. I explained that in the northeast, they were doing that procedure; I worked with a woman at the food company who was able to lose the tube but save the baby.

"No, ma'am, we do not do that here, and most babies that do go through that procedure are not born 100 percent right. It is too much of a chance."

What I heard him say between the lines was, "We are sorry, but you do not have insurance."

I woke up and the baby was gone. All remnants of the pregnancy had been sucked out of me. It had been a boy. "It was just a fetus," my husband said but I could tell from his eyes that he was hurt. He had wanted this son.

"I am sorry," I told him.

"I am sorry too," he said. That was it, we were sorry.

"How is Lynne?" I asked him.

"She is fine; I left her with Colleen."

I learned that he had been spending time at the casino instead of with my daughter for the last three days. I hated that he treated her like baggage but I could not do anything about it. I was glad that she was safe with the neighbors instead of with him.

He told me that, knowing I would be out of commission for a week, he had arranged for my best friend Becky to visit. "Thank God," I said. I missed my home and I missed my family. I was grateful. I hugged him and he left.

As he walked out the door, I wondered if I would regret my second marriage. I had been working my ass off trying to put him through his GED class so he could get a job. I was in the hospital after nearly dying and he did not have a minute to spend with my kid. Because I was not going to be able to clean, do the laundry or cook for him, he had arranged to have my best friend come down and help me. I hated him for his selfishness but I was glad that he had called my best friend. I missed her. I had not realized how much until I saw her.

Becky came and stayed with us for a week, cooking, cleaning, and keeping me company so I did not overdo it. We were sitting in the living room and a female comedian came on the television. She had a shtick where she talked about how much fun it was to clean up after her kids and try to time dinner to the exact minute her husband will want it, and then he comes home and says he has to go out and she says to him, "I love you honey. I love you so much I could killlllllll you." Becky and I cracked up. We could relate. She is back with her husband and they are doing well.

We had had good times over the years, sharing difficulties. Anytime of the day or night, I knew I could call her and she would be there for me. She knew she could do the same with me. Special friends like that take time to get to know, and friendships grow. I was glad she was in my life.

She and I talked about me losing this baby. It bothered me more than I wanted to admit. It felt like a piece of me had been ripped out and thrown away. I remembered how I felt when my mother lost Peter. I wondered how she had not gone insane after losing so many babies over the years. One loss was enough for me. If something were to happen to my Lynne, I did not think I could go on. Life was not fair.

At work, I was finally starting to make commission and Dick had gotten his GED and was now in training to become a sales associate at Met Life. We bought policies, and he began selling to friends and family, as well as making cold calls.

Lynne was sick all the time from daycare and it was hard for me to be a straight commissioned sales person and a mom. I felt guilty because she was the first one dropped off at daycare and the last one to be picked up. Sometimes, I paid the late fees that cost me $10 a minute but that was only when I was closing a sale and the rewards would be significant. One time I made $5000 by staying on the phone an extra twenty minutes with a customer and sold him half a million dollars of diverted goods. Spending $200 that night for another twenty minutes of care for my daughter was worth it, but the daycare counselors gave me dirty looks like I did not care about her.

I could buy many things with $5000. I told myself I was working hard to give her a good life.

Dick and I had set our wedding date, Valentine's day 1993. Most of our friends and family were in the Hartford, Connecticut area and we gave them time to plan the trip. We had joined Toastmasters to meet some of the local people in Fort Lauderdale and hone our public speaking skills. We were both in sales, and being able to speak in public was a skill we both wanted to learn.

Dick and I met Allison through Toastmasters. She was looking for somebody to rent her house while she took a job for a few years out of state. We agreed that it was the perfect arrangement and so we moved into her two-bedroom house in Fort Lauderdale.

We enjoyed meeting active members of the community and hob-knobbing with some of the more influential people in town. When we mentioned we were getting married and trying to figure out how we could accommodate some of our friends and family from out of town, several of them offered up their homes for the weekend. It was extremely generous and we took them up on it.

We felt welcomed into the community and we were starting to do well with our respective careers. Life was getting better.

Right before we moved to Florida, Dick's father had called our house in a drunken stupor and told Dick that he was afraid of his girlfriend. Not long after that, we got a call that Dick's father was found dead at the bottom of the stairway of his home. Dick was convinced his dad had been murdered, but after getting nowhere on the phone, he decided to make a trip out to Dallas, where his dad had died.

It turned out, his father had told people that he had no family because he was trying to dodge financial responsibility for child support payments long overdue. He owned a nice mini mansion that had a housekeeping cottage on the premises. During his trip, Dick did some snooping and found a hammer with blood on it under his father's bed. It took a long time but they eventually exhumed the body, did an autopsy, and found that Dick's suspicions were correct. His father had been hit with the hammer, which is what caused him to fall down the stairs.

Instead of the girlfriend getting Dick's father's estate, his sisters and he got the money after his dad's debts and the trial expenses were paid.

We got our first distribution of his estate about a month before we married. We had planned to spend about $10,000 for an elaborate affair. Since many of our friends and family were traveling to the area, we felt we needed to offer two days of activities. The day before the wedding, we planned a fishing trip for the people who were going to be in the wedding party and a final fitting for the girls who were bringing their custom dresses with similar themes from their local dressmakers. The day of the wedding would include, for the girls, makeup, and hair done by Glamour Shots' Affiliates. We would include accommodations with food and drinks for all who came. The only thing they needed to cover was getting to Fort Lauderdale, Florida.

Chapter Sixty-One

The Wedding That Shouldn't Have Been (1993)

Dick and I reserved an elegant stateroom for our wedding in Boca Raton at a prestigious place by the water. We met with the caterer and I had signed the contract after checking references and getting great reviews. Not a month later, the hall owner called and said he had had a disagreement with the caterer and that a new chef would cook our meals. He would not give me the name and I could not check references.

My first wedding had been all about saving money because Phil and I had wanted to buy a home. This wedding was going to be more of a *Miami Vice* kind of event. The wedding would be black and white formal.

When I went to buy my wedding dress, I went shopping for dresses with one of my co-workers. "Really, Kay," Xio told me, "You could pluck those, you know. And while you are at it, whiten up those arms."

I had no idea that my hairiness was so offensive, but apparently, it was. My husband thought I was a new woman after I bleached my arm hair blonde, tweezed the nipple hair, reduced the mono-brow, and tamed the mane. I had not cared about how I looked in a long time; working was where I put my focus.

With Xio's help, I was starting to feel feminine.

About a month before, Becky called and said she had wrenched her back and did not think she could make it to the wedding. I assured her I would send money for airfare so that she and her family could make the trip without the long car ride. Then my brother and sister said they were tight on cash and did not think they could make it. I told them I would cover all expenses for gas, tolls, and food, as long as they came.

I spent $700 on my dress and another $150 on my veil. We paid someone $1200 to have the wedding videotaped and photographed. We knew the meal was going to run about $5000 and the men's tuxedos and the material for the women's dresses were another $1000. With the bridal party gifts, the men's fishing trip, the dress rehearsal dinner, money was coming and going faster than we had anticipated. We were at the end of the cash and we had no money for a honeymoon or shoes to match my dress.

Three days before the wedding, the woman who was supposed to do my flowers fell down the stairs and twisted her wrist. She had only finished a third of the flowers. I assured her the wedding party and I would find a way to create the bouquets. I went to her house, picked up the materials, paid her for a third of the job, and released her of her services.

The beach party and wedding rehearsal were a nightmare in anybody's book. The charter boat lost track of time and returned hours late. I had spent the day trying to entertain the guests who had showed up at the beach, and many of us were sunburned and dehydrated. I was exhausted from months of planning.

As we dashed home from the beach to change and get ready for the rehearsal dinner, I received a call that the justice of the peace could not make the dress rehearsal because she had been in a car accident. She was not hurt but she was stuck with no vehicle. Instead, when we were ready, we would call her and practice the rehearsal over the phone.

The women enjoyed a table of sandwiches and refreshments at the hall while we waited impatiently for the men. When Dick and the rest of the wedding party finally got to the hall to go over the wedding rehearsal, we called the minister and she directed us on what to do over the phone.

As the rehearsal dinner party was winding down, Dick realized that our decorative arch would be facing a street filled with construction equipment. The town had decided to tear up the street next to the area where we were getting married. He tracked down the general contractor and offered him hundreds of dollars to move the equipment so that our wedding pictures would not be "ruined."

The night before our wedding, we had several people staying with us, some in beds, most on the floor. I was trying to get everyone comfortable and Dick was blustering around the house, making nasty remarks. We had overspent on our budget, and although my girlfriend had bought me shoes, and his best man had given us a honeymoon as a wedding gift so everything had been provided for, he was frustrated, and his ego was hurt.

Instead of being grateful for our friends who were coming through for us, he was bitching about everything. That night, both my sister and Becky told Dick to back off. His remarks were hurtful and deliberately abusive. Each of them solicited me individually and told me I did not have to go through with the wedding if I did not want to. I laughed it off but they recognized the verbally abusive behavior before I did.

We got married. The ceremony was beautiful, though calamitous. One of the girls ripped her gown getting into the limo, the wedding rings ended up in the bushes, and the food was not 100 percent cooked and some guests got sick and vomited.

By the time it was over, Dick and I were barely speaking. I wanted to dance and socialize with our guests. He wanted to leave and open our wedding gifts before we headed to the cruise. I said goodbye to my daughter, who would be traveling back up north with Becky on the plane so she could spend some time with her dad, and we went back to the house to pack.

We met Marty and his friend Marc at the dock in Fort Lauderdale at 4:00 a.m., and by 6:00 a.m., after clearing customs, we were on the water headed to Nassau. By 7:00 a.m., about 50 percent of the passengers were vomiting due to the high seas on the waters.

I tried to go below deck to avoid the winds but the putrid smell forced me to go back on deck. Dick, Marty, and Marc were gambling on the slots. I sat in a deck chair with a towel over my head to keep the ocean spray from dripping down my face. I did not feel like a gloriously happy bride, I felt more like a drowned rat heading toward the sea.

Ironically, Marty and Marc took the two-floored honeymoon suite with the heart shaped bathtub, kitchenette, and complimentary honeymoon gift basket. Dick and I got a small room with a double bed and a couch that barely allowed for walking room. I was happy to be on a honeymoon in the Bahamas, but it was definitely not happening how I imagined it would.

I went to get some sodas out of the vending machine and when I got back, Dick was on the phone with his mother. He beckoned me between his legs and I played with his penis while he talked to her. I hated doing it but it was something that had become part of our relationship already and was one of his frequent requests.

He talked to his mother for over an hour, and by the time he got off the phone, I was mad that he had talked so long. I made the mistake of calling him a momma's boy. He got mad and instead of fooling around, we decided to go out for dinner. We found a restaurant where there was no line, no waiting.

That is a big mistake, in case you do not know it. The food was horrible. We ate in about twenty minutes and then had the rest of the night to wait, since our friends had decided to go to a local place that was hopping and required reservations. We walked around the island as our food settled. We had been up for almost forty-eight hours and the weeks of stress before the wedding were taking its toll.

We did not have a lot of money, but when one of the locals asked me if I wanted my hair braided, Dick gave her $5 to braid my hair. We walked back toward the restaurant Marty and Marc had gone to and we saw them eating on the patio above.

We yelled to them and they said they were going dancing after dinner. That sounded like fun to me, but Dick copped an attitude and wanted to go back to the room. He made me feel guilty that I even wanted to go dancing, and started pouting. "We are on our honeymoon, Kay; I cannot believe you want to go dancing with those guys instead of going back to the room with me."

He was right, of course. He always had a way of being right. It was easier to agree than to fight with him. When we got back to the room, I got undressed in the bathroom and put on sexy negligee. When I came out, he was sitting on the couch, watching TV. I tried to sit next to him but he pushed me away and put me between his legs. I knew what he wanted and I started working him but he was not getting excited. When I looked up at him, I saw that he was still mad.

"You disrespected me, and you disrespected my mother." He was pulling my braid and it hurt. He forced me to crawl across the carpeting into the bedroom, leading me with my hair.

He sat at the foot of the bed, and told me to fetch his shoe. I knew what he was going to do. He had done it a few times before during sex. I retrieved his shoe and handed it to him and he pulled my braided hairpiece again and made me lie across his lap.

We had lived together for almost two years. He had spanked me as part of our sexual playing before, but this time was different. He held my hands behind my back and spanked my ass hard. At first, I was giggling, but he let me know he was serious right away. "This is not funny and I do not want you to forget it. You will not disrespect me, behind my back or in front of my face. You will not disrespect my mother. If I am talking to her for three hours, it is none of your business. If I want you to blow me the entire time, you will. Do you understand me? You are my wife, you will love, honor, and obey me."

He was hitting my ass hard with his shoe and it was starting to sting but he did not relent until I started crying and saying I was sorry. When he let me go, I was mad at him, telling him that he was a lunatic and had taken it too far. He thought we should both cool down and get some sleep. When I tried to get in the bed, he told me he thought I should sleep in the closet. I thought so too, and so it was that I spent my honeymoon night on the floor of a Nassau closet hotel.

The following morning, I woke up and he bid me to the bed, and we began our married life officially. He had drawn a line in the sand, menacing in some ways, and provocative in others.

When we got home, Dick and I slipped into our familiar routine before we had tied the knot. Our careers were going well, and we were starting to see the light of being able to unbury ourselves from debt and possibly even buying a house someday. I had been working in Florida for almost a year at that point, and I was finally bringing in decent commissions at Premium Sales.

Chapter Sixty-Two

Premium Sales (1993)

The office was located on Biscayne Boulevard, overlooking the inter-coastal next to the Hallandale Race Track.

When I got upstairs in the high-rise, I found a nice reception area with a friendly lady behind the desk.

On the day I went for my interview, she had called Steve on the phone, and he sent Pammy out to get me. Pammy had been one of the sales reps who called on me when I worked at Sweet Life, and I had casually said to her, "If I ever move down there, what are the odds that I could land a job?" She had assured me Steve would love me and hire me right out and that is exactly what happened.

Pam and I had had conversations over the phone when she called me to sell me grocery products. She told me of fun dates she had, and the things she did on the weekends in Miami. I wanted that lifestyle and she thought I could make it. She was a petite JAP, and proud of it. She wore four-inch heels and designer clothes; and made a decent living while looking for Mr. Right. Someday, she would get married and settle down but she was in no rush. We had met when she came on a sales call to the northeast that previous November, and we hugged like old friends when she came into the lobby. Then she ushered me into Steve's office.

Steve's hair was what I noticed first. It was black, almost as if he had taken a spray can and painted it; but it was frizzy and large, like an afro though he was pale white. He was dressed in an expensive gray blue pinstripe suit and he was wearing cufflinks and a Rolex. His shoes were also alligator, I noticed, as he came around the desk to sit next to me for the interview.

Pammy shut the door but the half wall of glass from Steve's office allowed the sales pit to watch us as we conversed. I had had job interviews before but none quite like this one. Steve started out by telling me how the company had come to be, with the two owners forming a partnership and providing funding for buys.

At first, it was a few family members but now the company was expanding. In the position I wanted, it would mean that I would be selling and buying diverted goods for straight commission. They would give me a $500 a week draw for six months. In six months' time, I should be able to pay back any debt that I owed for the draw and start pulling commissions. Some of the people in the office were making six figures. It was a hard job, but lucrative if you were good at it.

"How old are you, Kay?" I had worked in HR before and I knew that was something you are not supposed to ask.

"You are not supposed to ask that, you know, but I am twenty-eight." I was looking at him and wondering if he was stupid, obtuse, or feeling me out.

"Well, you are right about that, and there are some other questions I am going to ask you that I am not supposed to ask, but you do not have to answer them if you do not want to. All of our discussion is confidential. You know I have to make a good decision about who comes on board, and I need to know that people will match up. I can only do that by asking questions, but feel free, you know, at your discretion, not to answer anything that makes you uncomfortable. I will respect that."

"So tell me how you came to be here, asking me for a job?"

"I was working up at Sweet Life, working with Pam, as you probably know. I was buying from you guys and some of the other diverters and I was thinking I could probably do this and make some decent money at it. I made Sweet Life $4 million, dead net their first year. The guy before me was making them a quarter of a mil a year, believe me when I say they did not want to see me go."

"But they did not want to pay you enough to stay either, is that what happened?"

"Exactly, I was not asking for much, but to them, I was a female and a mother with limited potential. If I had been a guy and head of a household, I think they would have taken me seriously, you know, a Jewish mentality, not that there is anything wrong with that. It was a family business; they did not want to pay me what I felt I was worth. Anyway, I am ready to take a shot at going straight commission."

Steve laughed at my honest answer. "Well, we do not discriminate against females when it comes to wages; in fact, right now Pam is in the lead on the sales floor. That girl can sell the pants off anyone. Many of our people here are Jews and Cubans and we do not allow discrimination. We are all one big happy family. If you can cut the mustard, you will be very happy. If you cannot, you will know fast. I have watched many die in that pit, they cannot make it."

"So how did you get into the diverting end?" Steve stretched his feet, putting them on his desk as he leaned back in his chair. I had a skirt on and I noticed the stark difference in our attire. He was impeccably dressed and I was not. I had tried that morning to look great, and something had happened. I had gone to the interview almost in tears, with a spot of coffee on my outfit. I tried to add a scarf to hide it, not having time to change, but it only stood to accentuate the spot. I was hungry for what Steve, Pam, and the other sales people I spoke to in the diverting business had—unlimited earning potential and nice lives.

Steve looked me up and down. "If we hire you, you will have to get a new wardrobe. Those clothes are too drab for North Miami. We run a nice place here, Kay. If we agree, maybe we can give you a bonus to help you get on your feet and get you some Florida clothes."

I had noticed the women in the office dressed provocatively, more for a nightclub than an office, but I just assumed it was because we were in Miami. Steve was asking me if I thought I could fit in, and I told him I thought I might.

"So did you sleep with your boss in your last job?"

I was answering him before I even thought about what I was saying. "No, not technically."

"Not technically . . . what does that mean?" he was intrigued.

I knew I did not have to answer the question, but the fact that he asked it in a job interview and that he had the balls to say somehow that my answer to the question was in any way related to my current job possibilities was absolutely criminal and insane.

"Well, here is the deal," I shot it straight at him. "One guy wanted a blow job for his birthday; but technically, he was not my boss, he was just my first supervisor. I did not report to him and I did not actually blow him. Just my showing up at his place was enough to get him off."

"The other guy I played with for a while, I did not report to either. We both had a dotted line to the president of the company."

I was up front in what I had done, and I think he liked my answers. I asked him why he was asking me such personal questions.

He said he had learned that people with aggressive highly sexual appetites were usually the fiercest and most competitive in the sales pit. He did not have to worry about me, I laughed. I was still a tigress, just a little older and wiser.

I got the job after the three-hour intensively personal interview. By the time I got back to the car, Dick was livid. He had been waiting and wanted to know what had taken so long. I had a hard time relaying the interview verbatim so I talked a lot about the office and the other people there. They gave me a bonus check which I was supposed to use for clothes but I ended up spending the cash on my daughter and husband instead. I was still very unsure about Florida fashion, and every time I wore a shorter skirt, Dick would tell me I looked like a slut, asking me whom I was trying to impress.

My first day on the job, I had a desk in the middle of the pit, right in front where Steve could keep an eye on me. He gave me a list of things to sell and told me to go for it. My cubby was in front of Pam's and next to Lance's cubby.

A buyer sat in another glass office next to Steve's office. His name was Rob and he was a nephew to one of the owners. He was a nice person and built like a shit brick house. With the sun coming in over the window in Rob's office and his silhouette of dark hair, well muscled arms, and his slim stomach, sometimes I thought I had died and gone to heaven working there.

I picked up the phone, dialed a cold call, and tried to engage them in conversation. As I waited for them to pick up the phone, I imagined what I would do to Rob if he would ever let me. I was not used to having good-looking people notice me. I was a plain Jane, the girl who looked like she lived next door. My obsession with Rob was all in my mind. I never told anyone how sexy I thought he was.

After three months of obsessing about making my draw, I had begun pulling even. Another six months and I was bringing home a little money. A year later, by the time Dick and I got married, I was making six figures. I had made some successful speculative buys and been promoted to assistant buyer. I was paid to buy and sell and in the grocery business, it did not get any better than that. After getting my own budget for long-term buys, I was starting to roll in the dough.

One day, I got to work running late, as was my norm, and I was stopped at the reception desk as I got off the elevator. An armed guard told me that I had to sign in and be searched before I could go into the office. I asked him what was going on but all he could tell me was that if I went inside, things would be explained to me; and if I left the site, I would lose any rights I had to future compensation.

Premium Sales owed me $15,000 in commission, so I went inside. The long and the short of it was that the SEC had put the company into receivership. The owners accused of absconding with millions of dollars in an elaborate Ponzi scheme. Harry Tropin, the overseeing authority from the SEC, told us he was not even sure if we were employees or actors. He said that a lawyer would interview each of us on a one-on-one. We should take a seat and wait for them to call. For some of us, that took three days.

I was flabbergasted. I had been naïve. The things I had seen in the office had been a novelty, yes, but illegal? I did not think so. However, as I learned more about what they had done, I saw the red flags in hindsight.

We worked at a prestigious address overlooking Biscayne harbor. One time, Don Johnson and the *Miami Vice* cast had filmed scenes in our building, with a motorcyclist going up one side of our building stairs and down the other. We had watched the filming in spurts throughout the day.

In our office, the kitchen we had access to had two freezers and refrigerators, both fully stocked with sodas, juices, and snacks. There was bagel time in the morning around 10:00 a.m. and there was cake time in the afternoons at 2:00 p.m. where we celebrated birthdays. We ate well, were treated well, and it was fun to go to work.

I was a smoker, so sometimes I hung down by the lobby outside, catching my break. One day, one of the owners, Dan Morris, drove up in his limo. The rumor was he had lost his license due to a drunken driving accident, so now he had a driver who took him everywhere he wanted to go. When the driver opened the door, I expected to see his girlfriend, a no-name European model, but instead I saw a tiger on a leash. He brought his tiger upstairs to his office, and kept him there all day.

To me, that was weird, but these people were millionaires and lived exotic lives. I knew they went to Switzerland and the Bahamas over the weekends sometimes; at least, that was what was rumored in the office. They told us they were wining and dining international investors because we were doing so well. That was partially true. We were doing fine as a grocery diverting company but the owners had taken our company into a new realm when they started borrowing money from Peter to pay Paul.

I was devastated to learn that I had no 401k and my insurance would be cancelled in thirty days. Worse, I had no job and the FBI was accusing me and the rest of the employees of being part of the Ponzi scheme. Fortunately, within thirty days the SEC had gathered enough evidence to find out that only family and select friends were involved.

I was still out my commission, though I did end up filing a suit along with the other creditors and sales representatives. I worked another place for about six months, and as soon as I started making commission, they changed the commission structure. My husband thought that maybe what I was doing was not as legal as I thought it was, but I was sure what I was doing was legal. It was just the people I had worked for had been seedy.

Chapter Sixty-Three

Sexual Harassment Lawsuit (1994)

My friend Pam called me up. She was working at another place called Ocean Diverting. She heard what happened to me and wanted to know if I wanted a job.

I was glad she had reached out to me. "Sure, yes, thanks. I will be there on Monday." I had bills to pay.

There were eight sales reps in my new office and two traffic people, the manager, and the private investor, Dustin. Dustin had been in the garment industry for many years, and now played the stock market and invested his money in worthwhile causes for fun.

His home was ten thousand square feet, and he had friends amongst the rich and famous. He was often betting on sports or the stock market during the day while we made our trades. I told him my husband was like that. Every night looking at his winning tickets to see if he had won megabucks or the lottery or something. He knew the breakdown of annual earnings numbers in his head but I could not be bothered dreaming about winning big. I was somebody who would make my own destiny.

It took me about six months before I started covering my draw with Ocean Diverting. I had unearthed a few gold mines on the buying end; my tenacity toward taking abuse had paid off. I was soon the number one or two sales people in the office depending upon the week, and Dustin, and my supervisor, Brad, was happy with my work.

One day, Brad's phone rang. It was my husband asking him if I could leave early for the day. Dick had hit at the casino and wanted to pick me up and take me shopping. My boss waved to him out the window and let me leave. What was he going to say? I was straight commission.

Dick took Lynne and me to the store and told us we could buy whatever we wanted. She bought some toys, I bought some perfume, and he and I bought a set of luggage.

Through work for his sales efforts, he had won an all-expenses-paid trip to San Francisco and had planned to go there for the three-day trip alone. Now that we could afford it, we decided that we would all go and we would extend the trip to a total of ten days so we could see the region.

It was not long after Dick won the casino money that another distribution came from his dad's estate inheritance. He and I were each making six figures and we were getting along pretty well. Then after my trip to Ponca City, Oklahoma, we were not anymore.

One day, my manager, Brad, suggested I go on a business trip to visit some of my Midwest customers. I had visited other clients on my own in this job and others like it, but Brad said Dustin wanted to go with me to protect me in case one of the clients got out of hand.

I had flirted with Dustin in the office a few times, mainly behind closed doors in his office. He told me that he had bought sexy negligees for his wife and explained how she would dress up for him. He thought women should enjoy their bodies and capitalize on their assets. He thought maybe I should have a breast enlargement and I should wear high heels more often. I kidded him and said I was not that kind of foo-foo girl, but when I could afford it, I would buy myself breasts.

I had a bad feeling about going on a trip with him, and begged Brad to allow me to go alone but he was adamant, Dustin was going with me. When Dustin and I arrived in Dallas, we made our trip to the customer. The visit went well and Dustin was impressed with the size of the account.

Then we drove back to the airport and caught a puddle jumper. We were going to Ponca City the next day to visit another client. It was dinnertime by the time we touched down in the tiny town. Dustin thought we should have some dinner. We stopped at a fried chicken joint after we got our rental car and ate a cheap meal.

During supper, the conversation turned toward sex but I tried to turn it around and talked of antics from our office. Then we went to our motel. Dustin dropped me off at my room and continued to his. I was in my room about ten minutes later when there was a knock on the door. It was Dustin and he wanted me to let him in so we could chat and get to know each other better.

"I think it is better if you go to your own room, Dustin. We can talk in the morning."

"Don't be like that, Kay," Dustin urged me through the door. "We are both adults here. Open up the door."

I knew that his request to get to know me better meant he wanted to become physical. I was embarrassed that he had thought I would sleep with him. Yes, I had flirted with him but I had not meant anything by it. I had been naïve in thinking that he would not cheat on his wife. I could tell by his voice that he was mad that I would not open the door. He knocked one more time and I debated whether I should open the door, but I knew if I cheated and my husband found out, he would kill me. It was not worth the risk.

"Dustin, go call your wife. You can have phone sex with her. I am not opening this door." I had changed. I wasn't the slut that I was years ago.

The next morning, Dustin apologized to me and said he must have gotten different signals from me than the ones I was sending. It had been a mistake. I felt uncomfortable knowing I had rebuffed him. Men did not do well with rejection. I probably should have slept with him; given my past, what would it really have mattered? However, after my affairs on my first husband, I vowed I would never do that again. Now it was too late to undo what I had done the night before but Dustin seemed to take my rejection in stride. The plane ride home was uneventful.

When we got back to the office, I was going through my desk and getting ready to see what I could do about making a sale when Brad pulled me into his office. He asked me how the trip went and then he told me that Dustin had called him that morning before we boarded the plane and insisted that Brad turn a couple of my best accounts into house accounts. Brad explained that it would mean any commissions that they were supposed to pay me on those accounts would now go to the house instead of me. I had purchased eight trucks of coffee from a Puerto Rican source I had acquired, right before we went on the trip. The buy commission on the trucks should have been worth about $40,000 if we warehoused the coffee for a few months, but Brad told me now that these were house accounts, I would not get the commission.

I was so upset I did not know what to do. I left work early and went home. I told Dick about what had happened on the trip and he insisted that I file a legal sexual harassment charge and get an attorney unless it was my fault. He accused me of leading Dustin on by flirting with him, and I had to admit, in hindsight that was what I had done.

I had never intended for things to go this way but my behavior had gotten me into trouble again. I tried to go to work for a few days after that, but as soon as I filed charges, it was very uncomfortable for me to continue working there. I decided to quit the job and Dick thought I should stay home and become a homemaker. We had enough money to get by on his salary alone. He sold the car he was driving and began driving mine back and forth to work. I went from working sixty-hour weeks, watching the commodity market, and having high-powered teleconferences to having nothing to do and it began to drive me crazy.

I loved being home with my daughter and I walked her back and forth to school. At one point I became a Brownie Scout leader until they told me that wearing sleeveless shirts was unacceptable and setting a bad example for the girls. The shirt I was wearing had a collar, it covered my mid-drift, and it wasn't see through. I took offense and quit the group thinking that the rules were too archaic and closed-minded for me. In the interim, Dick was gambling more often and our savings account was dwindling, but I did not know it because he controlled the money and paid the bills.

Chapter Sixty-Four

San Francisco (1994)

Lynne was seven and Grandma and Grandpa had come to visit us from all the way across the ocean. They lived in Indonesia because of Grandpa's job. We talked to them on the phone occasionally, but this time, they were here for a weeklong visit.

When Grandma came for breakfast, she made scrambled eggs with cottage cheese. I was walking on eggshells as my husband pitched a fit because he did not like cottage cheese with his omelet. I normally gave into him because it was painful to deal with his whining, but my mother insisted that he try the eggs. The breakfast was uncomfortable. My husband contained himself with just a minor rumble.

We were in the bathroom, washing up after breakfast, when Lynne said, "Why does Grandma put her hands together and whisper before she eats?"

"She is praying to God, honey," I said.

"Why don't we do that, Mommy?"

"I do not believe in God, honey, but if you want to, you can. It is your choice. Many people do it and they pray for God to make them better people, or for God to take care of people that are sick or hurt."

I watched as she solemnly put her hands together, whispering, "I pray to God that Dick shuts up and that Grandma does not make omelets with cottage cheese anymore."

She was so damn cute. I wondered where my life would have been without her, probably in a not so good place. It had taken me this long to realize how much I loved her. I could hug her to death. My marriage was rocky and her smile was what kept me going.

Dick's tenacity and aggressive selling methods had earned him the trip to San Francisco and we were all going. On our flight out of Fort Lauderdale, one of the passengers agreed to swap seats so that Dick could sit with us. The flight attendant had made the usual announcements and had just put in the movie, but within ten seconds of the movie running, the screen went black and the cabin lights went out abruptly.

At 3,500 feet, the airplane was silent, and it was an odd sensation. Normally the air-conditioning system acted as a sound barrier, but without the white noise in the background, the silence was loud.

The fasten seatbelt sign came on just as the flight attendant ran up the aisle to where the wing was and she looked out the cabin windows. The pilot came over the intercom system and told us that we had lost an engine. Did it drop off the plane or seize? I guessed that that was what the flight attendant was checking.

He told us to standby, and immediately people began to pray, some silently, others in groups, reciting the Our Father, the Hail Mary, and the Apostles Creed. Twelve monks seated around us gave the passengers faith, and a man remarked that the airplane would not go down with the men on board. Another person said shush, and the airplane filled with murmuring. Dick decided he wanted his old seat back for identification reasons in the case of a crash.

I laughed at him and he got mad. I watched the flight attendant as she instructed us, and I taught Lynne the crash position. Dick had switched seats and I was grateful that I had lived my life with no regrets. If I died today, I was okay with that. I had tried to be the best person that I could be. I had made amends for the horrible things I had done to the best of my ability and I was trying to live a good life now.

The runway for our emergency landing in Tampa was covered in foam but our landing was uneventful. The pilot did a commendable job and we exited the defective plane unscathed in an orderly fashion. As we were standing in line to catch a connecting flight, Dick was angry with me for being calm. He saw his life flash in front of his face and it scared him. I saw the same thing and yet it gave me peace. We were at odds in so many ways. We caught the next available flight to Dallas then transferred to San Francisco, wondering if we really even knew one another.

We muddled through the first three days of the sales convention and toured the San Francisco area. It was my first trip out to the West Coast and I found it beautiful but strikingly different from the northeast or Florida. It was the Fourth of July and we took a cruise ship out on the bay to enjoy fireworks. We froze from the cold and we froze from the chill that had overtaken our relationship.

On July 5, we made up in Muir Woods. The vast redwood trees had the same effect on me as the ocean did. It made me and my problems seem miniscule, like a blip in time. I wondered how many people had appreciated that redwood forest as I had. I couldn't help thinking about the song, 'This land is your land, this land is my land'. I decided life was too short and apologized to Dick again. I always was the one to apologize because he was never wrong. He finally warmed up to me and we kissed in the woods.

The next day, we took a ride down to Santa Cruz, getting out walking on the pier and putting our toes in the water. My legs ached immediately from the cold temperatures of the sand and sea. I thought the water in Maine in the summer was cold but this was beyond tolerable for me. The next night, we took a ride through Yosemite.

We found a hotel that offered condominium accommodations and we enjoyed the Yosemite Mountains from the view of our own private hot tub. It was one of the better nights of our trip after Lynne went to bed in her choice of three different bedrooms. The next night, we drove to Lake Tahoe and booked a room at the Caesar's resort.

I was not a fan of gambling but Dick had just won the $30,000. It was because of that that we were able to be on this trip. Within fifteen minutes of us being in the casino, I had pulled on a dollar machine and won $1800. The hotel compensated the costs of our room but told me my daughter was not supposed to be in the casino. I could have been done with gambling but Dick cajoled me into hiring a babysitter so we could enjoy a nice dinner and go back on the casino floor.

During dinner, he saw somebody famous, bought him a drink, and sent it over. He was playing Mr. Big Shot again and it embarrassed me.

We gambled a bit more, and then, feeling guilty, I went and got Lynne and convinced him to come back to the room. She and I fell asleep watching TV, and he got up and went back to the casino. In the morning, he told me he had spent all the money I had won and then some. The ride back to San Francisco was quiet. We could have used that money for many different things. I told him he had no right to spend it, but he replied, "Easy come, easy go. At least I had not worked hard to earn it." Rather than continue to have a terrible time, I let it go and we enjoyed a nice room-service dinner back in our original hotel. He didn't want to hear it but his behavior worried me.

That August, my sister was planning her wedding. I was to be in the wedding party and I was excited for her. I flew up to Connecticut early since I was not working, and spent some time with my best friend, Becky, her family, and my family.

Dick arrived the night before my sister's original wedding date, now cancelled due to my sister having last minute jitters. I was glad she had decided to cancel it; I was not fond of the way her fiancé made her feel. Dick had decided to make the trip anyway to see his family and friends.

We had a nice room at the Sheraton at Bradley. Our friend Party Marty booked the room for us at his employee rate. Now that my sister had cancelled her wedding, Marty wanted us to go out to dinner with him instead. Dick and I had not seen each other in ten days and he was eager to have sex. When we were done screwing around, he rolled over and told me he has to tell me something.

"I know you are going to be upset, but I need to tell you I went to the casino last night."

He had been spending more and more time there and less time working. I was relying on him to keep our family afloat but it felt like he was letting me down with each casino trip.

"How much did you blow this time?" I pulled the sheet up over me, suddenly feeling vulnerable.

He paused for a minute as if he was not going to tell me after all, "Five grand."

"What the fuck! You blew five thousand dollars in one night. Do you know how long it takes us to earn five thousand dollars? What were you thinking?"

He tried to tell me that it was not that much money, but to me it was. Not only was the amount of money an issue, but the trust factor was also an issue. He had promised he would stop but he was not stopping.

We had already discussed his gambling on numerous occasions because I thought it was getting out of control. He was like any other addict, remorseful at first, but as I hammered him about the gambling and the fact that he needed to stop doing it, he got more and more defensive. I knew it was useless for me to yell at him. People had yelled at me about my drinking but I did not stop until I was ready.

We decided to spend the evening apart. I went to my friend's house and he went out with Marty to the casino. The next day, we were supposed to go back to Florida. I did not want to go back with him and told Becky I wished I could move back home. At least in New England I had a support network. Down in Florida, I was trying to make friends with the other mothers but it was hard and I was lonely. I had no one I considered a friend.

Back in Florida, I convinced Dick we need to buy another car. I was tired of being stuck at home and Dick relented because he was tired of me asking him to pick up Lynne here and there.

Chapter Sixty-Five

Gambling Addiction (1994)

By November, I was wondering how we were going to make rent. Dick had managed to blow $250,000 at the casino in about a year. The money we had set aside for a house was gone, and what was worse, we had no money for our bills. The dream of owning a home in the same Coral Springs neighborhood as Dan Marino, former NFL Miami Dolphins quarterback, was shattered. I told Dick we were in trouble, and he decided to borrow $2500 from his mother.

I told her that she should not loan us the money because I was not sure how we could pay it back, but she told me not to worry. I was grateful to her, but I was angry with Dick for putting us in this position. Running to my mommy was the last thing I would ever do.

Doreen served us a beautiful thanksgiving meal, and on our way out, handed us $2500 in cash. "Pay your bills and pay me back when you can." She worked herself to the bone for her kids.

I wanted to stop on the way home to deposit the cash so I can pay bills the next day, but Dick told me he would do it on his way to work the next morning. We got home and the stress level had temporarily subsided. I was relieved we would not be evicted this month. We made love and I fell asleep.

In the morning, when I reminded Dick that he needed to make the deposit, he told me that he had not been able to sleep and had gotten up and gone to the casino in the middle of the night. The $2500 was gone.

Ordinarily I did not raise my voice, but he was pushing me beyond my limits. I screamed at him, "How could you do that? What are we going to do now?" I was sobbing on the couch when he left the house, angrily slamming the door. Lynne woke up and told me she did not feel good, her stomach was upset. I felt similar but for different reasons.

After stewing and pacing for an hour, I called the bank and saw that we had a $450 balance. It was not enough to cover our bills but it was all the cash that we had.

Lynne threw up and then said she was feeling better. I sat on the couch with her for a bit, and then I got up and called the bank to check our balance. It was now down to $350. I wanted to go to the bank and take out the last of our money before he spent it. I paged him, and as usual, he was not returning my calls. I knew he was at the casino because I could see where he was making the withdrawals. I felt desperate.

As much as I hated myself for doing it, I packed my vomiting daughter into the car with a puke bucket and we drove to the bank. By the time I got there with her, there was only $150 left. I withdrew all but $5, and as we are heading back home, Lynne started upchucking again. I felt like a rotten mother and I apologized to her for having to take her out of the house when she was feeling so sick. She said, "It is okay, Mommy." She knew I was upset but she did not know why.

When we got back to the house, I was suddenly afraid to be there. I knew that Dick would be angry with me as soon as he saw that I had withdrawn our last $150. I went into his office and got the gun and bullets that he kept in his desk drawer. The gun was not loaded, I checked to be sure. I put it and the ammunition in a bag and carried it carefully out to the car and put it in the wheel well of the spare tire.

By rights, I should not have been transporting this gun as I did not have a permit, but it was a chance I decided to take because I was afraid that if I left the gun where it was, Dick would either try and hurt me or himself. It was not a chance I wanted to take.

I needed to get out of the apartment but I did not know where to go. I didn't want to squander the little cash I had left on a motel room. One of Dick's co-workers had been friendly, inviting us to his house for dinner to meet his wife Doreen and daughter Lauren. I was embarrassed to call them and ask for help but I was petrified to stay in the apartment and face Dick's potential wrath. I called and talked to Harry and he put his wife on the phone. I told Doreen I did not want to put them in the middle but I had no place else to go. She listened to what had happened and told me to pack up Lynne, come over, and spend the night.

I had tried to keep a positive face on all day, making light of our mad dash to the bank and then home again, but I was terrified. If Dick refused to get help, as he had in the past, our marriage was over. I could not live like this anymore. I wanted to get off the rollercoaster ride.

About ten o'clock that night, the Feingold's' phone rang. Dick asked them if they had seen me. They told him I was there. He wanted to come over and get me, and Harry told him to stay put for the night. "Kay is tired, you are tired. Sleep on it, and then come over in the morning."

At first, Dick was resistant and angry, demanding that he talk to me. When I got on the phone, he berated me for involving the Feingold's, as I knew he would.

"How could you go over there and complain about me?"

"I was not complaining about you but I did not know what else to do, Dick. I was afraid of you and afraid for my life. You have a gambling problem and you need help. You have not been able to stop on your own and I cannot live like this anymore. You have spent almost a quarter of a million dollars and we have nothing to show for it."

"Where's my gun?" He did not acknowledge what I had said.

"I have it. You can have it back tomorrow."

"I would not have hurt you, Kay."

"I don't know that, Dick, and I was afraid. You blew out the windows of your girlfriends' car with a gun back in the eighties and I thought this might have sent you over the edge. This seemed like the safest plan. Please, Dick. You need to stop gambling, you are out of control. Get some sleep, and we'll talk tomorrow."

Just the thought that he had checked to see if his gun was still there made me glad that I had grabbed it. I was positive I had made the right decision to get out of the house and take the gun with me.

The next day, I went home and Dick promised me he would get help for his gambling addiction. His sister loaned him another $2500, and that time I took possession of the money and we paid the bills with it.

Dick's paychecks covered a bleak Christmas, and in January, I told him I wanted to move back north. When he asked me if I meant with him or without him, I told him that that was up to him.

He said he wanted to make the marriage work, and I agreed that we should try. I did not want to be a second-time divorcee either, but I was done with the craziness. We sold half of what we owned at a tag sale and that gave us the money to move back north.

The plan was for Dick to accompany me back to Connecticut and help me settle in, then go back to Florida and live with his mother for a few months until he could get a transfer within his company. That way, he would not lose his 401K or future commissions, which he had estimated to be significant. It also would give us some time apart to do some thinking.

Chapter Sixty-Six

Moving Back North (1995)

When we moved back to Connecticut, I began hitting AA meetings again. I knew where they were but the people had changed and I did not feel that connection I had felt in my earlier years of sobriety. I knew that if I hung out more or devoted more time to helping others I could find a new support system, but I was content with my sobriety; and although I was going through trouble in my second marriage, I did not want to drink. I just wanted the rollercoaster ride to stop.

His mother's house was vacant again, so we decided to help her by moving in and paying rent. I got myself a temporary job right away, but I was making about a quarter of what I had made in Florida diverting. The first of the month, Dick's mother called me about the rent that she said was late. I told her I did not have the money because Dick was not sending me his paycheck. I thought he had paid her directly but she said he had not. I tried to get him on the phone but he would not return my calls.

While I was traveling for my job, I had gotten an American Express card, and when we made our trip out to San Francisco the year prior, I had added Dick's name to the card. I got a bill from American Express and suddenly I had a $25,000 debt that they were not willing to consider payment options on because they were not a credit card company. They wanted the money immediately. I did not even know what he had purchased for twenty-five grand.

I was beside myself; I really did not know what to do. In some ways, I thought it might be better if Dick and I just ended our marriage immediately; but in other ways, I hated to be going through a divorce again. I felt like such a failure. I was in the kitchen crying when Lynne came in to console me.

"Why do you let Dick do that to you, Mom?"

"Do what to me, Lynne?"

"Make you feel bad. He always makes you cry. You should be happy, Mom. Are you and Dick going to get divorced?"

"No, honey, we are just going through a rough spot right now." I could not give up yet, and a few weeks later, Dick was home.

I was still trying to go through with my sexual harassment lawsuit but my heart was not in it. My attorney had heard some things about my flirtatious habits and he knew if this went to trial, the defense attorney would bring up any and every bad thing I had ever done.

This was my second marriage and I had admitted to having affairs in my first marriage. It was not hard to see what kind of woman I was. The other girls that I worked with and that I had hoped would testify on my behalf had backed off and refused to speak with me. Working the case long distance was not panning out. I decided to give up the case against Dick's wishes, and chalked it up to experience.

I had lost $15,000 to Premium and another $40,000 of my earnings to Ocean Diverting but I had made about $450,000 in three years' time too.

I had eaten Sushi, sailed the inner-coastal, and swum by the light of the moon reflecting against the ocean. We had walked the beaches, enjoyed the sandcastle contests, and listened to jazz music by world-renowned musicians. We had danced in Miami Beach and dined at the Grove. We went to the Dolphins games, and ate caviar at parties. I had started with nothing, and after three years, left with less.

Even with Dick back in Connecticut, we still could not afford the $750 his mother needed from us to cover her mortgage. She said she wanted to sell the house, and we told her we were not in a position to buy it. My credit was ruined and I was in deep debt because of her son. She was sorry but we would have to move because she had a buyer for the house. She wanted to know if we could be out by the first.

We found a small duplex for $600 a month in Simsbury. I was still working for the same company and had gotten a promotion and a raise, but we were still broke. I was working forty hours and it was not enough, so I decided to work for my little brother, waitressing on the weekends in his restaurant in Hartford.

As young kids, my parents gave us chores such as cooking, cleaning, doing laundry, working in the garden, and cleaning windows. My brother started drinking around age seven and cooking around age eight and had managed to build a business around one of his passions. He was trying to go through the courts to see the son that he had lost in a custody battle, but things were not going his way. I felt bad for him because he had a huge heart when he was sober.

One day, my brother David and I were talking and I got the notion to start a rock band. I asked him if he would join me and he said he would. I talked to my girlfriend's husband Mike and he said he was in. We just needed a drummer and maybe a keyboardist or another guitarist.

Dick was not happy about me being in the band. He knew I loved to sing but he did not think I was very good. He accused me of starting the band as a ploy to look for lovers so that I could cheat on him. He said I was being selfish and a bad mother. Didn't I care about my kid?

I told him I was singing because I loved it and I needed to do something fun and positive with my emotions. I was tired of sitting on the couch feeling sorry for myself. I wanted more from life. Maybe I was just an okay singer but I was not looking to be a rock star. I just wanted to do something that involved music. If my daughter saw me going after my dreams, what was so bad about that? I did not think it was a bad thing and I was sorry to hear that he did.

I mentioned to one of the girls at work that I was starting a band and she talked to her committee, and then hired us for our company picnic. We had about twelve weeks to pull a band together and learn four hours', or about forty-five songs, worth of music.

It was crazy. That is how I met Bobby; he was one of the three drummers (the other two ironically named Vinnie). I told Dick we needed a drummer and he looked up his high school friend. Bobby interviewed with us and we hired him.

One weekend Dick, Lynne, and I went to his sister's house because her son was receiving his first communion. Lynne also wanted to go through the same ceremony. I asked her if she wanted to go to church but she said that she did not want to do that, she just wanted to have God in her life and she wanted to wear a cross.

Dick was a lay minister, so we had a small private ceremony at home. Lynne had chosen to believe in God. My minimal attempt at a ceremony displeased my mother but I told her when Lynne was an adult she would have the choice to be more formal about her faith if she so desired. I was happy she had made a choice. I felt successful in the fact that she felt comfortable exercising her right to choose and was grateful she felt comfortable enough with me to tell me that was what she wanted.

Dick and I decided to take Lynne and my best friend's daughter, Sarah, to Six Flags in New Jersey. On the way home, Lynne said her stomach hurt and she had a fever. I asked Dick to stop at the hospital because Lynne has had kidney problems before and I was worried. He argued with me but he finally relented. He thought the hospital trip was wasteful and he wanted to go home. While Lynne and I were in the emergency room for almost six hours, Sarah stayed in the car with Dick. She told him she had to go to the bathroom but I found out, after the fact, that he would not let her go. I wondered how I could be married to such an asshole, and I apologized to Becky and Sarah for his attitude. They understood it was not my fault, but it did not make the situation any better.

Then one day, Dick came home and told me he needed a new car and he wanted me to co-sign his loan. A few months previously, I had made him cash in his 401K to pay off our American Express bill. He was still gambling and I was working as hard as I could not to lose what we had left. That Christmas, it had been so bad my friend Becky had bought us a Christmas tree under the guise of a Secret Santa. We were barely hanging on. I was working three jobs and I did not think he needed a new car. I refused to co-sign the loan. I told him I had one child, not two and that I was tired of trying to support him.

Dick got mad at me and stormed out of the house, saying I did not care about him. He said I was selfish. I was sitting in the kitchen crying and Lynne, in her wisdom, told me for the second time he was not worth my tears or all my hard work. The band was helping my depression and I was starting to feel better about myself, but when I was around him, I was miserable.

Chapter Sixty-Seven

The Band (1996)

My relationship with Dick was getting worse but we still tried to manage. We could no longer afford the $600 a month rent so we moved to Andover and rented a small two-bedroom house across the lake for $400 a month. A long-ago owner had converted the summer cottage to a year-round home.

I held band practice at our house. In the evening, Dick was often out on a "sales call" or he would be playing a computer game like golf. He refused to help me with Lynne at all when I needed a babysitter to cover a gig or work, but he was quick to ask me for twenty bucks and pouted if I gave him a hard time about it.

One morning, after we had had a particularly rough week, he caught me as I was leaving for work and explained that one of his friends was in the hospital and could I loan him twenty bucks. At first I told him no but he started with the "C'mon, it is only twenty bucks" routine.

I was already running late for work. It was his way. He knew my routine and he knew I would try to avoid conflict with him especially as I was walking out the door because I would be afraid of getting in trouble for being late for work.

"Dick, this has to stop. I cannot keep giving you money. You need to help more around here and start earning more money." I gave him a check for twenty and he was out the door.

After he walked out, I put my checkbook away. And as I was doing that, my daughter came to me and said, "Mom, I thought you weren't going to give Dick any more money."

She had wisdom beyond her years. I just looked at her. She was right. I tried to justify my behavior to her but I could not. It was time I got out.

I talked to my parents and explained that I needed to get out of my marriage. I had stayed sober for over a decade now and I was responsible. I asked them if I could move in and save money to buy a house. They hated my second husband and they were glad we were divorcing. They had not liked the way he treated my daughter or me but had never told me because they did not want to interfere.

Lynne and I moved in but I could not change my ways. Before long, I was back in the saddle again. I needed to keep my vagina open, but I did not want to be in the meat market with a new man every night.

Chapter Sixty-Eight

Friends First (1997)

Bob and I were friends for a year and a half in the band and I never once thought of him as a possible boyfriend. I thought he was in a long-term relationship, and although I knew he was not happy, I assumed he was committed, as I had never seen him hit on anyone other than his girlfriend when our band played out. I had already been down the affair route once before and I was not interested in repeating that situation.

It was not until after I left Dick that I had any indication that Bobby was interested in me.

In 1997, Chainsmoker was born. Dick had introduced Bobby to the band and we had hired him for my company gig. After our first gig as Vicarious Moments, playing cover tunes, we decided we wanted to do only originals.

We changed the band name to Chainsmoker because it was controversial, and it was something we all had in common. The name Chainsmoker was a name that you either loved or hated, and we felt that people would remember it.

We began writing and practicing our own music and gradually we learned to complement one another. We got our first gig as Chainsmoker through a card my brother posted in a Laundromat. Another band was looking for an opening act, were we interested?

I was so nervous that night my stomach kept me in the bathroom before, during, and after the show. We did it, the bar owner liked us, and we had brought fans, which was a plus. Our name had made the local *Advocate* in the entertainment section. When you are hot, you should ride the wave. My brother took the opportunity to call a few bars and he soon lined up several gigs.

During our second year, we played Thursday, Friday, Saturday, and even sometimes, Sunday nights. We participated in battle of the bands, we played for tips or for the "door" which was up to us to collect, and sometimes we actually got paying gigs. We were an all-original act, so we would never claim the big money.

We played in places people said never booked bands. We played at Toad's Place in New Haven and we played the Webster Theater in Hartford. We played all over the Hartford and Springfield area in bars. As we continued to book, I got more and more comfortable on stage and started to learn how to work a crowd. I was becoming a front lady and a lead singer to my band.

At one time in my life, after I made the porn movie, I could not bear to have people look at me. I hated being the center of attention, and my feelings of inadequacy were so bad, I absolutely knew everyone was staring at me and saying mean things. Maybe they were and maybe they were not, but what changed for me, was my attitude. I stopped caring so much about what they said, and instead I began working on what I said and how I said it.

My confidence came to me when someone said to me, "I cannot believe how brave you are standing up there, working that stage. I could never do it." The fact was, she was a much better singer than I was but she could not get over her fear of public speaking. I had done it with the help of AA, Toastmasters, and voicing my opinion in meetings at work. My life's experiences were finally working in my favor, and because I had not given up, and was continuing to learn new things, I was becoming a more valuable member to society, to my family and friends, and to myself as a whole.

Chapter Sixty-Nine

Mommy for a Decade (1997)

I was starting to listen to what Lynne said by what she did not say. Like when she started the sentence with, "You probably will not let me, but . . ." I knew that she was looking for me to tell her no, but even then, I still did not normally come out with a straight no. I would say, "You are right, honey, I do not think it is a good idea because of X, Y, and Z, but the choice is up to you." She would get on the phone and say, "My mom does not think it is a good idea," but there was not a lot of confrontation between us because she knew she could use me as the fall guy for what she really wanted anyway.

Other times, she would say, "Please, Mom, I want to do this." Like when she wanted to get a second piercing in her ear. I told her she had to demonstrate her ability to debate the topic and give me reasons why she should get her ears pierced.

She said, "You are a bitch." I laughed at her attempt, took her to get her ears pierced, and on the way home we discussed how she should approach the next big decision in her life. I explained she needed to examine the pros and cons and we used the ear piercing as an example.

I would make her justify why, including her answering who, what, when, where, and the how questions. Then we would discuss the possible and likely outcomes and talk about the risks.

Most of the time, she came to the appropriate conclusions herself, while I acted as devil's advocate and cheerleader. She needed a sounding board more than a gatekeeper. I tried to listen to help her work through things rather than being the one to tell her no, without her understanding the thought process behind it.

She knew I was different in some ways, and I did not try to hide it from her. I preferred to go to work and be the primary wage earner rather than take care of a house. I was not comfortable doing things women traditionally did, nor was I comfortable relying on a man for my financial well-being.

It was not that I could not do those things; I had taken care of other people's homes in my teens. I had babysat for years. I just preferred to work in an office and earn a good wage. Sometimes, my need to succeed was hard on her and we would talk about it. Some of the mom's were craftier, more sensitive, or better homemakers than I was. I encouraged her to follow her interests and not look to me to be the perfect mom. That was not what I was good at, and I would have only hurt her if I had tried to pretend that I was.

Instead, I brought her into my life in other ways. When she was three, I had a produce stand with my second husband. She would go with me on the weekends and we would pick through moldy strawberries in the morning before we put out the display. We discussed the need to show up for work every day, on time. We discussed how to talk to customers and what not to say, like talking about the moldy strawberries we had picked through earlier that day.

Lynne would sit on the stand counter eating watermelon, looking cute, and the next thing you knew, our sales would double for watermelon. She learned to run the register and talk to the customers while batting her eyes.

Michael J. Fox stopped on his way home one time, and after learning that he was on TV, she remarked that it was her first time ever meeting a movie star. We had Radar from MASH and the NRBQ bassist come through on occasion too. It was a rural community with some affluent members. Lynne was friendly with the customers and learned how to talk to people as if she had been doing it all her life.

Later, with other side businesses, Lynne helped deliver balloons, clean offices, and airport hangars. One year, we sold Christmas trees, Christmas cactus, Poinsettias, and other local crafts. I took her with me and exposed her to business transactions such as making deposits, paying suppliers, and dealing with customers. I talked about finances and investments, as well as costs.

All business aside, the fact was, making money was a big part of my life. While with my parents, we had learned the value of hard work, they said we were poor when we knew we were not. We ate hotdogs on occasion because my parents were trying to balance their income with their outgo and plan for today, tomorrow, and someday. But that was not talked about in our house. Money was adult business, a private matter. Consequently I thought we were poor until I realized how well off we actually were compared to other people I met, for example, in A.A.

Chapter Seventy

An Affair (1998)

One time, we had band practice at my house in Andover and after practice Bob was walking down the sidewalk when he looked up at the stars and yelled to me to go wake up Lynne. There was a galaxy event happening that would not happen again in our lifetime and he thought she should see it. I was amazed that he seemed to care more about my kid than my own husband did, and it just reinforced to me how abusive my relationship had become.

After I moved out of the house in Andover and began proceedings for my divorce, Bob made a comment about liking my ass at a gig. I had no idea he even liked me. While Mike and even my own brother would make jokes about me needing a dick up my ass when I became bitchy, Bob was always reserved and polite. I was surprised to hear it from him after all that time, and he piqued my curiosity all of a sudden. Why was he with a woman that was twenty years older than he was?

He explained to me that she had tamed him. I said, "What do you mean?" and he had laughed. He explained that she had turned him into a submissive sex slave, making him work to take care of her and support her. He also shared that the relationship had started out as a sexual one, but the sex part had faded, and the relationship was now about how much money he could earn to support her habits. He told me that he thought she was cheating on him and he felt taken advantage of by her.

Bob is a talker, probably because he grew up as an only child and his mom doted on him. In the band, we often called him Blah Blee Bob because he could talk for hours about nothing. Beneath the constant chatter, however, he was actually a nice guy who had some good things to say. Bobby and I had a few things in common, like the fact that he had been adopted when he was ten days old. I told him I knew a bit about adoption as I had friends and family on both sides of the adoption situation.

At age thirteen, they admitted Bob into the hospital after an almost fatal sledding accident in which his head was tangled in a tree. His mother thought he would die. I knew what that felt like from my operation at the same age; we both had seen the white light they say you see when you are on the operating table and you die. It was a life changing moment for him, as it was for me. His incident had left him feeling spiritual. He felt the white light had been the hand of God. I just thought it was the overhead lights in the operating room because the anesthetic had worn off too early. Who really knew? But we were both glad we had lived when the odds were against us.

Bob's mother got divorced when he was ten and by the time he was fourteen, he was often out for most of the night partying with his friends. One of his mom's boyfriends paid him to disappear. While she loved him with every part of her and gave him opportunities that many kids did not have materially, she was working and playing so hard herself, she did not have a lot of time for him. It was not unlike the situation that Lynne was in, only I was going to school in my bedroom online, rather than frequenting the bars.

Bob had been overweight and the kids at school made fun of him. He found that through drugs and alcohol, a) he did not care what people thought and b) he had what they wanted, so it gave him some control and power.

For a period in his teens and twenties, he dealt drugs. He was never caught but he had friends that had served time in jail. In terms of brushes with the law, he had been lucky, and so had I.

Bob ended up in a situation where he lost his drum set (his most prized possession) during a cocaine bender when he was in his mid-twenties. That made him wake up to the fact that his life was spiraling out of control. He stopped drinking alcoholically, stopped doing coke, and tried to regain control of his life. It had taken him longer than it had taken me. I was seventeen and a half when I quit and he had been twenty-eight.

We were another couple that had "the addiction beast" in common. Both of us understood how crazy life could be living under the influence. However, I did not meet Bob through AA; I met him through the band. We had our love of music in common, and we started out as friends.

The night we started flirting, we were at a gig in East Hartford. It was a sports bar with a dance floor and several televisions tuned to the local UCONN Husky game. After a while, twin girls who were dancing and flirting with him started hitting on him. He made a plea for me to "save him." They were coming on to him during a break and he did not want any part of it.

We were friends by that point. We knew a lot about each other as we had shared many conversations at band practice during breaks in the previous two years. Since band practice had been at my house a portion of the time, he had seen the way Dick treated my daughter and me and he did not like it. In fact, one time Bob tried to intervene and suggest my husband do something for my daughter, and that did not go over very well. After that, Bob held his tongue but I could tell that he did not like Dick's ways.

We were tearing down the set and packing up the equipment as we always did when we broke down at the end of the night. We positioned the equipment at the edge of the stage so that we could carry the gear to our vehicles. The other two guys were off talking to our fans and trying to line up another gig.

Bob mentioned something about going to a New York sex club when he was in his early twenties and being surprised at the live sex shows. While I considered myself rather knowledgeable on the sex front, I had never been to a sex show and I was curious.

Bob explained to me how there were different rooms for different kinks. Some people had foot fetishes; others were into bondage, others into submission or humiliation, and others into dressing up and role-playing. He said he and his friends had walked through the rooms and ended up watching a couple getting it on. I had watched porn and participated in my own movie, but I had never been to a live sex show.

I was just getting out of a divorce and the last thing I wanted was to get into a relationship. I was done with long-term relationships, they were nothing but trouble and I would never get married again, but that did not mean I would forgo having a sex life.

Bobby was not married (because his girlfriend was still married to her husband), but he was in a committed relationship. I knew he had not been happy in both the years that I had known him but I did not want to be the "other woman."

I knew his mother hated his girlfriend, which made it difficult for all involved. She had told me once at a gig, "Laurie is a piece of shit.

She does not deserve my son. He should get rid of her. She does not appreciate him."

That night, Bob said he had been thinking of splitting up with Laurie because he suspected she was cheating. She was spending a lot of time at the beach while he worked to support her. They had "grandchildren" that he was fond of and they had bought a home together that he did not want to lose.

We played a few other gigs and had practices when I realized he was starting to joke with the others. Separated from my husband now, I guess he was loosening up with me. Our band held our first annual bash and I discovered, after talking to Bob's mom, that he had arranged through her to have a date that night after our gig.

In fact, I met the girl and she told me she and Bob had dated at one point a few years back. I made the conscious decision at that point that I was "single" and if he was going to have an affair on his girlfriend, I was just as good as the next girl.

As we were packing up that evening, I asked him unexpectedly if he wanted to get laid. It was apparently a surprise to him as he was not sure that I had actually asked him that question. He made me repeat it.

"What did you say?"

"Do you want to get laid tonight?" It was a simple question.

"Yeah, I do" was his enthusiastic reply but he told me he had to say goodbye to his mother before we could leave. We had half the band gear with us but we had arranged with the other band members to unload the following day so we were "free."

Bob's girlfriend was at the beach probably "Getting some right now," he said, but he would have to go home early in the morning to take care of his dogs. On the way to the hotel room, we stopped at a convenience store and got some condoms. I told him I had herpes, and although I was not contagious, I did not want to risk the chance of giving it to him. He thanked me for my honesty and we continued on to the hotel.

It was a bit awkward when we first entered the hotel room until he sat on the bed, pulled me into his arms, and kissed me. He literally swept me off my feet and very slowly undressed me. We held each other and I was instantly afraid. It was not supposed to be like this. It was not supposed to feel this good. He was making love to me when all I had asked for was a quick lay.

I felt alive with a rush of energy I had never felt before. It was not like a thunderbolt of energy but more like a buzz. The kind of buzz that reduced my blood pressure, relaxed my heart, and gave peace to my mind.

"BZZ," he whispered to me as he held me in his arms after we had both come and were exhausted. He felt it too!

"BZZ," I whispered back, knowing I was on a road I should not be on, doing things I should not be doing. I did not want a relationship; I did not want to care for somebody else besides my daughter at this time. I should not be involved with a guy who was not single. This was not supposed to be happening, but it was.

I wanted to get on my own two feet and build a solid foundation. We said goodnight the next morning and joked about our one-night stand and the fact that we had broken a band rule.

It took him three days before he called me, and when he did, I was so happy to hear from him. We knew we would see each other during band practice but we had left it as it was supposed to be. Just a one-night stand, and by day three, both of us knew we wanted more. We met again and had a quick lunch. A few times, we fooled around in his car after gigs for a bit before we went to our respective homes.

Then, about eight weeks after we started seeing each other, the band did a television spot that included us playing some tunes and a band interview on a local college station. We had a blast doing it and felt like local rock stars. People had told us that as an original band, we had a tough road ahead of us, but we were making it.

Bob was kissing me during break times, but because my brother and our guitarist Mike did not know we were dating, we had to sneak. Afterward, we went behind the local grocery store and fooled around in his van. That night, my brother ended up calling Bob's house and talked to his girlfriend. Dave told her that he was surprised Bob was not home yet since our interview had been hours ago. Then Laurie called my house and found out I was still out, and it did not take much for her to derive a conclusion.

When Bob got home, she accused him of having an affair and he could not deny it. She kicked him out and threw his work clothes and tools out on the front lawn for him to retrieve. He ended up at a hotel in the town next to where I lived. He called me and told me what had happened and I told him to hang in there. The following morning on my way to work, I swung by the hotel, and when I spotted his van, I left him a note telling him that things would get better.

He stayed with his mother for a week until he could collect his paycheck and then put a deposit on an apartment. The only problem was that the apartment was the same place he and Laurie had previously rented before they bought their house, and it was about five miles from where they had lived together.

Bob worked in Ellington, and I was living in East Granby. I would stay at his apartment with him on nights that I did not have my daughter, or sometimes I would drive there after she went to bed around 8:30 at night, leaving her in the care of my parents. It was a forty-five-minute trip one-way. I would come home before dawn and get ready for work. It was an exhausting time but I was running on adrenalin; I was in love.

One night, Bob asked us to meet him at his apartment so we could go out to eat after he got through with work. My daughter and I were there when he pulled in the driveway. Within a minute, his ex-girlfriend pulled into the driveway and they were talking.

The next thing you know, Bob got in the car with Laurie, and she peeled out of the driveway with him in her car. There I was in his apartment and I was not sure what to do. He did not have a phone installed and I did not own a cell phone back then. I was not sure if he had been willing to go in her car, or if she had just surprised him and taken off without his permission. He was a grown man. Should I be worried for his safety? I did not know, but I knew she was pissed off.

Laurie was an ex-biker bitch who could have kicked my ass with one hand tied behind her back. She was a big girl and did not take kindly to me stealing her man. I stayed in the house and waited for about fifteen minutes but he did not come back. Then I decided to drive to their house, which was less than ten minutes away. Bob had showed me where they had lived one time.

I drove to their house and parked at the end of the driveway, honking my horn. I thought Bob might come out and tell me what was going on, but I found out later, she had locked him in with the deadbolts and unless he wanted to break a window, he was stuck. Laurie had seen me in the window but did not tell him I was out there.

Next, I went to the local pizza parlor, and using their public phone, I called their house. Laurie answered, and when I asked to speak to Bob, she told me to fuck off. I was not ready to do that yet, so I called back again and this time she hung up on me right away.

I decided we were not going for dinner and drove home. He had made his choice, and although I was mad at myself for getting involved, I was glad I had not invested any more time. I went home and Bob called me later that evening and said he was quitting the band and that he was going to stay with Laurie.

I told Bob it was his choice and that I could understand where he was coming from, but if he wanted to take a chance with me, I would do my best to make sure our life would be different. I also said we did not need to continue our relationship, and that we could keep that separate from the band. I did not want our relationship to be the cause of the band's break-up. He apologized and explained that Laurie would not be cool with him being in the band anymore with me.

When Bob hung up, I called Mike and David in the band, and explained that Bob was quitting. Then I called his mother and told her what had happened. Each of them called his house and tried to talk to Bob, trying to convince him to stay with the band and leave Laurie.

The next day, Bob called me again. He was so upset he was crying. He said he and Laurie had discussed it and he really was not sure what to do. He was afraid of her son because of his mafia connections, but he was also afraid to keep living a life without love and certain freedoms.

He told me he was walking to his apartment while he was talking on his cell phone, and needed some time to sleep and think about things. I think I might have fallen in love with him then. He was honest and vulnerable with me, and I gained a tremendous amount of respect for him that day. "You never know where things will go with us," was all that I could promise him but I hoped he would take a chance with me. We both deserved to have someone who appreciated us, and I knew I would appreciate him.

Chapter Seventy-One

Kidnapped (1998)

It was enough to take the plunge. He was going to keep his apartment but end it with Laurie. I was uncomfortable with his decision but I had no choice. As it was, I was living at my parents and had most of my things in storage. Therefore, one day when he asked me to swing by his apartment to get his pants, sneakers, and toothbrush so we could go to the Six Flags amusement park after he got out of work, I told him no problem.

The plan was that he would change at my house, which was near where he was working. I asked Becky to go with me and to bring her truck.

When we got to Bob's apartment, we packed up all of his belongings in the boxes we had brought, setting aside the pants, sneakers, and toothbrush by putting them on the front seat of the truck. We hauled his things to my storage area and dropped the stuff off there before I went to his work to pick him up.

He was happy to see me and was excited to be bringing Lynne and Becky's daughter Sarah to Six Flags. He asked me how my day had been, and I replied that it was very busy. Then I explained that I was holding his stuff hostage in my storage bin until we could find a place to live together and that I was kidnapping him.

I think he thought I was kidding until I drove him by the storage bin on the way to Six Flags to show him where his stuff was and to give him a key in case he needed something. I was serious. If he was going to be with me, he was not going to be near Laurie.

The next day, we began looking for an apartment. He stayed at his mother's for about a week until we could find a place. He had a dog and that was a problem for many places.

My parents were not happy that I had stayed at their house a total of two months and I was already gallivanting off into another relationship. They wanted me to provide a stable home for my daughter, and they felt this was not a very good start. Lynne was not happy about it either. She wanted time with me, alone. I felt terrible that I could not do it, but I liked sex too much and I did not want to be single.

I could not explain how I felt about Bob except that I loved him and that it was easier to live together than it was for us to live apart. Driving for miles, spending money on separate apartments did not make sense when we wanted to be together and share our lives.

As we began building a life together, we realized that we had a lot of debt. Both of us had been the breadwinners in our previous relationships, and we had borne the cost of our significant other's bad habits. When we tallied it up, we both owed about $25,000 each to various debtors. We also were in the band together, but we were not making a lot because we were doing original music instead of covers.

Even though we were not married, we shared everything. We created a budget and shared our finances, gradually paying off our debts together. On the weekends that we had my daughter, we did family things—watching movies, visiting friends, doing laundry, and spending time with neighbors and family. On the weekends Lynne went to her dad's, we played adult games.

Although we had talked about BDSM when we were first flirting, we did not really talk much more about it until after we started living together. We bought some sex toys and constructed others. We both knew we did not want a real 24/7 BDSM relationship but we enjoyed role-playing. We were kinky. We knew sex was important in our relationship and we knew that we would not be content with a traditional, monogamous relationship. We decided to define ours as an "open relationship."

Chapter Seventy-Two

Marriage Contract #3 (1999)

Bob and I examined our previous relationships together and talked about what we had liked and hated in each. The reasons for getting married were simple. There were tax advantages, social advantages, and insurance advantages. The things that led to divorce were complacency, financial issues, and sex.

It was easier for us to identify what we did not want in a relationship than it was for us to identify what we did want, so that is somewhat how we went about it. Honesty and trust had been the foundations of our relationship so far, and we both felt we needed to continue those attributes as building blocks. We agreed we would rather hear the ugly truth than be lied to, no matter how bad it might be.

Bob grew up Catholic as well, and unlike me, is a strong believer in God, although he was not a churchgoer. He told me he had a special relationship with God, and I believed that he did. I respected his beliefs and he respected the fact that I had mine.

I believed in spirits, energy, and karma, but I did not believe there was a supreme being overseeing all. I believed in the power of hate just as strongly as I believed in the power of love. I told him all I saw with religion was hate and prejudice, and he agreed that in many cases diversity had caused disparity.

On television, we watched George Carlin's comedy act as he talked about the Ten Commandments. I had always wondered what all the Christian soldiers formerly thought about commandment number five, thou shall not kill, and how they reconciled that with their jobs, which required them to kill others. This is probably the main reason for separation of church and state in our country. George managed to get his "thou shall not" list down to two commandments, but my list is even simpler. Though shall not lie. Anything else is up for debate, based upon situational circumstances.

With this rationale, we talked about sharing chores, sharing money, sharing old age. We discussed dreams and desires. We talked about family dynamics and in-laws. There was nothing we could not talk about, though some conversations proved more animated than others did. We decided that we would be open-minded about each other's needs and desires, and that we did not need to be monogamous to establish a marriage contract.

Sometimes when people are told they can't have something, it makes them want it even more. We wanted to avoid a situation where our marriage would end instantly if either of us was ever attracted to someone else, or debilitated and unable to have sex. We decided we could be friends and lovers and that meant we might swing on occasion.

Because he had been an only child, Bob connected with Lynne in ways I could not. Driven to work and earn money, I was more passive about nurturing and housekeeping. Bob was social and kind hearted and could work, but did not necessarily want to drive himself into the ground. He was quite happy staying close to home. I asked him if he wanted a child of his own because I was sure I did not want any more kids. He said he did not want children. I told him if he ever did, I would be okay with him having a child with someone else. His mother thought I was crazy, but when you love someone you do not want to hold them back from their dreams, and that was how I felt. I loved him but if he wanted to have a kid, I would not stop him. He said he loved Lynne as his own and that was good enough.

Bob and I balanced each other out financially, emotionally, and socially. He was the Yin to my Yang. Physically, our house became home to band equipment and house painting equipment, as he was a painter. We pushed the couch into the middle of the room so that behind it we could pile ladders, a sprayer, a drum set, some amps, and microphone stands. Back then we were playing often enough that we needed the equipment to be easily available; but we soon got tired of living without a living room, so we convinced the band that if we booked gigs often enough, we could pay for a practice space.

We rented an office next to the local carwash and set up the band equipment there. We played from 7:00 to 10:00 p.m. when everyone else in the office building had gone home. Sometimes, we had kids hanging outside of our window, listening. Drawn by the sound coming from the open windows, they heard the music at the carwash and from the fast food restaurants across the street.

The band had long forgiven us for breaking the band rule about not screwing other band members. What could they do? We were half the band. Besides, as long as we got along, who cared? We kept band business separate from our house business and Bob and I each reserved our rights as full individual members. I did not speak for Bob and he did not speak for me when it came to band business.

One weekend, I was feeling frisky and I asked Bob to marry me. I was not sure what I expected to happen but he said yes. He had already given me a pre-engagement ring and was willing to take the next step. I wanted to elope because I was embarrassed that I had already been married twice. He wanted a wedding because it was his first and his parents would want it that way.

I agreed to a big wedding provided I could have a wedding planner. Honestly, I just wanted to show up and not have to worry about the details. We joked with people that the reason we were getting married was so that our band could play a gig. We played at our own wedding and had a DJ too. We had a justice of the peace perform the simple ceremony. The location was nice, the food was delicious, and everyone had a good time. This time around, I was putting my energy into the marriage instead of the party.

Our wedding vows were simple. Bob promised to treat me like his Queen, and Lynne as his Princess, and we promised to treat him like our King. I also vowed I would try to keep things interesting.

After our wedding, I was laid off after working as a customer service manager in a small foundry. We took my 401K, bought OSHA compliant equipment, and after I could not find a job, decided we would go into business together in 1999. Bobby and I worked well together; he had the construction experience and I had the business skills.

We made barely enough to survive the first year, and when I got sick the second year, we decided we could not afford to live without health insurance. I eventually found a "real job" working for a "real employer" that provided "real benefits."

Life gradually got better for us as we worked hard and paid off our debt. Our band continued to play here and there, and although I missed working with my husband 24/7, I enjoyed the 9-5 routine where I did not have to worry about working nights and weekends.

Chapter Seventy-Three

Making Time (2000)

Many things changed for us around the same time. We got married in September 1999. The following June, I began working at a large aerospace firm, I started school the same week, and we moved to Bob's dad's house.

Joe, Bob's dad, had originally given us his house as a wedding gift, but due to a change in circumstances, he ended up living there with us for seven years before he passed on from prostate cancer.

During those years, we did not have a lot of privacy. When we got married, we bought ourselves a week's worth of timeshare as a wedding present. That guaranteed when we moved in with his dad that we would at least have a one-week vacation. Later, we bought another week so that we could have two weeks to get away periodically. I worked on average 60 hours a week and I went to school on average another 30 hours a week. Sometimes, Bob and I chatted on Yahoo or AOL to each other late at night. He would be downstairs and I would be upstairs. Sometimes, we would use our cameras and masturbate together just as lovers would do. It stimulated our sex life, and at the same time, kept it quiet as the house had thin walls.

Joe was a dick to his son and my daughter. I had a strong work ethic and Bob's dad and I clicked, but he would constantly berate Bob and Lynne for not doing enough around the house or not working hard enough. He called my daughter fat and would not allow her to have her "colored" friends over to play. Joe got mad when Bob did woman's work, and I did men's work, but to us, it didn't matter. We pitched in and got the job done together and neither of us had a problem with how we worked but it bothered his dad. The way we spent our money was also a cause of disagreement.

Lynne was miserable and I felt terrible because I had brought her into another abusive household. One time, her dad got so mad at the situation that he called me up and said that he did not think that the way Joe was treating our daughter was right. I agreed with him and told him I was very sorry but that it was temporary, Joe was dying and he did not feel good. I reminded my ex that he had grown up in just an abusive household and the fact was we could not change others. We could only change ourselves. I assured him I was not justifying Joe's behavior but I did not know what else to do. I hated having to choose between my husband and my daughter. I told my daughter to ignore her step-grandfather and to avoid him as much as she could.

One day I got home from work after an exhausting day and Joe was sitting in his wheelchair, blocking the walkway to the rest of the house.

"I want to talk to you about your daughter," he started in.

"What about *my* daughter, Joe?" I sighed, knowing this was going to be a painful conversation.

"Your daughter is rude and you need to talk to her about it."

"What did she do?"

"Today she came in from school and walked right past me without even saying a word. She needs to learn some manners."

It was one of those rare times when my brain was actually working and I replied, "Well, Joe, you are going to have to take that up with me. I have tried to raise her so that if she had nothing nice to say, then she shouldn't say anything at all."

His jaw dropped when he realized what I was saying, and he did not respond. What could he say?

After that, he made an effort to show her some affection. He had grown up in a tough love Italian home where girls were secondary and submissive. I had raised my daughter to be strong and independent. It was tough for the generations to live together and I felt like I was stuck in the middle, not unlike how I had felt during my marriage to Phil with his son Collin, only this time I had matured enough to not give up, not run away and to try and stick it out, and turn it around

I had to ask myself what really mattered in a relationship to me. At that point, I wanted someone I could trust emotionally, someone whom I could cuddle with and fool around with, someone whom I could entrust the care of my daughter to, and someone who would not be a financial or emotional drain on my life. Just as I had carefully taught my daughter to debate the pros and cons, and examine the risks, I was doing the same thing. While in-laws were important, they shouldn't make or break my relationship.

Before my involvement with Bob, I had kept Lynne very sheltered. We were not around alcohol or drugs, and therefore she did not see the effects of them on a person until our band had a family-type gig that served alcohol.

Lynne saw her uncle and his friend weeping and carrying on, drunk out of their minds and barely able to stand; it frightened her. By that point, she was in sixth grade. Some of her friends might have seen their parents in the same condition but she had not ever seen me under the influence, and I was glad I had put off her exposure until her teens.

Chapter Seventy-Four

Choosing to Drink (2001)

I took my first drink after seventeen years of sobriety at Christmas time. My husband had never known me in my drinking days, and at first, he was very nervous that I would go off the deep end. I was nervous too but it was not a spontaneous decision. I had examined my life for the last two decades and I felt that I had changed significantly and that I was not the same person I had been when I was seventeen.

Then in February, we went on vacation to Florida and I ordered a piña colada out by the pool. When my daughter asked me if she could have a sip, I told her 'no' as it had alcohol in it. She was surprised to find out that I was drinking again and became worried. I told her I had had a few drinks since Christmas and that I was fine.

I explained to her, and was fully aware for myself that the YETs could still happen to me. The difference was that when I was a kid, I lacked confidence and drank to erase how I felt. Through the years, I had learned how to face my fears head on and had overcome many obstacles and challenges. I had no desire to go back or lose what I had worked so hard to achieve.

Chapter Seventy-Five

Raising a Teenager (2002)

The hardest points of raising Lynne had been over issues relating to sex, relationships, and the female's role in society. I had raised her to speak up and be independent. At times, that has caused her to be in conflict with her teachers, her grandmother, and even her mother, but I was still proud of whom she had become because she had her own voice.

During her sixth grade, the whole time I was telling her she was going to get her period; in the back of my mind, I was petrified there might be something wrong with her and that she would not get it.

When Lynne finally did get it, I had no idea what to tell her about tampons. I could not use them and was jealous of those who could. I was stuck with the cursed pads. Fortunately, my sister and my best friend were close enough to my daughter where she could ask questions and feel comfortable with the discussion.

When it came time for her physical exam, I made an appointment with a regular doctor. When Lynne found out the doctor was a man, she was so upset she screamed at me and said she would not go. She was uncomfortable seeing a male doctor and refused to go for an appointment until I switched her to seeing a woman. The concept of male doctor versus female was so foreign to me; I did not really understand it, and I am sorry to say, I laughed it off at first. That was until I could see the desperation in her eyes. She was afraid, of what I was not sure, but I acquiesced and respected that she felt uncomfortable with a male doctor and I found her a female one.

I never gave it a thought. I had been in and out of hospitals my whole life and my physicians were often male. The sex of my doctor made no difference to me, but it obviously made a huge difference to her.

When she told me she wanted to go on birth control, I took her to the doctor. I did not want her to have an unwanted pregnancy. She told me she was afraid of date rape and I was afraid for her. I felt like a hypocrite telling her she should not have sex, but I tried because as a mom I thought that was what I should do. When I learned she was sexually active, I was grateful she had waited a lot longer than I did. I was also glad she felt she could talk about uncomfortable situations with me. We had no taboo subjects. I never wanted her to feel alone, and I told her no matter what, I would always love her.

Chapter Seventy-Six

A Career (2003)

At work, I had come up with a solution to a million-dollar problem and solicited management support. I got the support and began creating a workflow system for the company that would affect 1900 people. It was a big deal, it included oversight for Sarbanes Oxley compliance issues, and it effectively merged five companies into one.

My co-workers thought I was nuts and I agreed that I was. I had been called "la loco chica" before. I was learning about the way the company worked and resolved conflicts as they arose. I had learned project management skills over the years, but had never managed a project of this magnitude. I worked day and night for three years, developing forms, workflow, and a database that connected information to several different company systems.

I was gaining a reputation for getting things done and it felt great. People looked to me to resolve problems and I began learning how to apply lean six sigma principles to administrative work. The company recognized me as their worldwide expert on continuous improvement activities and I reached a new high in my career.

I spent an average of eighteen to twenty hours a day working and going to school but we had a roof over our heads, good food, and money for extras. Life was good.

Chapter Seventy-Seven

Gays, Queers, and Other Sentiments (2004)

Lynne began questioning certain relationships of friends. It was no secret. We had friends and family members who were gay. She had questions and I did my best to answer them. Then I revealed that I was bisexual. I did not flaunt it, and I did not hide it. She gave me a direct question and I gave her a direct answer, as I always had and always would. I did not feel it was my place to judge other people's sex life, it was as simple as that; nor did I feel they had the right to judge mine.

Emotionally, on some levels, I knew I was not as sensitive as I should be. I did not discriminate against people because of their sexuality and it angered me when others did it.

When we moved fourteen times in ten years, I got rid of things I did not think I would need or use again. It was easier to pitch than pack. Unfortunately, I threw out things like my daughter's first outfits and her special baby blanket.

I learned later that I had hurt her feelings through my actions and felt terrible about it, but what could I do to fix the situation? I had committed the crime and the damage had been done.

As parents, we have regrets. We do things we should not do or we don't do things we should. For the most part, though, I am satisfied with the paths we took because of where we ended up. I tried not to worry or waste energy projecting negative outcomes unless I had reason.

For a while, Lynne came home in tenth grade always tired. Her eyes were droopy and I thought she might be high. She denied it but I later learned that she had been. I was afraid that she might get into drugs or alcohol abuse because both her father and I had had problems, not to mention her two step-fathers and they say it ran in families. The only thing she had going for her was that she had not grown up with it around her.

For her entire life, she had seen me work two or three jobs consistently, getting up for work, doing a good job, being responsible, and paying my bills. I did believe kids emulate what they saw whether they wanted to do it or not. It was the easiest path as it was what they know. I was glad that during her formative years I was sober. I was also glad that she was taking responsibility. She babysat and worked at my brother's restaurant. She understood the value of money.

Chapter Seventy-Eight

Reputation and Repercussions (2005)

I did not know what they said behind my back to my family members, but I did know that rumors flew. The repercussions of my actions did not fully hit me until about thirty years later when my husband joined a local pool team and one of his team members, someone who had gone to school with my brother, called me a whore to my husband's face.

It did not go over very well; my husband was protective, and although he knew of my past, I was sure it hurt him. I was glad I had not lied to him. That would have been much worse. He defended me but he talked about it to his other friends, so I knew it bothered him. What could I say? It was true. I enjoyed sex and had had a lot of it, with many different people. I thought of myself as an empowered female, but not everyone thought that way. There were double standards and they sucked.

Another one of my brother's friends told me that as a kid my brother had not had a very good opinion of me either. He never said anything to me, but my sexual indiscretions must have had repercussions for him too.

After Lynne was born, I had completed my fourth to twelfth steps over a period of about five years. I found it hard to share all the bad things I had done with another person. Honestly, it was and always has been easier for me to have sex with someone than to share my intimate feelings and thoughts with them, but I kept at it. I made amends as best I could for the things I had done wrong, examining each situation to see where my motives had been. In some cases, where it would have been more hurtful to open up old wounds, I let those situations lie. Even though I could not change who I had been, I tried to move forward in my life without hate and without anger, and to accept those around me as they were. We all had baggage. The trick was to learn from our mistakes.

In September of 2005, Joe became so sick he could no longer drive. He had been vocal about not wanting to go into a nursing home, mainly because he did not want to give a home his money. I approached my boss about working remotely and he agreed that I could as long as I met my work commitments. Joe was not able to eat very much anymore and it was very hard to watch him die.

He was making an effort to be nicer to my daughter, but by that point, she had written him off. We had hospice aides and a visiting nurse who came to the house almost daily to provide him with conversation and medical support.

Joe needed a wheelchair to get around the house and we kept a baby monitor in our bedroom so we could hear him call if he needed anything, but he never would ask for help. One time we heard him fall and went down to find him stuck behind the toilet on the floor. Bob and I got him up but he was embarrassed that I had seen him naked. About a week later he fell again, this time, in the hall; and this time, he had broken bones. When we called the nurse, she came over and told him he could no longer get out of bed. That was the end for Joe. He did not want to use the port-a-potty we set up in his room and he told us he was done.

He asked my husband to go to the bank and withdraw some cash he had set aside. He called his friends and family to his bedside one at a time and said goodbye. I had the baby monitor going in my bedroom upstairs at one point, and when one of the guys came over and said, "I'll see you up there, Joe," it made me bawl. I did not believe in heaven or hell but I believed in an afterlife. Joe agreed with his visitor. "Yeah, I'll see you on the other side."

I told the nurse what he had done, and she handed me a booklet explaining the last days of life and how patients often get a burst of energy right before they die. I knew the end was near.

Bob and I were exhausted and I convinced him to go out for a few hours and play pool with some of his friends. He needed a break from the emotional strain.

The last night of his life, Joe refused painkillers and was so demanding, wanting me to get him up in the bed that I called my sister to help. He was perturbed and difficult and I was completely exhausted. I had been working almost around the clock for the last two months and I had very little left to give. My sister left when my husband got home. Joe and Bob got into an argument.

I called my mom and I told her how tired I was and how difficult it was to watch someone that you love die. I told her it was time to send the angels. I don't know what made me say that to her, except for the fact that I was desperate. I knew that she prayed for people and that she had friends who were connected to her that would gladly do the same. She called me back around 10:00 p.m. and told me she had started a prayer chain and there were about 300 people praying for Joe that night.

I told Bob what I had done and we agreed we would sleep in the back bedroom, next to Joe's room, on the twin bed that we had set up in the room. Bob passed out right away but I could not sleep. I went into Joe's room and he was in pain. Had I been his daughter, I would have lain on the bed next to him, but he wasn't my dad and I didn't want to make him uncomfortable. Instead, I lie on the floor and put my hand on the bed, and he held it for several hours. I didn't want him to die alone. I tried to give him pain medication, but he would not take it, so finally I gave up, went into the guest room, and fell asleep in Bob's arms.

When we woke up around six, we knew. Even before we went in, we knew. Bob went in first and he screamed. His dad had managed to get his feet off the side of the bed, something he had not been able to do for weeks alone, and he was lying back with his arms crossed across his heart as if he had hugged himself to death. The angels had come.

Bob was upset and I told him to leave, I would take care of it. He called the nurse and explained that his dad died. Lynne was upstairs, and when she woke up, we told her Joe had passed. She wasn't sure if she wanted to go to school or to stay home. I told her it was her choice, and that if she decided to go to school and then later changed her mind, she could come home. She said she felt weird that there was a dead body in the house and decided to go to school.

I explained that we were going to have a wake for Joe at the house during the day, and when she got home, his body would be gone. She decided to go to school, and I accepted her decision. Later, she called the house and asked if she could come home, and I told her absolutely. When she got home, she made her way into Joe's rooms and paid her respects but she was still hurt and very angry.

Then one of the visiting nurses came by, gave her a hug, and said something about how sad Lynne must have been to lose her grandfather.

"Hardly," I said. "He treated her like shit." I should not have been speaking ill of the dead, but at that moment, my heart was with my daughter and I felt for her.

Startled by my reply, Tracy, the nurse, looked surprised. "You can't mean that. Every day after school, he would get excited. He would tell me *his* girl was coming home."

My daughter was in the room and she and I looked at each other with disbelief, *his girl*?

He *had* loved her! She came to me and I held her in my arms. Our tears were happy ones.

Why do we always hurt the ones that we love the most? Life was not fair.

Chapter Seventy-Nine

On Gender, Roles, and Socialization (2007)

Work was not going so well. I had gotten my bachelor's degree in marketing and I felt good about it. I was working as an imbedded consultant at the aerospace company, teaching six sigma and lean principles to the management team and the more than four hundred staff. Because of my extensive business experience, it was easy for me to see business processes that were failing.

I was proud of things I had accomplished, but I felt as if I should be doing more with my life. I was more aggressive than the average employee was. I made progress but I also made enemies. I was at odds with my own values and the values of corporate America. I saw things happening that made me question management and I did not know how to make them right.

My supervisor recognized signs that I had job burnout, and it was true. I was frustrated with my job, but I was more frustrated with people and their prejudices. I felt like I could not truly be who I was at work. Corporate America is conservative and I was more liberal.

My husband and I began to remodel our home. It had been our plan when Joe was alive, but we knew he would not have been comfortable during the major renovation, so we stalled it. We had money to renovate and we began to discuss our plans. We wanted a house that felt like a home. We wanted a place where we could entertain and enjoy family and friends.

Remodeling a home could cause a bad marriage to end. We managed to get along well, even while living without a kitchen for six months. It took a year to complete, but we had spent our money wisely and we were happy with the results.

I invited my management team to come for drinks after work one day to see my remodeled home. One of my female associates made mention that in another building on campus one of the men had come back as a woman over the holidays. He had had a sex change. Some of the employees had made a big stink about a man using a woman's restroom.

That forced corporate to put out a memo to the effect of people who dressed as women could use the ladies room and people who dressed like men would use the men's room. My co-worker thought this was hysterical. She made some rude comments about the person's sex change and how much trouble it was causing people in the office.

I did not know why, but as I listened to her making fun of this guy, now girl, I wanted to scratch her eyes out. I was on the fence with her before, trying to decide whether I liked her or not; but as soon as she was done laughing and giggling about this person's sex change and the dilemmas he/she would run into, I instantly hated her, and for a while, I did not even know why. I just knew she made my skin crawl.

I found out that one of my friends was having an affair. That part did not bother me as much as the fact that her daughter was involved, and was forced to keep the secret because she knew her mother was being unfaithful. How do we become empowered as women if we continue to lie about what it is we want from our partners?

How do we become effective managers when we believe our organization is unethical and we know they lie to their customers? I was starting to get angry and short-tempered but I didn't know why.

Chapter Eighty

Career Counseling and a Direction Change (2008)

I went through career counseling, including personality testing at work. I discovered that I was not in the best career for my personality. I had spent much of my life working in conservative, patriarchal settings where innovation and new ideas were not rewarded. The feedback I received was that I was a Research & Development, inventor, an idea type.

My Strong Interest Inventory Profile (SIIP) said I am enterprising and artistic, though conventional. My career counselor wanted to know why I had avoided becoming an entrepreneur full time. I told her it was fear of success that held me back.

She suggested that perhaps the only way I would ever be truly happy was to work for myself. I decided to pursue my MBA for international management. I hoped someday to write and do some public speaking about my life experiences, but I also wanted to be successful financially so that I did not have to work for someone else. I had become spoiled working those few months at home, and I liked it. I did not want to go and have to rely on a "job" given to me by an employer that might renege my paycheck at some point in the future. That meant that I needed to understand business in a way that I never had before.

I begin thinking about what I have to offer and what skills I need to hone.

Chapter Eighty-One

How Do You Define Success (2009)

Lynne bought a car by herself. She went online and looked at the different options in her price range and then she took a friend to test drive several cars at a few dealerships. She knew exactly what she wanted. She negotiated the car contract and insurance quotes all by herself. At first, I was nervous for her, afraid she would make the same mistakes I made; but after I reviewed the contract and saw what she had done, I was very proud of her.

I was meeting commitments at work but I had become bitter. I did not plan to stay there for much longer. Obtaining my advanced MBA degree was easier than I thought it would be. I realized I had been doing the work as a manager for many years.

I thought about my life and the struggles I have had and felt profoundly grateful to have come so far. I was at a point in my life where money did not matter as it had once. The void inside of me was not being satiated. I thought it was time for me to give back.

I felt a calling to tell my story to others. Instead of focusing on making money as I had for so long, I started to focus on feelings and connections with others, and it felt fantastic.

Lynne moved out and I went through the empty nest syndrome. For a few months, I wondered if I had any reason to go on living anymore.

The things I had done so long ago seemed like pebbles on the path of my life and yet they still haunted me sometimes. I still could not go to work and talk about my life because of the secrets I had and the way I lived.

I did not share with people that I worked with that I had sex with my husband and another friend over the weekend. Most people could not fathom the idea. We were celebrating our ten-year wedding anniversary. I never thought I would be able to stay committed this long, but our open marriage contract had worked out well for the both of us because we never felt trapped. We agreed to modify our contract as necessary throughout the years. It was such a simple way to look at marriage, but it changed everything. We were still in love and we trusted each other. We had no reasons to lie.

I told my husband all the time that if he ever decided to divorce his wife to let me know because I wanted to be next in line. We kept our marriage alive by making it feel like an affair, and it worked for us.

I still battled with depression. Sometimes I was manic and other times suicidal. My husband was accustomed to my mood swings and helped me to keep it real. He gave me ample space when I was in my creative moods and he was tender and attentive when I was needy. Some of my family members took medication for depression. I did not want to do that.

The work situation was escalating. My job was to improve our processes and our management had decided to outsource work instead of making it better internally. I knew that financially this was the right decision, but it undermined the employee morale and conflicted with what I taught. Making the quarter was more important than making the right decisions.

I got tired of keeping my mouth shut, and in a moment of self-destruction, I spoke publicly about questionable ethics in a division meeting. I knew what I had done was career breaking but I didn't care.

If I had been smart, I would have kept records and become a whistle-blower. I struggled with the dilemma. I knew that was probably what I should do, but I could not bring myself to do it. I made vague references to quality but I provided no facts and disgraced myself. It was easier.

In September, my boss told me regretfully that he had to let me go. I tell him thank you, and I meant it. I was thankful I was done there. For almost ten years, I walked across that parking lot feeling as if I had sold my soul. Yes, I had a great paying job with excellent benefits but I had had no time for me. I had felt bought and more used and abused than I had in any of my previous relationships, personally or professionally. I had an education and experience, but I hated my life.

Chapter Eighty-Two

What Is Normal Anyway? (2010)

I was looking for a job but I was restless. I had never been normal. I felt like a square peg trying to fit in a round hole. I realized I was not the only one who felt this way; other people shared with me similar feelings.

I had written a few articles for the web and on some of my articles, I had struck nerves. People were responding and I realized I had something to offer. Maybe I was not the best mother, the best writer, the best singer, the best employee or employer, but I did have a voice and a message. Life was worth living. Being best is not all that it is cracked up to be. Being is better than not being.

A poem by William Ernest Henley (1849-1903) entitled *Invictus* inspires me. The last two lines of the poem most powerful, *I am the master of my fate: I am the captain of my soul. (Henley, A book of verses)*

In June 2010, while surfing the internet one day, I read the *Missing Vagina Monologues* and I cried. Diane had taken me to the Hartford Bushnell to see the *Vagina Monologues* back in the mid-eighties but I never knew there was a segment written about those who were born without their sexual organs intact.

Esther Morris related her own story about discovering that she had MRKH. Mayer Rokitansky Kuster Hauser Syndrome is a condition that involves congenital absence of the vagina, fallopian tubes, cervix, and/or uterus. Some women have uterine remnants or horns. External genitalia are normal. Chromosome karyotype is 46XX (normal female). The incidence rate is approximately one in five thousand. Other symptoms involved, to varying degrees, are kidney abnormalities, skeletal problems, and hearing loss. The cause is somewhat unclear, but the syndrome occurs sometime during the fourth to sixth week of fetal development.

Although I have never been formally diagnosed, Esther's story was more similar to mine than any other person I have ever encountered. I am thankful for the internet and the fact that I searched out "missing vagina." Esther's notes say that when she became sexually active at seventeen, she realized men were not that particular about where they put their penises. I could identify with how she felt when she said that the medical need for feminization sterilized her soul.

I could not get away from my body. I was in pain again but I had been ignoring it, choosing to work and go to school with my every waking hour. It seemed like my vagina was closing up and vaginal intercourse was almost impossible and very painful.

In August, my husband and I agreed to share our two weeks of timeshare time for a family reunion. It was the first time in about twenty years that my immediate family had spent time together for more than an hour or two and we were all nervous and excited. Each of us still harbored pain from those early days. We loved each other and we hurt each other. There was no other way to say it. It is hard to say what went wrong, but obviously something did when you consider my brother, sister and I all moved out of our parents house by age 17. When we were all of legal age, our parents moved out of state and then out of the country. We felt they were embarrassed by our actions and they probably were. We had not been the perfect children but we had grown up and survived.

Thankfully, we were all still alive. I was extremely grateful for the chance to spend some time together with our family, my parents, my siblings and their children. While we may not be able to fix the wreckage of our past, we could certainly build bridges toward a better future. I wrote this memoir with deep regret for the mistakes I made as a youngster, already knowing that my family loves me for who I am and what I have now become.

After vacation, I had vaginal reconstruction surgery. The DaVinci robotic surgery took almost two hours longer than anticipated because I was not normal inside. The doctor removes three and a half inches of scar tissue and fibroids that have been the cause of pelvis pain for several years. I would be a fully functional woman once more in just a few months.

I felt glad that I was with a man who knew my history and loved me no matter what. I was thrilled that my daughter did not have to go through what I did and yet she understood enough of my history so that I did not have to keep secrets. I was thankful for my own mother.

She came to take care of me and I shared some of my past with her and found that she still loves me. How was it possible that I had not trusted her, and in fact, thought she hated me? For many years, I wanted her and my dad's approval and felt like I would never get it, so I lied and distanced myself to protect everyone. It hit me like a ton of bricks. They had only wanted what was best for me and I had not given them the chance. Somewhere along the way, fear took hold of me and turned into anger and rage.

I think back to the day that my sex tape aired to friends of friends and I remember how humiliated I felt. I could have easily jumped in front of a speeding car as I ran on the highway that day, just as Tyler Clementi from Rutgers University jumped off the George Washington Bridge when his roommate used YouTube to out him. Back then, my tape was on VHS not YouTube but I was mortified just the same when I walked into AA meetings and people began whispering or pointing at me. I thought everyone knew.

I realized that my anger towards my co-worker for making fun of the transgendered was actually anger I felt towards myself. I did not have the guts to stand up to my co-workers and tell them to not make fun of those born knowing they had been born the wrong sex or been born in between the sexes. I had not shared my own secrets, which might have helped educate them. Instead, I stayed silent and it still bothered me a year later. Why couldn't I just be honest about who and what I was?

As is the case for most of us, we are a product of inherited genes and our environments. At any moment in time, if our development is interrupted or influenced by things outside of our control, such as a traumatic event, strange things can happen. Our thoughts are just that, thoughts; our actions and reactions are what could make or break us.

Conclusion

I am sitting in a chair on my back porch, talking on the phone with my cousin. It has been twenty years since we lived together in my parents' house. We had been close at one time, but life got in the way and we hardly ever talk anymore. One summer, we spent the entire time making a list of every song we could think of. We had over five hundred songs between us. It was a fun project, something to make the summer days pass.

I think about the time my first husband wanted me to make a list of all the people I had slept with and the list topped two hundred. I was a bad girl back then but since then, I had changed some of my ways. I was no longer out to hurt myself, and I no longer felt I had something to prove. My heart had changed and unlike Anne Frank, I was willing to wear it on the outside on occasion.

"You are amazing," Carolyn says to me.

"What? Why do you say that? I am a fuck up." I am back on the porch, breaking away from the memory.

"No, you are not. You have had a lot of adversity in your life, but you do not let it stop you. You just keep going, and you overcome it. I cannot do that. Many people cannot do that, Kay."

"Yes, they can," I tell her. "I realized when I was in rehab that I was a perfectionist with an inferiority complex. I do not like to try things unless I can be good at them. The problem is, we cannot become really good at anything unless we try."

I continue, "If we allow our feelings to keep us from moving, then we will always feel bad. Yet if we can channel that fear into action, we may find that things we once thought were impossible, are not only possible, but also attainable."

"Do you remember that old story about the little train that thought he could? It was a story my grandmother told me as a child. What I discovered through therapy is that we have to train our brains to change the old negative tape in our heads. When we think, 'I cannot do that,' we set ourselves up for failure. Instead, we have to put out there, what we want to have happen. By changing our mental thoughts, consciously at first, to something like "I can do this," we change our destiny. To not participate and not try means that we are choosing to give up living life to the fullest."

I realize as I am talking that we have to choose to live our life with no regrets, and sometimes that means accepting what we did or said was wrong, and then moving on. Beating ourselves over the head for things we failed to do or for things that we did wrong years ago gets us nowhere now. Wisdom comes from accepting the things we cannot change.

She tells me there are things she wishes she could say. Things she has kept stuffed, secrets she is afraid to tell. "Let the demons out, Carolyn," I want to shout. "Do not keep the secrets in if they are hurting you. Fight back and be who you want to be. It is okay to be afraid, and it is okay to have made mistakes. That is what life, living, and becoming experienced is all about."

For many years, I felt alone and lonely; but with the help of others, I was able to change the way I thought about myself and stopped thinking like a victim. Instead, I became a fighter, a survivor.

Today, I have a strong support system of friends and family, and I use music and writing to help me express my emotions. Fortunately, there is always something to sing about and I realize we cannot appreciate the good without the bad, the happy without the sad. Look for the album on my website, *Paths* that will be simultaneously released with this book to hear the songs that meant something to me as I struggled through growing up.

A little bit about the characters, these people I have called friends and family:

Diane committed suicide at home on November 27, 2009. She could never get past her demons.

Alex continued his sobriety and is now working on his twenty-eighth year. Recently, we re-acquainted on Facebook and I invited him to dinner to meet my husband. Bob, Alex, and I spent the night laughing as we spoke about some of the crazy things we had done in our past. It was one of the happiest nights of my life. I felt incredibly lucky and special.

Alex tried to make amends to me for our crazy times, but I told him I had been a willing accomplice. He credits our BDSM relationship with showing him that he could live out his dreams and still stay sober. I feel much the same way.

Jenny and Tim both met their birth parents. Jenny had a good experience and Tim did not. When Tim met his blood related siblings, he discovered they too had struggled with alcohol, drugs, and many of the same legal hassles. Even though Tim's environment in his adoptive home had been stable, he was amazed to see how much genetics played a role in his life's path. Jenny works for a Fortune 500 company and is moving her way up. Tim has struggled with heroin addiction and has a year's sobriety under his belt at this time. I wonder why most of the adopted kids I know choose not to have children.

Dick called me a few years ago in a drunken stupor and said he still loved me. He had apparently won some money at the casino and it had reminded him that he owed me thousands of dollars from our divorce. He promised to send the money but never did.

Becky and I are still friends. I know that if she called me in the middle of the night or if I did the same to her, we would be there for each other, no matter what. I am so lucky to have a friend in her.

Lynne graduated high school early and is pursuing a career that fits her personality. We are emotionally close. I am proud of her accomplishments and I look forward to seeing her life unfold as she continues her journey.

In 1993, the SEC shut down Premium Sales and the owners convicted of being involved in an international Ponzi scheme.

My sister Cathy was able to meet her birth son and was pleased to find out she was a grandma. My brother David also has re-acquainted himself with the son he lost as a teen. Both of them have two additional boys from later relationships. My husband has never searched for his birth parents.

If you are in a position, where you feel all alone and you do not think you can live one more minute, please pick up the phone, and call someone. The suicide hotline, the AAhotline, the police are all there to help and they will help you if you just reach out your hand. Minutes make up hours that make up days that make up weeks, months, years, and lifetimes. Know that this too shall pass. Give it a minute or two. Walk away from what ails you, and give yourself a chance to succeed. I believe in you. You too can be the captain of your soul.

Citations

AA Twenty Questions: Lifeline, Retrieved on 9/20/2010 at
www.a-lassociates.com/aa/20Questions

AA 12 Steps: Retrieved on 9/20/2010 at
www.serenityfound.org/steps

Sound of Music

Diary of Ann Frank

Missing Vagina Monologue and Beyond, Esther Morris, Retrieved on
7/20/2010 at www.mrkh.org

http://www.skeptic.ca/george_carlin_ten_commandments.htm

Invictus
Premium Sales

Edwards Brothers,Inc!
Thorofare, NJ 08086
20 December, 2010
BA2010354